Give me my
My staff of i
My scrip of
My bottle o.
My gown of glory, hope's true gage;
And thus I'll take my pilgrimage.

Sir Walter Ralegh

To the Christians who still remain in the Holy Land.

PILGRIMS
TO
JERUSALEM

Fisher Press

Published by Fisher Press, Post Office Box 41,
Sevenoaks, Kent, TN15 6YN, England

Pilgrims to Jerusalem was first published as a Fisher paperback in
1999
Copyright in the compilation © Antony Matthew
Copyright in the illustrations © Mary Tyler
All rights reserved

British Library Cataloguing in Publication Data.
A catalogue record for this book is available from
The British Library

ISBN 1 874037 15 9

Printed by Antony Rowe Ltd., Wiltshire
Cover: Sol Communications Ltd., London

CONTENTS

ACKNOWLEDGEMENTS

W̶E̶ are most grateful to Dr Greville Freeman-Grenville, who not only drew to our attention the important letter by Bishop Bonifacio OFM reporting on the opening of the tomb of Christ in 1555, but also provided valuable help for certain other accounts, as well as pointing out some pitfalls; to my cousin, Dr Henry Emeleus, who researched information about the railways of Palestine; to Anthony Collings-Wells, who offered us the benefit of his extensive experience in the Near East; to Joan Bond, the Librarian of the Catholic Central Library, who helped locate some sources for pictorial material; and to many friends who have encouraged us in the preparation of this book.

INTRODUCTION

IT is nearly two thousand years since the first pilgrims went to see the infant Jesus. This book offers a selection of pilgrims' accounts of journeys to places in the Holy Land associated with His life. The authors include lay people and religious, men and women, the highly sophisticated and those of simple faith, who wrote from the early centuries of the Christian era until the end of the nineteenth century. Each text is linked to the next by historical and biographical background.

Most are first hand travel accounts. But I have included a fourth century catechetical lecture by St Cyril of Jerusalem, which shows what pilgrims would have been taught, had they sought instruction for baptism at that time, and the continuity of belief and practice down the ages. I have also included a letter from the Franciscan Prior of the Holy Land, in which he gives an eye-witness report of the opening of the tomb of Christ in 1555, as this was the principal physical objective of a pilgrim's spiritual quest.

For the first three centuries Christian pilgrims could face the death penalty in the Holy Land for their faith, as elsewhere in the Roman Empire. Yet even when Christianity became its official religion, pilgrimage by the sea or land route remained hazardous. From the seventh century until after the First World War the land of Jesus was under Islamic rule, except in the twelfth and thirteenth centuries when the Crusaders established the Latin kingdoms. Yet the conditions for Christian pilgrimages under Islam varied greatly, depending on the nature of Arab or Turkish rule at any particular time, and on the wider political situation. The extracts show how individual pilgrims responded to the hardships and joys. They also provide insight into the way in which religious sensibility has changed over almost two millennia, even though the purpose of the journey and the underlying faith have remained the same.

ANTONY MATTHEW

CHAPTER ONE

THE FIRST PILGRIMS

Wise men came as pilgrims to the place where Christ was born.

NOW when Jesus was born in Bethlehem of Judea in the days of Herod the king, behold, wise men from the East came to Jerusalem, saying, "Where is he who has been born king of the Jews? For we have seen his star in the East, and have come to worship him." When Herod the king heard this, he was troubled, and all Jerusalem with him; and assembling all the chief priests and scribes of the people, he inquired of them where the Christ was to be born. They told him, "In Bethlehem of Judea for so it is written by the prophet: 'And you Bethlehem in the land of Judah, are by no means least among the rulers of Judah; for from you shall come a ruler who will govern my people Israel.' "

Then Herod summoned the wise men secretly and ascertained from them what time the star appeared; and he sent them to Bethlehem, saying, "Go and search diligently for the child; and when you have found him, bring me word that I too may come and worship also."

When they had heard the king, they went their way; and lo, the star which they had seen in the East went before them, till it came to rest over the place where the child was. When they saw the star, they rejoiced exceedingly with great joy; and going into the house they saw the young child with Mary his mother, and they fell down and worshipped him. Then opening their treasures, they offered him gifts, gold, and frankincense and myrrh. And being warned in a dream not to return to Herod, they departed to their own country by another way.

St Matthew

The parents of Jesus went from Nazareth to Jerusalem every year for the Passover. One year when Jesus was a boy they were perplexed by what happened during their visit.

NOW his parents went to Jerusalem every year at the feast of the Passover. And when he was twelve years old, they went up according to custom; and when the feast was ended, as they were returning, the boy Jesus stayed behind in Jerusalem. His parents did not know it, but supposing him to be in the company they went a day's journey, and they sought him among their kinsfolk and acquaintances; and when they did not find him, they turned back to Jerusalem, seeking him. After three days they found him in the Temple, sitting among the teachers, both listening to them, and asking them questions; and all who heard him were amazed at his understanding and his answers.

And when they saw him, they were astonished; and his mother said to him, "Son, why have you treated us so? Behold, your father and I have been looking for you anxiously." And he said to them, "How is it that you sought me? Did you not know that I must be in my Father's house?" And they did not understand the saying which he spoke to them.

And he went down with them and came to Nazareth, and was obedient to them; and his mother kept all these things in her heart.

St Luke

After the death, resurrection and ascension of Jesus, and the foundation of the Church at Pentecost, there are no detailed accounts of pilgrimages to Jerusalem dating from the period when Christians were a small sect persecuted by the Jews and the Roman administration. St Paul went up to Jerusalem to see the disciples of Jesus. But his letters show him as largely concerned with the apostolic task of spreading the Gospel and keeping the Christian communities unified. He must have been acquainted with the sites of the events in our Lord's life since these took place only twenty or thirty years before. But in the letters we have he does not mention these specifically.

The Christian communities were likely to have met in many of the houses belonging to those whose family traditions went back the two or three decades to the time of Christ. Yet to many early Christians, although well acquainted with the sacred places where our Lord dwelt, taught, and suffered during His passion, this knowledge might initially have seemed somewhat marginal to the exciting apostolic task which He had bestowed on the early Church. The siege and devastation of Jerusalem by the Romans in 70 AD destroyed buildings, such as the Temple, which had been important in the events of our Lord's life. This terrible disaster, predicted by Christ, may well have encouraged the Christian community to take a more precise interest in the sites which provided the historical and material testimony to the reality of their Faith. Most Christians went into exile in Pella after the destruction of Jerusalem. But within a few months some returned to their ruined homes amid the rubble.

The unbroken continuity of a line of leaders of the Christian community in Jerusalem and its environs, as recorded by the historian Josephus, makes the accuracy of the tradition relating to the sites very probable. Jesus was crucified outside Jerusalem. About ten years later the places of the crucifixion and burial were incorporated within its walls as part of an expansion of the city. The hill of Golgotha, being a highly visible natural feature, would have been easily identifiable, and was still being pointed out inside the city when Christianity had ceased to be a persecuted Faith three centuries later. When, on the order of Constantine, excavations were carried out in the fourth century, to lay the foundations for suitable churches to celebrate Christianity, now the official religion of the Empire, a number of tombs were discovered near the hill of Golgotha. One of these was immediately identified as the tomb of Christ. The reasons were not put into writing at the time, but were evidently convincing to those of the Christian community who lived in Jerusalem and were heirs to its tradition. The archaeologist, Martin Biddle, in his book 'The Tomb of Christ', published in 1999, quotes with approval the view of the Jerusalem city archaeologist, Dan Bahat, who has said: "We may not be absolutely certain that the site of the Holy Sepulchre Church is the site of Jesus' burial, but we certainly have no other that can lay a claim nearly as weighty, and we really have no reason to reject the authenticity of the site." In the same way, knowledge of the other sites is likely to have been handed on within Christian families, rather as the knowledge of the Faith, its shrines, chapels and mass centres, was passed on in Catholic recusant families in Britain during the almost three hundred years of their persecution.

The first visitor who provides a useful detailed account of the Holy Places is the Bordeaux pilgrim, who went to Palestine in 333, twenty years after the Emperor Constantine, by the Edict of Milan, granted religious freedom to Roman citizens throughout the Empire. We do not know the pilgrim's name. A great many of the churches in the Holy Places were then being built by order of the Emperor, and under the supervision of his mother, St Helena. Some of this building work was incomplete at the time of this pilgrim's visit. His brief comments on what he saw at Golgotha and the surrounding area suggest that building work was still in progress—some of the cisterns and water works which he notices may be connected with the architectural plans for the later complex structures on the sites.

Much of the early part of his account is simply a list of staging posts on his journey. He travelled mounted from Bordeaux to Milan, then down through the Balkans to Constantinople. He records the total distance travelled as somewhere between 2,100 and 2,200 miles, with about a hundred overnight stops. He then followed the land route, having crossed the straits of the

*Bosphorus by boat. His first mainland halt in Asia Minor was at
Pandik. His route then took him across what is now Turkey,
through the Roman provinces of Bithynia, Galatia, Cappadocia
and Cilicia, with stops at Ankara, Colonia, Tyana, and Pylae.
From Tarsus he followed the coastal route, through Antioch,
Tripolis, Sidon and Tyre, past Mount Gerizim to Sichem, then on
to Caesarea and Jerusalem. His account becomes more detailed at
this point.*

IN Jerusalem beside the Temple are two large pools, one to
the right and the other to the left, which were built by
Solomon. Further on in the city are twin pools with five porticoes, which are called Bethsaida. Persons who have been ill
for many years are cured there. The pools contain water
which becomes red when it is disturbed. There is also a crypt
in which Solomon used to torture devils. Here is also the corner of a very lofty tower. The Lord climbed this and the
tempter said to him: "If you are the Son of God, throw yourself down from here." And the Lord said to the tempter, "You
shalt not tempt the Lord your God, and Him only shall you
serve." And there also is the great corner-stone of which it
was said, "The stone which the builders rejected has become
the head of the corner."

Below the pinnacle of this tower are very many chambers,
and here it was that Solomon had his palace. The actual
chamber where he was living when he wrote of Wisdom is
there, and is roofed over with a single stone. Below ground
there are some vast water cisterns and pools built with a great
deal of labour.

In the sanctuary itself, where the Temple which Solomon
built stood, there is marble in front of the altar which has on
it the blood of Zacharias—you would think that it had only
been shed today. All around you can see the marks of the
hobnails of the soldiers who killed him, as plainly as if they
were pressed in wax. Two statues of Hadrian stand there, and,
not far from them, there is a perforated stone which the Jews
come and anoint each year. After mourning and rending

their garments they depart. There too is the house of
Hezekiah, king of Judah.

As you leave Jerusalem to climb Sion, you can see, down
in the valley on your left beside the wall, the pool called
Siloam. It has four porticoes, and there is a second pool
outside. The water is allowed to flow for six days and nights,
but the seventh day, which is the Sabbath, it does not run
either by night or day. Ascending Sion from that point you
can see the place where the house of Caiaphas, the priest,
once used to stand. The column where they fell on Christ
and scourged him with rods still remains there.

Inside, within the walls of Sion, you can see where David
had his palace. Seven synagogues used to be there, but only
one is now left—the rest have been "ploughed over and
resown" as was foretold by the prophet Isaiah. As you leave
there and pass through the walls of Sion towards the gate of
Neopolis, down in the valley on your right, you have some
walls where Pontius Pilate had his house, the Praetorium,
where the Lord's trial was held before his Passion. On your
left is the small hill of Golgotha where the Lord was crucified, and, about a stone's throw away from it, the vault
where they laid his body, and he rose again on the third
day. By order of the Emperor Constantine there has now
been built a "basilica" of remarkable beauty—I mean a
"place for the Lord". Beside it there are cisterns and a bath
where the young are baptized.

Arriving at the gate of Jerusalem which faces east, and
on your way up to the Mount of Olives, you come to
what is called the Valley of Jehoshaphat. On the left
there are vineyards. Here there is the rock where Judas
Iscariot betrayed Christ; and on the right, the palm-tree,
from which the children took branches and strewed them
in Christ's path. Nearby, about a stone's throw away, are
two memorial tombs of beautiful workmanship. One of
them, formed from a single rock, is where the prophet
Isaiah was laid, and in the other lies Hezekiah, King of
the Jews.

On the Mount of Olives, where the Lord taught before his Passion, a lovely basilica has been built on Constantine's orders. And not far off is the small hill where the Lord went up to pray, taking Peter and John away with him, and where Moses and Elijah appeared to them. A mile and a half to the east is the village called Bethany, where there is the vault in which Lazarus was laid, whom the Lord raised from the dead...

Four miles from Jerusalem, on the right of the highway to Bethlehem, is the tomb of Jacob's wife Rachel. Two miles further on, on the left, is Bethlehem, where the Lord Jesus Christ was born, and where a basilica has been built by command of Constantine. Not far away are the tombs of Ezekiel, Asaph, Job, Jesse, David and Solomon. Their names are written in Hebrew characters low down on a wall as you go down into the vault.

Fourteen miles away is Bethsur, with the spring where Philip baptized the eunuch. It is nine miles on to Terebinthus. Here Abraham lived and dug a well beneath the terebinth tree, and spoke and ate with angels. Another exceptionally beautiful basilica has been built there on Constantine's orders. Two miles on from there is Hebron, where there is a remarkably beautiful tomb, square and made of stone, in which are laid Abraham, Isaac, and Jacob, and Sarah, Rebecca, and Leah.

Some fifty years later a nun, Egeria, wrote an account of her pilgrimage to the Holy Places of the East. It includes her detailed description as an eye witness of the way religious services were conducted at the principal places of our Lord's life in Jerusalem and the surrounding districts about three hundred and fifty years after His death. The scholar, P. Devos, dates her pilgrimage to the East to the early years of the 380s, and her actual stay in Jerusalem from Easter 381 to Easter 384. She includes the arrangements for services held daily, on Sundays, and on other major days of commemoration. Those she describes for Holy Week still form the basis for the services

for Maundy Thursday, Good Friday, and the Easter Vigil—
the Easter triduum—as celebrated in the Roman Catholic
Church today. Egeria also includes details of the fasting cus-
toms, and the preparation of candidates for reception into the
Church by baptism.

Following Constantine's edict of religious toleration in 313,
and the Council of Nicaea in 325 which clarified Christian doc-
trine, membership of the Church grew rapidly, and it was a
time of considerable fervour. Egeria writes for the benefit of her
religious community at home in northern Spain. Her account
was actually written while she was in Constantinople, after she
had completed her visit to Jerusalem, but she still had further
travel plans.

IT is from Constantinople, ladies, ever lights of my life, that I offer you the following details to encourage your devotion. My current plan is to go as a pilgrim of Christ our Lord to Asia, in particular to pray at Ephesus because of its association with the Holy Martyrs and the blessed Apostle, John. If, after that, I am still "in the body", and am able to go on to see other places, I will provide you with an account, either in person, if God so wills, or, if I change my plans, by letter. In any case, please keep me in mind, whether I am "in the body" or "out of the body!"

I must now give you first-hand information about the daily services in the Holy Places to inform your devotions. I know how glad you will be to learn about these.

Every day, before cock crow, all the doors of the Church of the Resurrection are opened, and the "monazontes" and "parthenae", as the monks and consecrated virgins are called here, come down to the Church. And they are not alone; there are also lay people, men and women who are willing to get up early. From then until dawn they sing hymns and the responses to the psalms, and the antiphons. In between each hymn there are prayers. Two or three priests and deacons take turns with the monks to recite the prayers. When it begins to be light, they start to sing the morning hymns.

At this point the bishop arrives with his clergy. He goes immediately into the cave within the Church of the Resurrection (Anastasis), and from behind the screen he begins the Prayer for All. He mentions personally by name those whom he specially wishes to recall; in this way he blesses the catecumens (those of them who have been accepted to be prepared for baptism). Then he says another prayer and blesses the faithful. Finally he comes outside the screen and everyone comes up to him to kiss his hand. He blesses each one individually, and then departs. It is daylight by the time the service ends.

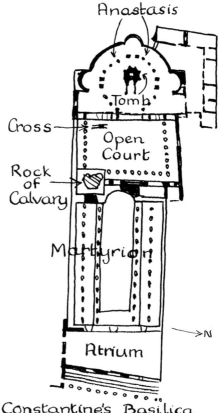

Likewise at noon everyone comes down again to the Church, and they sing psalms and antiphons, until the bishop is sent for. He comes down again, but does not take his seat. He goes behind the screen in the Church (and thus into the cave where he went earlier). Then, likewise after some prayers, he blesses the faithful, comes out from behind the screen and the people come up to kiss his hand.

At three o'clock there is the same ceremony as at noon, but at four o'clock they have "Lychnicon", which we call the Service of Lights. For this, all the congregation comes together in the church, the lamps and candles are lit, and everywhere is full of light. The flame for the lights is not brought from outside, but from beyond the screen near the cave within, where a light burns night and day. The psalms for the Service of Lights are sung, and the antiphons as well, and this takes some time. Again the bishop is summoned, descends, and this time sits in the chief seat. The priests also arrive and sit in their places. Hymns and antiphons continue.

Then when they have completed singing what is appointed for the day, the bishop rises and stands in front of the screen before the cave. One of the deacons mentions by name each person whom it is customary to recall on this occasion, and every time he says a name a large number of boys standing by make the response, "Kyrie eleison," (or, as we say, "Lord, have mercy"), and everywhere is filled with the sound. When the deacon has completed what he has to say, the bishop says a prayer and the Prayer for All.

At this point both the faithful and those preparing for baptism are all praying together. But then the deacon addresses each of these "catachumens", wherever he is standing, by name, and he bows his head. The bishop stands and gives his blessing. There is another prayer, and then the deacon raises his voice to require the faithful also, wherever they are standing, to bow their heads. The bishop then blesses them, and this is the signal for the dismissal. The congregation then comes forward to kiss the bishop's hand. Then, as they sing hymns, the bishop is escorted by the whole congregation from the Church to the Cross which is across a courtyard and faces the colonnaded Martyrion, the Great Church, which is in front of the Church of the Resurrection.

When they have all arrived there he says a prayer, then blesses the catechumens and the faithful. Then the bishop and the whole congregation go behind the Cross and do what they did in front of the Cross. The people likewise go up and kiss the bishop's hand as they did in the Church, both before and behind the Cross. A great number of enormous glass lanterns and candelabra are hanging there both in the Church, and in front of and behind the Cross. When all these ceremonies have been completed it is dusk.

This is the routine of services held every weekday at the Cross and in the churches. But before cock crow on the seventh day, the Lord's Day, all the crowd gathers as if it were Easter, as many as can fit into the courtyard of the Church of the Resurrection. The courtyard is the "basilica" outside the Church. Lights are suspended there to illuminate the neighbouring church building. Those who are afraid that they may not arrive before cock-crow come early, and sit down there. They sing hymns and antiphons, with prayers between each piece, since there are always priests and deacons present for the vigil to say these. Large numbers gather early. It is not the custom to open up the Holy Places themselves until cock-crow.

But as soon as the first cock crows, the bishop comes down immediately and enters into the cave within the Church of the Resurrection. All the doors are opened, and the whole congregation comes into the Church where countless lamps are already lit. As soon as the people have entered, one of the priests sings a psalm and all make the responses. Prayers follow, then a deacon sings a psalm, and this is also followed by prayers. A third psalm is sung by one of the clergy, followed by a third set of prayers with the Commemoration of All. After these three psalms and prayers the censers are taken into the cave within the Church, and the whole Church is filled with the smell of incense. Then the bishop, who is then standing inside the screen, takes the book of the Gospel and goes to the entrance and himself reads the account of the Resurrection of the Lord. But when he begins to read it, such a moaning and groaning arises from all those present because of everything that the Lord suffered for us, that even the hardest heart would be moved to tears. When he has read the Gospel, the bishop comes out and is led by the entire congregation with processional hymns to the Cross. There is one psalm there and a prayer, then he blesses the faithful, and that is the dismissal.

As the bishop departs, all the congregation come to kiss his hand. He then goes immediately to his residence. The monks then return to the Church and sing psalms and antiphons until daybreak, with prayers between each item. The priests and deacons take turns each day to keep the vigil with the people. Some lay men and women like to stay on until daybreak, while others prefer to return home to catch up with some sleep.

At daybreak, since it is the Lord's Day, everyone makes his way to the Great Church which Constantine built on Golgotha, and which is beyond where the Cross stands. Here they do what everyone does everywhere on the Lord's Day. But you will want to note that it is customary here for any priest who takes his seat and wishes to preach to do so. When all the priests have had their say the bishop preaches himself. The reason why there is always this preaching on Sundays is to ensure that the people will be both learned in the Scriptures and in love for God. Because of all this preaching it is a long time before the dismissal, which does not take place before ten or even eleven o'clock. The Service of Lights takes place on Sundays in the same way as on week days.

These are the customary services which are held each day, except on days of special solemnity, which we shall describe below. What I found particularly impressive in the way they do things is that the psalms and antiphons always suit the occasion, whether at night or early in the morning; and the same is true of all that is chosen for the services at noon, three o'clock, or for the Service of Lights. Everything has been thought out, and is relevant to the hour and occasion of the service.

Throughout the year the services on Sunday are in the Great Church which Constantine built on Golgotha. On only one day, that of Pentecost, which is the fiftieth day after Easter, does it take place on Sion. On that day the congregation goes there at nine o'clock after the dismissal at the Great Church.

Egeria now describes the ceremonies for the main solemnities, beginning with the Epiphany. Christmas was not celebrated at this time at Jerusalem. The 25th of December was kept as the commemoration of St James and King David. An Armenian lectionary of the period notes that in other towns the birth of Christ was celebrated, and it is reasonable to assume that Bethlehem was one of these.

A page of manuscript is missing at the very beginning of the Epiphany section. It seems likely that there was some kind of processional journey which began outside Jerusalem, and included Bethlehem. As we have seen in St Luke's account, the Wise Men were said to have travelled both to Bethlehem and Jerusalem. The importance of the celebration of the Epiphany derives from the fact that their visit was seen as foreshadowing the extension of Christ's redemption to those who were not Jews.

..."Blessed is he who comes in the name of the Lord, etc.". The procession has to go slowly because the monks are travelling on foot. In this way they arrive at Jerusalem almost at daybreak, at the moment when people can just recognise each other, but before it is light. When they arrive, the bishop goes staight into the Church of the Resurrection, and everyone goes with him. Extra lamps have already been lit. A psalm is sung, and then there is a prayer. The catechumens and the faithful are blessed by the bishop. The bishop retires, and everyone goes home to rest at the place where he is staying. But the monks remain in the Church and sing hymns until it is light.

Just after seven o'clock, when the people have rested, everyone comes together in the Great Church on

Golgotha. As with the Church of the Resurrection, the Cross, and the Church at Bethlehem, it is decorated on this day in a way to which it is impossible to do justice. Wherever you look you see nothing but gold, jewels and silk. All the awnings and curtains are of gold-striped silk. Everything brought out to be used for the services on this day is made of gold and jewels. It is not possible to calculate or describe the number and weight of the candles, tapers and lanterns and the other things used for the services.

Yet what can I say about the decoration of the building itself? Under the direct supervision of his mother, Constantine honoured it with as much gold, mosaic and marble as his empire could provide. He did this not only for the Great Church, but also for the Church of the Resurrection, the Cross and the rest of the Holy Places in Jerusalem.

But to return to my subject. On the first day of Epiphany the service takes place in the Great Church on Golgotha. All the preaching, readings and hymns are appropriate for the day. Then, after the dismissal, the congregation goes in procession with hymns to the Church of the Resurrection in the usual way, and the dismissal follows there at about noon. On the same day the Service of Light follows the usual daily pattern. On the second day they assemble in the Church of the Resurrection, as they do on the third day. Throughout the three days the celebrations last until noon in the Great Church. On the fourth day they beautify the Church on the Mount of Olives (the Imbomon), and celebrate a liturgy there in a similar way. On the fifth day the celebrations are at the Church of Lazarus, about a mile and a half from Jerusalem; on the sixth day it is at the Upper Church on Mt Sion; on the seventh day at the Church of the Resurrection, and on the eighth day at the Cross.

The celebrations thus continue for eight days, and each church is specially decorated for the occasion as I have indicated above. But at Bethlehem the decorations remain up for eight days, and the festival is celebrated by the priests and clergy of the village itself, and by the monks who are resident there. So from the time when everyone returns from Bethlehem with the bishop at the beginning of the festival season, all the local monks keep vigil in the Church at Bethlehem, and sing hymns and antiphons until morning. The bishop, however, is required to keep the rest of the festival season at Jerusalem. During the solemnity and celebration of the first day of the festival vast crowds gather in Jerusalem, not only monks, but also lay men and women.

I should tell you that the fortieth day after Epiphany is celebrated here with particular dignity. On this day the people come together in the Church of the Resurrection, and everything is performed with all the joy of the celebrations held at Easter. All the priests preach first, and then the bishop. They usually take as their text that part of the Gospel which describes how Joseph and Mary take the Lord to the Temple; and which records the words of Simeon and the prophetess Anna, the daughter of Phanuel, which they use when they see him; or they treat the matter of the sacrifice itself which his parents offered. When everything has been celebrated according to custom, the Sacred Mysteries take place, and the people are dismissed.

Egeria now describes the details of the services during Lent. Besides those held regularly there were some extra ones, with an all night vigil on Friday evening, and communion very early before sunrise on Saturday morning. The arrangements for fasting were voluntary, as Egeria explains below. Those who observed the strictest regime had their main weekly meal after Communion on Saturday, with one further meal for the week after the services on Sunday.

These are the customs for fastings which are followed in Lent. There are some who fast during the whole week from Sunday after Mass until the meal they have on Saturday after the vigil service at the Church of the Resurrection. These are called hebdomaries who keep the week. On

Saturday they eat early, and do not eat again until the next day which is Sunday, when they dine after Mass at 11 o'clock or later. After this they do not eat again until the following Saturday, as I have said above. Those who are called apotactites have a general rule of eating once a day throughout the year, and not just in Lent, whether they are men or women. If any of the apotactites cannot sustain a week's fasting throughout Lent, they eat an extra meal half way through Thursday, or on two days a week, or else they follow their usual practice of eating a meal every evening. No one requires anyone to have a particular fasting regime, but everyone does what they can. Those who have a strict regime are not praised, nor is anyone who does less criticised. That is the way things are observed here.

During Lent this is the diet they follow: no bread unless it has been soaked in water and strained; no oil, and nothing which grows on trees. They have water and a little gruel made with flour. The fast is for forty days ...

On the Saturday before the Great Week of Easter, as it begins to be light, the bishop offers the Holy Sacrifice, as is usual on Saturday. Then, at the dismissal, the archdeacon makes the following announcement: "Today at one o'clock everyone should be ready for the service at the the Lazarus church."

And so, as the seventh hour approaches, everyone arrives at this church, which is at Bethany and about two miles from the city. As you travel to the church from Jerusalem, about half a mile before you reach your destination, there is a church by the road. It is on this spot that Mary, Lazarus' sister, met the Lord. There, as soon as the bishop has arrived, he is greeted by all the monks, and the people enter the church. They have one hymn and one antiphon, and the passage of the Gospel is read which tells of the meeting between Lazarus' sister and the Lord. After a prayer and a blessing, they process, singing hymns, to the church of Lazarus itself.

When they reach the church, a great crowd has gathered there, not only in the building itself, but already all the fields round about are full of people. Hymns and antiphons are sung, all fitting for the day and the place. Then, at the dismissal, the feast of Easter is proclaimed.

A priest mounts on a raised platform and reads the passage from the Gospel which says: "Then Jesus, six days before Passover came to Bethany" etc. When this passage has been read, and Easter has been announced, they are dismissed. They have this service on this day because it is written in the Gospel that it was six days before the passover when these events took place in Bethany. From Saturday it is six days till the fifth day of the week, Thursday, when, after the Last Supper, the Lord was arrested. Once this service is over everyone returns to the Church of the Resurrection for the Service of Lights as usual.

The next day, which is Sunday, begins Easter week, which here they call the Great Week.

Egeria now describes the services for this day. In the morning they were similar to those of other Sundays. But the afternoon services took place on the Mount of Olives, first at the Eleona Church, built on a site where the Lord used to teach his disciples; and then at what was called the Imbomon, which Egeria gives as the place of the Lord's Ascension. There appears to have been no church here at this time, but it must have been suitable for open air services. In late afternoon there was a Palm Sunday procession back down to Jerusalem, which Egeria now describes.

At about five o'clock in the afternoon the passage from the Gospel is read which describes how the children met the Lord with palm branches, saying, "Blessed is he who comes in the name of the Lord." Then the bishop and the whole congregation set out on foot from the top of the Mount of Olives. All the people go before him with hymns and antiphons, to which the response is always, "Blessed is He who comes in the name of the Lord." All the children

of the district take part, even those not old enough to walk, who are carried on their parents' shoulders. All carry branches, some from palm and some from olive trees. In this way the bishop is led down in exactly the same way as happened with the Lord.

The route is from the top of the Mount of Olives and then on down through the city to the Church of the Resurrection. Everyone is on foot, even the older men and women. They escort the bishop, singing the responses and walking slowly so as not to tire those in the procession. As a consequence it is evening by the time they reach the Church, yet they still have the Service of Lights, then the prayer at the Cross, before the dismissal.

On the Monday in Holy Week Egeria explains that the services were held in the Church of the Resurrection and the Martyrion, with appropriate readings. The services were the same on Tuesday; except that late on that night, after the dismissal in the Martyrion, the congregation reassembled at the church of Eleona, on the site where the Lord used to teach his disciples. The bishop then read the whole of the passage from the Gospel according to St Matthew where the Lord says, "See that no man leads you astray." The Wednesday services were like those of Monday and Tuesday, except that, just before the end of the last service, a priest read, from the front of the screen in the Church of the Resurrection, the passage about Judas Iscariot arranging with the Jewish leaders to betray Jesus for money. On Maundy Thursday, the beginning of the Easter Triduum, the dawn and morning services followed the pattern of the first days of the week, but before the dismissal in the Martyrion, the archdeacon made the following announcement: "Let us meet tonight at the church of the Eleona at 7 o'clock. We have a great work to do this evening!" Mass was celebrated by the bishop behind the Cross (the only time this took place here during the year), and everyone received Holy Communion.

Egeria records the rest of the events of the Triduum as follows:

After Mass everyone hurries home to eat, since as soon as they have had their meal they all go up to the Eleona; here is the cave where the Lord was with his apostles on this very night. There, until about eleven o'clock, they have hymns, antiphons and readings, all appropriate to the occasion. Those passages from the Gospel are read which tell what the Lord said to his disciples on the day when he sat in that very cave, which is now within the church. At about midnight they go in procession singing hymns up to the Imbomon, the place where the Lord ascended into heaven. Again they have readings, hymns and antiphons there, all suitable for the day. The prayers too which the bishop pronounces relate to the events of the day. At cock crow, they descend, singing hymns, to the place where the Lord prayed, as is written in the Gospel, "And he withdrew from them about a stone's throw…and prayed etc." In that spot there is an elegant church into which the bishop and the congregation enter. Again there is a suitable prayer and a hymn, and the reading is from the Gospel where the Lord says to his disciples: "Watch and pray that you may not enter into temptation." When the whole passage has been read, there is another prayer.

Then, singing hymns, they all processs on foot—even the smallest children—to conduct the bishop to Gethsemane. The choral procession to Gethsemane moves very slowly, since the vast crowd, exhausted by the vigil and weakened by fasting, has to descend what is a large steep hill. Hundreds of church candles have been prepared to light the people's way. Once everyone has reached Gethsemane there is a suitable prayer and hymn, and then the passage from the Gospel is read which tells of the Lord's arrest. When this is read in this particular place everyone is sobbing and moaning so much that the noise of their wailing can probably be heard in the city.

When the dawn light makes it just possible for people to recognise each other, they go in procession to the city gate singing hymns. Then, every single one of them, young and old, rich and poor, processes through the middle of the city. Everyone is prepared for this. For on that day each person makes a special point of not leaving off the vigil until morning. They conduct the bishop to the gate, then on across the whole length of the city to the Cross.

By the time they arrive there it is bright daylight. There the passage of the Gospel is read in which the Lord is brought before Pilate, including all the recorded words which Pilate said to the Lord and to the Jews.

After this the bishop addresses the people to keep up their morale after all the effort they have put in throughout the night, and to offer encouragement for the further effort needed in the day ahead. They are not to tire, but to place their hope in God who will reward them for their efforts.

Having given them as much encouragement as he can, he says to them: "Each of you should now go home to your rooms to rest a little. Then, at about eight o'clock, you should be here again and stay until midday to look on the holy wood of the Cross, believing as each of us do, that this is for our salvation. And from midday onwards we need to gather here, that is at this place of the Cross, to devote ourselves to readings and prayers until nightfall."

Before the sun rises they are dismissed. But those who remain undaunted go off to pray at the column where the Lord was scourged. Then they return for a short break in their houses and all quickly get themselves ready for the next stage.

The bishop's chair is now placed on Golgotha, behind the Cross, which is standing there now. The bishop sits in his chair. A table covered with a cloth is set before him. The deacons stand around him, and a gilded silver box, in which is the wood of the Cross, is brought to him. The wood of the Cross is placed on the table, with the inscription. When it has been placed on the table, the bishop sits with his hands resting on the ends of the Holy Cross. The deacons around him keep watch. It is guarded in this way because the people come up to the table one by one, the faithful as well as the catechumens, and, bending down, kiss the sacred wood, then move on.

Once, I don't know when, it is reported that someone took a bite out of the sacred wood and got away with it! So now the deacons who stand there are on guard to ensure that no-one dares do this again! So all the people come up, one after another, bend down, and touch the Cross and the inscription, first with their forehead and their eyes, then kissing the Cross in this way they pass on. But no one puts out his hand to touch the Cross. And when they have kissed the Cross there is a deacon standing there who holds the ring of Solomon and the Horn with which the kings were anointed. These are also venerated with kisses.

The ceremony starts at about eight o'clock in the morning, with the people all entering by one door and going out at another. All this takes place in the place where Mass was offered the previous day, Thursday.

But at noon they go before the Cross—whether it is raining or sunny. It is a very large and beautiful courtyard, out of doors between the Cross and the Church of the Resurrection. All the people congregate there in such numbers that moving through the crowd is impossible. The bishop's chair is set up before the Cross, and from noon till three o'clock they have nothing except readings from scripture: first, the psalms wherever they speak of the Passion; then the writings of the apostles, the Epistles or Acts, where they speak of the Passion, and then those passages from the Gospels which describe His actual suffering.

Thus they read the prophets which foretell that the Lord would suffer; and then the Gospels where the Passion of the Lord is itself recounted. And so for these three hours the whole congregation is taught that nothing which happened had not been foretold, and that everything foretold had now been fulfilled in every respect. The prayers between the readings are all chosen as appropriate for the day.

It is wonderful how moved they are by the readings and prayers, as the sobbing of the whole congregation shows. It is difficult to credit that there is not one person, old or young, who does not weep on that day for all that the Lord suffered for them. When three o'clock comes, they have the reading from St John's Gospel where He gives up the spirit, then a prayer and the dismissal.

After this dismissal before the Cross, they go to the Great Church, the Martyrion, and have the same liturgy as on every weekday between three o'clock and the evening. Then, after the dismissal, they go to the Church of the Resurrection, where, once inside, the passage in the Gospel about Joseph asking Pilate for the Lord's body and placing it in a new tomb, is read. After this lesson and a prayer, the catechumens are blessed and the congregation dismissed.

On this day there is no announcement about keeping watch in the Church of the Resurrection, because everyone is so tired. Nevertheless it is the custom to keep a vigil there. As many as wish, or rather as many as are able, do this. But those unable to last out until morning do not stay. The vigil is kept by the clergy, or at least those young enough to do so. Throughout the night until morning there are hymns and antiphons. A great crowd does in fact manage to keep vigil, some beginning in the early evening, and some from midnight.

The following day is Saturday, and there are the usual services at nine o'clock and midday. But at about three o'clock they leave off the Saturday services and start to prepare for the paschal vigil in the Great Church, the Martyrion. The Paschal Vigil is kept by them as we do. There is only one additional element. As soon as the young have been baptised and clothed and have left the font, they are first led, along with the bishop, to the Church of the

Resurrection. The bishop goes behind the screen; a hymn is sung, and the bishop prays for them there. Then they return with him to the Great Church where all the rest of the congregation is continuing to keep vigil. The service which follows is similar to ours, with Mass being offered. Then after the Vigil Mass in the Great Church they go in procession with hymns to the Church of the Resurrection, where the Gospel of the Resurrection is read. There is further prayer, and then the bishop celebrates Mass. These ceremonies are not, however, drawn out, so as to avoid detaining the people too long. The dismissal is at about the same time as the Vigil Mass ends with us.

Egeria goes on to describe the services during the first eight days of Easter. The decorations and arrangement were similar to those for Epiphany; the services were held at all the main centres of worship: the Church of the Resurrection, the Great Church, at the Cross, on the Eleona, at the Lazarium and at Bethlehem. She particularly mentions, on the eighth day of Easter, the reading of the passage about the Lord rebuking St Thomas for his unbelief.

During the remainder of the Easter season until Pentecost not a single person fasted, even if they were one of those, like the apoctactites, who followed special fasting regimes. Fasting resumed after Pentecost. The Sunday of Pentecost began like a normal Sunday, but, after the dismissal at the Martyrion, the people went in procession singing hymns with their bishop to Sion where they arrived about nine o'clock. Egeria continues her account in this way.

When they arrive, there is a reading of the passage from the Acts of the Apostles which describes the descent of the Spirit, and how everyone speaking different languages could understand what was being said. The service then follows the normal pattern, with the Acts of the Apostles being read there. For this is the very spot on Sion where a church has now been built where the crowd once gathered with the Apostles after the Passion of the Lord. The service continues, and Mass is celebrated. At the dismissal, the archdeacon gives out this announcement. "Let us all meet at the Imbomon on the Eleona immediately after midday." Everyone returns home for a rest, then, after a meal, they ascend the Mount of Olives to the Eleona, going however, first to the Imbomon, the place from which the Lord ascended into heaven. Here the bishop takes his seat, together with all the priests and people. They have readings interspersed with hymns and prayers, all suitable for the day and the place. The passage from the Gospel is read about the Lord's Ascension into heaven after the Resurrection. Blessing of the catechumens and the faithful follows.

By now it is three o'clock and they go down the hill singing hymns to the church at the Eleona. This is where the Lord used to teach his apostles in a cave. By the time the procession arrives it is four o'clock and they have the Service of Light.

Egeria then describes the further services at the Martyrion, the Church of the Resurrection, and on Sion. The ceremonies ended at midnight after what Egeria decribes as a very hard day for them. The final section of Egeria's account which we include here describes the way in which catechumens were prepared and instructed for baptism at Easter.

Anyone wishing to be baptised gives his name in before Lent, and a priest makes a record of all the names. As I have explained, this is eight weeks before Easter. Once the priest has all the names, on the second day of Lent at the beginning of the eight weeks, the bishop's chair is placed in the middle of the Great Church, the Martyrion. The priests all sit around him; all the rest of the clergy stand. Each one seeking baptism is then brought forward, men with their fathers and women with their mothers.

As they come in one by one, the bishop asks their neighbours questions about them: "Is the person living a good life? Does he obey his parents? Is he a drunkard, or a boaster?" He also asks about other vices which are more serious. If his enquiries of the witnesses reveal that the person is free of these sins, the bishop himself notes down the name of the person. But if the witnesses sustain an accusation against someone, that person is told to leave. The bishops says that the person needs to make amends before he comes to the font. He makes the same enquiries of men and women. If someone is a stranger it is not easy for him to be prepared for baptism unless he has testimonies from those who know him.

Now my lady sisters, I must write something to prevent you reaching the conclusion that baptism is given to the candidates without adequate preparation. It is the custom during Lent that those who are accepted as candidates for baptism are exorcised by the clergy first thing in the morning, immediately after the early service in the Church of the Resurrection. After this the bishop's chair is set up in the Great Church of the Martyrion, and everyone under instruction for baptism sits around the bishop, both men and women. There is a place too where their mothers and fathers can stand.

But not everyone who wishes to listen can enter and sit down: only those who are already of the Faith. Catechumens who are not yet under instruction for baptism are not allowed in when the bishop teaches the others the law.

Throughout Lent the bishop teaches them the whole of scripture, beginning with the book of Genesis. First he explains the literal meaning of the text, and afterwards expounds its spiritual significance. Throughout the period he not only teaches them about the Resurrection, but everything else about the Faith. The instruction is known as catechising.

After five weeks of teaching they are given the Creed. The bishop explains the reasoning behind each of its articles, and, as with the scriptures, he first explains the literal sense, and then its spiritual significance. In this way the

Creed is explained in its entirety. And so when the scriptures are read in church all the people in this part of the world follow closely, since they have all been taught three hours of catechism a day (from six o'clock to nine o'clock) during Lent. God is my witness, my lady sisters, when I tell you that the faithful are more ready to speak up on points when they attend catechism classes, than when the same points are raised or expounded by the bishop when he is seated and preaches in church.

At nine o'clock the catechism class is dismissed, and the bishop is taken in a choral procession to the Church of the Resurrection. The teaching thus lasts for three hours a day for seven weeks. But in the eighth week, known as the Great Week, there is no time for them to have their catechism if they are to follow all the services described above. So when the seven weeks are over and Easter week is about to begin, the bishop comes at an early hour into the Martyrion. His chair is set up at the back of the apse behind the altar. One by one the candidates for baptism come forward, a man with his father, a woman with her mother, and they recite the Creed to the bishop.

When they have done this the bishop addresses them as follows: "During these last seven weeks you have been taught the whole of the law of scripture. You have heard about the Faith, and the resurrection of the body. You have also heard as much explanation of the Creed as you are capable of understanding as a catechumen.

But the teaching about baptism itself is a deeper mystery which should not be revealed to you while you are still a catechumen. Do not think that this is something which will not be explained to you. You will hear all about it during the eight days of Easter *after* you have been baptised. But while you are catechumens you ought not to be told about these deeper mysteries of God."

Then Easter comes, and on each of the eight days after this, once Mass has been celebrated, there is a procession with hymns to the Church of the Resurrection. After the bishop has offered prayer and given his blessing to the faithful he stands leaning against the screen in front of the cave and explains everything which has been achieved by baptism. No catechumen who has not been baptised may come here at this time, only the newly baptised and the faithful who wish to hear the mystery explained.

The doors are closed in case any catechumen tries to enter. While the bishop relates what has been done and explains its significance, the sound of the applause of the audience is so loud that it can be heard outside the Church. Indeed the manner in which he expounds the deeper mysteries of God cannot fail to touch all who hear him.

In this province there are those who know both Greek and Syriac, and some who only know one language or the other. The bishop may know Syriac, but he always uses Greek and never Syriac in services and teaching. So, when the bishop is speaking, one of the priests always translates into Syriac to ensure that everyone can understand the sense of his homily.

The lessons read in church also need to be in Greek. But there is always someone standing by to translate for those who do not know Greek, so that everyone receives instruction. Of course there are people here who speak neither Greek nor Syriac, but Latin. But they need not be put off, since some of the brothers and sisters who speak Latin as well as Greek will translate for them into Latin.

Egeria concludes this section of the account of her travels with a description of the ceremonies which commemorate the original consecration of the Martyrion and the Church of the Resurrection. The feast was called the Encaenia, and Egeria says that it was kept on the anniversary of the day when the Cross on which the Lord was crucified was discovered earlier in the fourth century. The feast lasted for eight days and ranked with Easter and Epiphany in the splendour of its celebration. She remarks that large numbers came to Jerusalem for this, from Mesopotamia, Syria, Egypt, and other provinces.

By a marvellous act of providence the text of a number of talks given to catechumens being prepared for baptism by a bishop of Jerusalem has survived from this period. Any unbaptised pilgrim who came to Jerusalem and was able to find sponsors to attest to his or her character and so be accepted as a catechumen, would have received instruction along these lines at this period, in the same way as the local catechumens.

St Cyril, who is believed to be the author of these lectures, was made bishop of Jerusalem in about 349. He was banished three times for his opposition to the Arian heresy. Those who endorsed this heretical teaching claimed that Jesus Christ was not equal to the Father, not eternal, and not divine by nature. St Cyril's last banishment, by the Arian Emperor Valens, was from 367 to 378. By the time of Egeria's pilgrimage St Cyril had returned to Jerusalem from his last exile, and he would have been in his late 60s. He died in 386, and was made a Doctor of the Church in 1883.

In her account of the liturgical ceremonies, Egeria gives no details about the Mass or the reception of Holy Communion. There are several possible reasons for this. First, the broad structure of the service was probably one with which she and the sisters to whom she was writing would have been familiar. Secondly, she was probably still reticent about committing to a letter some of the most sacred aspects of Catholic belief and liturgy. It should be recalled that the Church still had considerable reserve about telling non-Christians all the details of the Sacred Mysteries. In part this may have been influenced by natural caution arising from three hundred years of Christian persecution which had only ceased in the early part of the century. It is also possible that Egeria's command of Greek may not have been sufficiently proficient to pick out any significant elements where the rite differed from the one which would have been in use in her homeland and religious community.

The text below is from St Cyril's Catechetical Lecture XXIII on the Sacred Mysteries. As can be seen, it is the last in the series, and was almost certainly given to catechumens after they had received baptism at Easter, and hence had become part of the *community of the faithful. The text of this actual lecture was probably delivered early in St Cyril's episcopacy, but the nature of the catechetical teaching was likely to have been very similar in his later years as bishop. The version is freely based on a translation made by R W Church, and edited by Cardinal Newman before the latter was received into the Roman Catholic Church.*

WHEN we met earlier, God's loving-kindness enabled you to learn what you needed to know about Baptism, Chrism, and the receiving of the Body and Blood of Christ. Now today we need to move on to the next topic so as to complete your spiritual education.

You saw that the Deacon gave the celebrant and the other priests who stood around God's altar water with which to wash. He did not give this to them because their bodies were unclean. Not at all! For we did not set off for church with our bodies unclean. But the washing of the hands is rather a sign that one should be pure and free from all sinful and unlawful acts. For, since the hands are a symbol of action, by washing them we represent the purity and blamelessness of our conduct. Have you not heard how the blessed David revealed this mystery when he said, "I wash my hands in innocence, and go about Thy Altar, O Lord"? The washing of hands is therefore a sign of freedom from sin.

Then the Deacon cries aloud, "Greet one another, and let us kiss each other." Do not think that this kiss is equivalent to those kisses exchanged in public among ordinary friends. It is by no means the same. This kiss blends souls to each other and seeks a complete mutual forgiveness. This kiss is therefore the sign that our souls are mingled together, and that all remembrance of injuries has been banished. It was for this that Christ said, "If you are offering your gift at the altar, and there remember that your brother has something against you, leave your gift there before the altar, and go; first be reconciled to your brother, and then come and offer your gift." The kiss then is an act of reconciliation, and for this reason holy Blessed Paul in his Epistles encouraged us to do this: "Greet one another with a holy kiss", and Peter spoke of "a kiss of charity."

The Priest then cries aloud, "Lift up your hearts." At that very solemn time we really should raise our heart high up to God, and not leave it below, concerning itself with the world and worldly things. The Priest then in effect bids all at that moment lay aside every worldly thought or household care, and set their heart in heaven and on the merciful God. Then you make the response, "We lift them up unto the Lord." By this we indicate our agreement and commitment. No one should come here, who says with his lips "We lift up our hearts to the Lord," yet keeps his mind occupied with thoughts about the business of the world. God should certainly be kept in mind at all times. But, if this proves impossible because of our human weakness, we should at least make an earnest effort to do so at this time.

The Priest then says, "Let us give thanks to the Lord." It is really right that we should give thanks because He has called us to this great grace, unworthy as we are, and has reconciled us who were His enemies, and has bestowed on us the Spirit of adoption. Then you say, "It is meet and right." For in giving thanks we do something which is fitting and right. What He did was not simply something right, but something that was more than right, since He did good for us and counted us worthy of such great benefits.

After this, we make mention of heaven and earth, and the sea, the sun and the moon, the stars and all of creation, rational and irrational, visible and invisible; of Angels, Archangels, Virtues, Dominions, Principalities, Powers and Thrones; of the Cherubim with many faces. In effect we are repeating that call of David, "Magnify the Lord with me." We also mention the Seraphim, whom Isaiah, through the power of the Holy Spirit, saw encircling the throne of God. With two of their wings they were veiling their faces, and with two their feet, and with two they were flying; they were crying out, "Holy, Holy, Holy, Lord God of Sabaoth." This is why we repeat this acknowledgement of God, which was passed down to us from the Seraphim, so that we may join in hymns with the Hosts of the world above.

After we have sanctified ourselves with these spiritual hymns, we call upon the merciful God to send forth His Holy Spirit upon the gifts lying before Him, that He may make the Bread the Body of Christ, and the Wine the Blood of Christ; for whatever the Holy Ghost has touched, is sanctified and changed.

Then, after the spiritual sacrifice is perfected—that is the bloodless rite made over that sacrifice of propitiation—we pray to God for the general peace of the Church and for the tranquility of the world; we pray for kings, for soldiers and allies; for the sick, and for the afflicted. In brief everyone present prays for and offers this Sacrifice for all those who stand in need of help.

Then we call to mind all those who have in the past fallen asleep: first, Patriarchs, Prophets, Apostles, and Martyrs, so that, following their prayers and intervention, God may receive our requests. Afterwards, we also call to mind the holy fathers and bishops who have fallen asleep before our time, and indeed all who have fallen asleep among us. We believe that this will be of very great advantage to the souls for whom our prayers are offered, when these prayers are made while the Holy and most Solemn Sacrifice is being presented.

I would like to persuade you of this point by an illustration. I know that many question how it can help a soul which leaves this world, either burdened with sins or without sins, if it is commemorated in this prayer? But surely, if a king had exiled some people who had offended him, and their close friends wove a crown and offered it to him on behalf of those from whom he was seeking revenge, would he not be likely to alleviate their punishments?

When we offer Him prayers for those who have fallen asleep, even though they have been sinners, and rather than weaving a crown and offering it to Him, we offer up Christ, who was sacrificed for our sins, we are doing something similar. In this way we propitiate our merciful God on their behalf, and on our own.

After this, we say, with a pure conscience, the prayer which the Saviour bestowed on His own disciples, in which we call God our Father. We say, "Our Father, who art in heaven." O most surpassing loving-kindness of God! For to those who have broken away from Him, and were in the depths of misery, he has granted a full pardon for their evil action, and such a share of grace as to be able to call Him Father. "Our Father, who art in heaven." They too are in heaven who bear the image of the heavenly. God is "dwelling and walking in them."

"Hallowed be Thy Name." The Name of God is of its very nature holy, whether we say it or not. But since sinners abuse it—as Scripture says, "Through you My Name is continually blasphemed among the Gentiles,"—we pray that God's Name may be kept sacred among us. Of course it does not become holy simply because we become holy and act in a way worthy of holiness!

"Thy kingdom come." The uncorrupted soul can boldly say, "Thy kingdom come;" for he who has heard the words of Paul, "Let not sin reign in your mortal body," but has cleaned himself up in his actions, thoughts and words, will say to God, "Thy kingdom come."

"Thy will be done as in heaven so in earth." The divine and blessed Angels do the will of God, as David has said in one of the psalms, "Bless the Lord, O you His Angels, you mighty ones that do His word." So you mean by your prayer. "As Thy will is done by the Angels, so be it done on earth also by me, Lord."

"Give us this day our super-substantial bread." Ordinary bread is not super-substantial bread. But *this* Bread has been ordained as food for the soul. For this Bread "passes" not "into the stomach and so passes on," but is diffused through all your being, for the benefit of the body and soul. By "this day" our Lord means, "each day," as Paul has confirmed.

"And forgive us our debts as we forgive our debtors." For we have many sins since we offend both in word and in thought, and very many things we do are worthy of condemnation; and "if we say that we have no sin," we lie, as John says. So we enter into an agreement with God, asking Him to pardon our sins, while we also forgive our neighbours their debts to us. If we consider what we ourselves receive, and what it is in return for, let us not omit nor delay our forgiving of one another.

The offences committed against us are slight and trivial, and easily settled. But those which we have committed against God are enormous. They call for the mercy which only He offers. Be careful that you do not allow those unimportant sins of others against you to block out God's forgiveness of yourself for your most serious sins.

"And lead us not into temptation, O Lord." Does the Lord teach us then to pray like this so that we may not be tempted at all? How then is it said elsewhere, "the man who is not tempted, is unproved;" and again, "Count it all joy, my brethren, when you have various trials"? But does not entering into temptation rather mean being completely overwhelmed by temptation? For temptation is like a winter-torrent, difficult to cross. Some then, being very skilful swimmers, get across, and are not sunk beneath temptations, nor swept away by them. While others who have not acquired this ability, enter into them and sink.

For example, Judas entering into the temptation of greed, did not swim through it, but sank beneath it, and was drowned both in body and soul. Peter entered into the temptation of denying Christ, but having entered it, he was not drowned by it, but vigorously went on swimming through it, and was rescued from the temptation.

Listen to another example from Scripture where those who held out give thanks for their rescue from temptation, "For Thou, O God, hast tested us; Thou hast tried us as silver is tried. Thou didst bring us into the net; Thou didst lay affliction on our loins; Thou didst let men ride over our heads; we went through fire and through water; yet Thou broughtest us forth to a spacious place." You see them speaking confidently, because they have passed through the test and their integrity was not damaged. Being brought out to a spacious place, is what is meant by being delivered from temptation.

"But deliver us from the evil." If "Lead us not into temptation" had implied not being tempted at all, He would not have said, "But deliver us from the evil." Now the evil is the Wicked Spirit who is our enemy. We pray to be delivered from him.

After completing the prayer, you say "Amen." By this Amen, which means "So be it", you set your personal seal to the petitions of this prayer which the Divine has taught us.

The Priest then says, "Holy things to holy men." The gifts presented are holy, since they have been visited by the Holy Spirit. You are holy also, since you have by grace accepted the Holy Spirit. The holy things then correspond to the holy persons. Then you say, "One is Holy, one is the Lord, Jesus Christ." For truly the One is holy, by nature holy. We too are holy, but this is not by nature, only by participation, and discipline and prayer.

After this you hear the cantor begin a sacred chant inviting you to the Communion of the Holy Mysteries, with the words "O taste and see that the Lord is good." Do not base your experience of this on the perception of your palate, but on your unswerving faith. For when we taste, we are invited to taste not bread and wine, but the sacrament of the Body and Blood of Christ.

When you come forward do not do so with your palms oustretched or your fingers open, but make your left hand a throne for your right, which is about to receive your King. Once He has hallowed the palm, take up the Body of Christ, saying as you do, Amen. Then when you have carefully blessed your eyes by the touch of the Holy Body, consume it, taking care that you do not lose any of it. For what you lose is rather like losing one of your own limbs. For tell me, if any one gave you gold dust, would you not carefully treasure it, and guard against losing any of it and suffering such loss? How much more carefully should you ensure that you do not let slip a crumb of what is more valuable than gold and precious stones!

After you have partaken of the body of Christ, approach the Cup of His Blood. Do not stretch out your hands, but bend down and say in worship and reverence "Amen". Be hallowed too when you partake of the blood of Christ: so while the moisture is still upon your lips, touch this with your hands, then hallow both your eyes, your brow and your other senses. Then wait for the prayer, and give thanks to God, who has accepted you as worthy of receiving these great mysteries.

Hold on to these traditions exactly, and keep yourselves free from offences. Do not cut yourselves off from Communion, nor, by the stain of sin, deprive yourselves of these Holy and Spiritual Mysteries. And may the God of peace completely sanctify you, and may your spirit, soul and body be kept spotless until the coming of our Lord Jesus Christ: to whom be glory and honour and might, with the Father and the Holy Spirit, now and forever, world without end. Amen.

Egeria mentions that there were some Latin speakers at Jerusalem at the time of her pilgrimage. St Jerome was one of these. He came to Jerusalem in 385 and settled subsequently in Bethlehem, following earlier visits by his friends Rufinus and St Melania the Elder. St Jerome had been in the East in the 370s when he had lived in Syria; and later he spent time with hermits in the desert east of Antioch, where he learnt Hebrew from a rabbi. He was subsequently at Constantinople. From 382-385 he acted as Secretary to Pope Damasus I in Rome, who asked him to revise the Latin version of the New Testament. Here he became the spiritual director of a group of pious Roman women, who had renounced the pleasures of society, disposed of their wealth, and devoted themselves to serious Christian study and practice.

After the death of Pope Damasus, St. Jerome returned to the East, and eventually settled at Bethlehem. Some of his Roman

*women friends joined him there, including St. Paula and her
daughter, St. Eustochium. From Jerusalem St Paula wrote a letter to their friend, Marcella, who had stayed on in Rome. The
letter conveys something of the spirit of those who made the journey to the Holy Places at that time, and made their home there.
It is in part a justification for their own pilgrimage, and in part
an exhortation and encouragement to Marcella and others in
Rome to make the journey themselves.*

I F, after the Passion of our Lord, this place is accursed, as the
wicked say, what did St. Paul mean by hastening to
Jerusalem, that he might keep the day of Pentecost there?
Why did he address those who would have held him back,
saying: "What are you doing, weeping and breaking my
heart? For I am ready to die at Jerusalem for the name of the
Lord Jesus." What did all those other holy and famous men
mean, when, following the teaching of Christ, they sent alms
and oblations to their brothers who were in Jerusalem?

It would be a long task to mention, year by year, from the
Ascension of our Lord to the present day, how many bishops, martyrs, and men eloquent in ecclesiastical learning,
have come to Jerusalem, thinking themselves to be lacking
in religion and in learning, and not to have received, as the
saying is, a full handful of virtues, unless they had adored
Christ in the very places from which the Gospel first shone
forth from the Cross.

Indeed, if even a distinguished orator (Cicero) thought
somebody worthy of criticism because he had learned
Greek, not at Athens but at Lilybaeum, and had learned
Latin, not at Rome but in Sicily,—since of course each
province has something peculiar to itself, that another cannot possess in the same degree—why should we suppose
that anyone can reach the highest pitch of devotion without the help of *our* Athens? Yet we do not say this because
we deny that the kingdom of God is *within us*, or that holy
men exist in other regions too. But because what we specially affirm is this, that those who are the foremost men of

the whole earth all alike flock here together.

We have come to these places, not as people of importance, but as strangers, that we might see here the leading
men of all nations. Indeed, the company of monks and nuns
here is a flower and a jewel of great price among the ornaments of the Church. Whoever happen to be the first men
in Gaul hasten hither. The Briton is cut off from our world,
yet, if he has made any progress in religion, he leaves the
setting sun, and seeks a place known only to him by its reputation and the narrative of the Scriptures.

Do we need to mention the Armenians, the Persians, the
nations of India and Ethiopia, and the neighbouring country of Egypt, which overflows with its monks; Pontus and
Cappadocia, Coele-Syria, and Mesopotamia, and all the
many peoples of the East? All these are fulfilling the words
of our Saviour when he said, "Wherever the body is, there
the eagles will be gathered together." For they flock here to
these sacred places and display for us exemplars of their
diverse excellent virtues.

Their languages differ, but their religion is one. There are
almost as many choirs of psalm-singers here as there are different nations. Here in this place will be found what is perhaps the greatest virtue among Christians—a lack of arro-
gance, and no overwheening pride in their chastity. All of
them rather vie with one another in humility. Whoever is
last is reckoned first. In their dress there is no distinction,
no ostentation. The order in which they walk in procession
neither implies disgrace nor confers honour. Fasts fill no
one with pride, abstinence is not commended, nor, being
moderately full, condemned. Every man stands or falls by
the judgement of his own Lord. No one judges another, in
case he should be judged by the Lord. Here the practice of
spiteful criticism, so common in most countries, finds
absolutely no place. Nor are luxury and self-indulgence
found here.

There are so many places of prayer in the city itself, that
one day is inadequate for visiting them all. As to the village

of Christ and the inn of Mary (for everyone praises most
where he lives himself), how can I find the language and
forms of expression to describe to you the grotto of the
Saviour? The manger, too, where the Baby cried, is better
honoured by silence than by imperfect phrases.

Yet where are the spacious porticoes which you have
where *you* live? Where are the gilded ceilings? Where are
the houses decorated as a product of the suffering and
labours of miserable condemned men? Where are the houses, built through the wealth of private men on the scale of
palaces, through which the corrupt body of a man may
move among costly surroundings, and gaze at his own ceiling rather than at the heavens? As if anything could be
more beautiful than creation itself! See, in this little nook
of the world, the very Founder of the heavens themselves
was born! Here He was wrapped in swaddling clothes, was
gazed on by the shepherds, pin-pointed by the star, adored
by the wise men. This place, I believe, is holier than the
Tarpeian Rock in Rome. The fact that it is frequently
struck by lightning shows that it is pleasing to God!

Read the Revelation of John, and consider what he says
of the scarlet woman, and the blasphemies written upon
her brow. Consider the seven hills, the many floods, and
the fall of Babylon. "Come out of her," saith the Lord;
"come out of her, my people, lest you take part in her sins,
lest you share in her plagues." And turning back to
Jeremiah, listen to a similar quotation from Scripture.
"Flee from the midst of Babylon, let every man save his
life." John warns us: "Fallen, fallen is Babylon the great! It
has become a dwelling place of demons and a haunt of
every foul spirit."

True, *there* (at Rome) is the Holy Church, and the tri-
umphs of the Apostles and Martyrs, *there* is the true confession of Christ, the faith preached by the Apostle and
despised by the Gentiles, *there* the name of "Christian" is
daily exalted. But *there* too is worldliness, authority, the life
of a great city, meetings and exchanges of greetings, praise

and blame of one another, listening or talking to other people, or even, against one's will, meeting vast crowds of people! All this is quite foreign to the ideal of quiet seclusion set before *monks*. Yet *there*, if we do venture to make visits, we are accused of pride. Yet when we return the calls of our visitors, and go to the doors of their proud houses, we are sometimes the butt of patronizing remarks from the servants as we enter their gilded doorways!

But *here* in the village of Christ, as we have written to you before, all is the simple country life and, except for the singing of psalms, *silence.*  Wherever you turn, the ploughman, holding the plough-handle, sings *Alleluia.* The sweating reaper entertains himself with psalms, and the vine-dresser sings some of the songs of David while he trims the vines with his curved knife. These are the ballads of this country, these are their love-songs, as they are commonly called. They are whistled by the shepherds, and serve as the past-times of the farmer. Indeed we do not reflect on what we are doing or on how we look, but we only see that for which we are longing.

Oh, how I long for the time when a messenger, out of breath, shall bring us news that our Marcella has reached the shore of Palestine! Then all the choirs of monks and troops of nuns shall shout out in rapturous joy. We are already eager to set off, and though no vehicle is expected, yet we want to run off to meet one. We shall grasp your hands, we shall gaze on your face, and shall hardly be able to break free of your embrace!

When will that day come on which we shall be able to enter the grotto of our Saviour at Bethlehem and weep there with our sister; and, with our mother at our side, in the

Sepulchre of the Lord at Jerusalem; and afterwards kiss the wood of the Cross, and, on the Mount of Olives, with our ascending Lord, lift up our hearts and fulfil our vows; and see Lazarus come forth bound with his grave clothes, and the waters of the Jordan, made more pure by the baptism of the Lord? And then go out to the sheepfolds of the shepherds, and pray in the tomb of David! And see Amos, the prophet, even now sounding a lament on his rock with his shepherd's horn! And hurry off to the tabernacles or tombs of Abraham, Isaac and Jacob and their three noble wives! And see the fountain where the eunuch was baptised by Philip! And go to Samaria, and adore with equal fervour the ashes of John the Baptist, Elisha, and Abdia! And enter the caves, where in time of persecution and famine, troops of prophets were fed.

We shall go together to Nazareth, the flower of Galilee, as its name signifies. Not far from there we shall see Cana where the water was turned into wine. We shall go to Mount Tabor, and there see the tabernacles of the Saviour, not as Peter would have built them, with Moses and Elijah, but with the Father and the Holy Spirit. From there we shall come to Gennesareth, and see where the five and four thousand men were fed in the desert with five and with seven loaves. Before us will then appear the city of Naim, at whose gates the widow's son was raised from the dead.

We shall see Hermonium too, and the brook of Endor, where Sisera was overcome; and Capernaum, that familiar witness of the miracles of our Lord; and indeed the whole of Galilee! Then, accompanied by Christ, after passing though Silo and Bethel, and the other places where the banners of the Church have been raised to celebrate the victories of the Lord, we will sing constantly on our return to our grotto at Bethlehem. We will weep often, and pray without ceasing; and, wounded by the arrow of our Saviour, we will repeat together, "I have found Him whom my soul sought for; I will hold Him fast and will not let Him go."

As it happened Marcella resisted this impassioned plea from her friend to make the long journey to the Holy Places. She remained in Rome occupied with her work for the Roman poor. And there she died in 410 from injuries that she received during the sack of Rome by the Gothic king, Alaric.

Barbarian invasions continued in much of Western Europe and North Africa during the fifth century. Visigoth kingdoms were established in Gaul and the Iberian peninsular. Rome was taken by the Vandals in 455, and, by the end of the century, the Ostrogoths had established their kingdom in Italy. The British monk, Pelagius, who denied the doctrine of original sin, was condemned by a synod at Rome under Pope Innocent I in 416.

In 431, the Council of Ephesus condemned the teaching of Nestorius, bishop of Constantinople, who had argued that there were two natures in Jesus Christ as a man, and that the Blessed Virgin Mary was only the mother of Christ as a man and not the mother of God. The Council then triumphantly proclaimed Mary as the Mother of God. In 451 the Council of Chalcedon further refined the Church's understanding of Christ: it declared that while Christ was one person there was in Him not one nature but two. This was a condemnation of Monophysitism (one nature of Christ). But it was never accepted by the church in Alexandria and the rest of Egypt. Chalcedon also freed Jerusalem from the jurisdiction of Caesarea and elevated it to the fifth place in honour after the great sees of Rome, Constantinople, Alexandria and Antioch.

The fifth century also saw the further development of monasticism in the Holy Land, with St Sabas being given oversight of all the monks in Palestine in 493. Justinian was emperor of the East from 527-565: he provided a garrison to protect Palestinian monasteries and destroyed the power of Vandals in North Africa. In Jerusalem he built a new hospital for pilgrims, and completed a church in honour of the Mother of God which was dedicated in 543.

CHAPTER TWO

CROSS AND CRESCENT

*T*HE *early part of the seventh century witnessed the birth of Islam, and conflicts between the Persians and the eastern emperors. The prophet Muhammad appeared in Mecca in 610. Persian armies took Anatolia and Syria from the Eastern Empire: Antioch fell in 611 and Damascus in 613. After the capture of Jerusalem by the Persians in 614, most of the churches in the Holy Places were burned. Only the Church of the Nativity in Bethlehem was spared, reportedly because a mosaic over the entrance depicted the Wise Men from the east in Persian costume, which allegedly softened the invaders' hearts.*

During the siege of Jerusalem the Christian inhabitants refused to surrender the city. It was finally taken because the Persians were assisted by the Jews within the city. When it was captured, Christians were indiscriminately massacred, some by Persian soldiers, and many more by the Jews. 60,000 Christians were said to have been slain, and a further 35,000 sold into slavery. The part played by the Jews in the fall of Jerusalem was never forgotten.

But the Persian triumph was short lived. Heraclius, the Greek Emperor, who ruled from Constantinople, rallied his forces, and after a major Greek success at the battle of Niniveh in 627, and the murder of Chroeses II in 628, the Persians sued for peace. The Holy Cross and instruments of the Passion, which had been sent for safe-keeping by the Patriarch of Jerusalem to the Queen of Persia, who was a Nestorian Christian, were brought back to Jerusalem in triumph. Many Jews were now massacred in their turn by the Christians because of the part they had played in the capture of the city by the Persians.

Some rebuilding of the Jerusalem churches took place after the city was recaptured. But in 637 the city was again taken, this time by Arab followers of the prophet Muhammad under

Caliph Omar I. The Bishop of Jerusalem had vowed that he would only hand over the city to Omar personally, and not to any of his generals. So Omar came himself, riding into Jerusalem on a white camel. But the holy relics of Christ had already been taken for safe-keeping to Constantinople. Within twenty years Antioch and Alexandria had also fallen to the Arabs, and the Persians had been defeated by them at the battles of Kadesiah and Nekhavend in 637 and 638. By 651 the Arabs had reached the Oxus and the frontiers of Afghanistan, and by the end of the century the whole of North Africa was under their control.

Arculf, a French bishop, went to Jerusalem in 670 during the first thirty years of Arab rule in Jerusalem. While returning from the Holy Places to France, his ship was blown completely off course in the Atlantic. A landing was finally made at one of the western-most points of Scotland. After many dangers he reached Iona, where he became the guest of Adamnan, the Abbot of the Monastery of Hy. St Adamnan, as he was known later, was fascinated by Arculf's story of his nine month visit to the Holy Land, and wrote a detailed account of what he was told. The Venerable Bede had a high regard for the usefulness of Adamnan's work.

IN the name of the Father, of the Son, and of the Holy Spirit. I am about to write a book about the Holy Places.

Arculf, a holy bishop and native of Gaul, was well acquainted with many far distant lands. He is a truthful and judicious observer. For a period of nine months he lived in the city of Jerusalem and examined the Holy Places during daily visits. He told me, Adamnan, all that is written here, when I pressed him to tell me all about his experiences. I then wrote down his trustworthy and accurate account, first on wax tablets as he dictated it to me, and now briefly on parchment. As to the topography and facts about Jerusalem, we shall include here the details which the saintly Arculf dictated to me, Adamnan. But what is found in the books of others about the plan of the city we shall omit.

In the great circuit of its walls, Arculf counted eighty-four towers and six gates, which are placed in the following order around the city: the Gate of David, on the west side of Mt Sion, is reckoned the first; the second is the Gate of the Place of the Fuller; the third, the Gate of St. Stephen; the fourth, the Gate of Benjamin; the fifth, a little gate from which steps descend to the Valley of Jehoshaphat; and the sixth, the Gate Thecuitis...

On the 15th of September every year a large crowd of people of every nationality assemble from all over Jerusalem, and from further afield, to buy and sell. The city plays host to the crowds for some days. Great numbers of the visitors' camels, horses and donkeys, as well as mules and oxen, which carry baggage and produce, fill the city streets. The dung produced is prodigious, and the smell much in excess of what the citizens ordinarily have to bear! Even walking about becomes difficult! What is extraordinary is that on the very night when the various beasts of burden owned by the traders and visitors leave, clouds bring heavy rain on to the city and this washes all the filth from the streets and completely cleanses them.

The special setting of Jerusalem, which has its outskirts on the northern tip of Mount Sion, has been well arranged by God, its founder. There is a steep slope, which descends to the lower level where the northern and eastern walls are. As a result heavy rain does not settle in the streets as stagnant pools. Instead rainwater rushes down like a river torrent from the upper to the lower parts of the city. This torrent from heaven flows through the eastern gate and carries all the filth down into the valley of Jehoshaphat and swells the torrent of Kidron.

Once Jerusalem has been baptised in this way the rain always ceases! We should therefore be careful to note how much the Eternal Father honours the glorious city He has chosen, since He does not permit it to remain filthy for long. But, to give honour to His Only Begotten, He cleans it quickly in this way, for the very reason that, within the compass of its walls, are contained the honoured sites of His sacred Cross and Resurrection.

In the famous place where once the magnificent Temple of Solomon stood, on a site near the east wall, the Saracens now frequent a four-sided house of prayer. They have built this in a crude way by raising boards and great beams on what is left of the ruins. The structure is said to be able to hold three thousand men at once.

When we asked him about the buildings in the city in which ordinary people lived, Arculph's response was: "I remember that I saw and visited many of the city's buildings. A good many of those I saw within the city walls were large houses of stone. The walls themselves were constructed with wonderful skill." But we must, I believe, omit a description of these. But I make an exception of the marvellous construction of those buildings built in the Holy Places, that is on the sites of the Cross and of the Resurrection. We questioned Arculf very carefully about these, especially about the Sepulchre of the Lord and the Church built over it. Arculf himself drew a sketch for me on a wax tablet.

This very large church is entirely made of stone and is totally round. It rises from its foundation on three walls. There is a broad passage between each wall and the next. In three cleverly constructed spaces on the middle wall three altars have been built: one faces south, one north, and one west. This round and lofty church is supported by twelve columns of amazing width. There are eight doors or entrances in the three walls which are set in the gaps between the passages. Four of these doors face south-east, and four, north-east.

In the centre of this circular church there is a round chamber, cut out of a single piece of rock, within which there is a space for nine men to stand and pray. The vaulted roof is about a foot and a half above the head of a man of reasonable height. The entrance to this little chamber faces east. The whole of the external surface of the chamber is covered with choice marble, and on the highest part of the outer roof, which is ornamented with gold, there is a gold cross of considerable size. The Sepulchre of the Lord is in the north part of the chamber, and is cut out of the same rock as the chamber. But the pavement of the chamber is lower than the place of burial. The burial tomb is about the width of three palms up from the pavement of the chamber. The Sepulchre, as it is properly called, is in the north part of the monumental chamber, where the body, wrapped in linen clothes, was deposited. Arculf measured this with his own hand as seven feet in length. The Sepulchre is not, as some erroneously believe, shaped in a double form so as to follow the contours of a body with a projection of solid rock between and separating the legs and thighs. But it is simple and plain from head to foot. It is a couch which provides space for one man lying on his back. It is in the form of a cave, having its opening at the side opposite the south part of the monumental chamber. The low roof above it has been artificially carved. In the Sepulchre there are twelve lamps burning, according to the number of the twelve Apostles. They are kept burning day and night. Four are placed in the inner part of the tomb and the other eight up on the right hand side. They shine brightly because they are regularly supplied with oil.

You should also be aware that the Mausoleum or Sepulchre of the Saviour, that is the chamber which is often mentioned, may be properly called a grotto or cave. It was about this place, and the burial of our Lord Jesus Christ in it, that the Prophet foretold when he said, "He shall dwell in a most lofty cave of a most strong rock." And a little later, to bring joy to the Apostles, he includes this passage on the Resurrection of the Lord, "You shall see the King with glory"…

At this point it seems appropriate to say something in brief about the stone which was rolled into the entrance of the tomb of the Lord, after He was betrayed by many, crucified and buried. Arculf relates that this stone was broken and divided into two parts. The smaller piece, which was roughly worked with tools, can be seen as a square altar in the round church described above. It is placed before the entrance of the chamber which forms the Lord's tomb. The larger piece of stone, which is likewise worked, is fixed in the eastern part of the church as a four sided altar under linen cloths.…

The chamber of the Lord's monument is not at this time adorned with any ornaments. To this day it exhibits the marks of the workmen's tools with which it was excavated. The colour of the rock of the monument and the Sepulchre is not uniform, but a mixture of red and white.…

I should add some details about the other buildings of the Holy Places. The four-sided church of St Mary, the mother of the Lord, is nearby on the right side of the round church mentioned above—the latter is known as the Church of the Resurrection because it was built on the spot where the Lord rose from the dead. Another very large church, which faces east, has been built high up on that place which in Hebrew is called Golgotha. In this there is a great chandelier of brass, with lamps suspended from it by ropes; and below this there has been set up a great silver cross, fixed in the same spot where the wooden cross was fixed on which the Saviour of the human race suffered. In this church, below the site of the Lord's Cross, a cave has been cut out in the rock, where the sacrifice is offered for certain specially honoured people. While this occurs their bodies are laid in a court before the gate of the Church of Golgotha until the Holy Mysteries on their behalf have been completed.

Nearby, to the east of this four-sided church built on the site of Calvary, there is a stone basilica. This was built as an act of devotion by the emperor Constantine. It is called the Martyrion, since it was built on the site where the Cross of the Lord, which had been hidden under the earth, was found, along with the two crosses of the robbers. The Lord allowed this to be found two hundred and thirty-three years after his death.

Between these two churches lies the famous place where the patriarch Abraham built an altar. Here he laid the pile of wood and seized a drawn sword to offer his own son, Isaac, in sacrifice. At the present time there is a wooden table of considerable size here on which alms for the poor are offered by the people. Between the Church of the Resurrection, that is the round church, and the Basilica of Constantine, the Martyrion, lies a small square extending to the Church of Golgotha, where lamps always burn day and night...

The sacred and honoured place where the Lord was baptised by John is always covered by the waters of the river Jordan. Arculf recounts that he went back and forth to the very spot through the river. A wooden cross of great size has been erected on the sacred spot. When the river is flowing normally it is at a point where the water comes up to the neck of a very tall man. In time of drought it would come up to his breast. At flood tide the cross is completely covered. The site of the cross is on this side of the bed of the river. A strong man could sling a stone from there to the Arabian bank of the river.

...On the river bank there is a small church, on the spot where, it is said, the garments of the Lord were taken care of during his baptism. It stands over the water, so that it is unusable as a church. Water flows under it on both sides, and it is supported on four stone vaults and arches. On higher ground, a great monastery for monks has been built on the brow of the opposite hill. Within this is a chapel in honour of St John the Baptist built of squared stones.

The city of Nazareth is situated on a mountain, according to Arculf, who stayed there. Like Capernaum, it is unwalled. It has large houses built of stone, and two very big churches. One of these, in the middle of the city, is built upon two vaults; it is on the site of the dwelling where our Lord the Saviour was brought up. Along the banks at the foot of the church is a very clear spring. This is frequented by all the citizens who draw water from it. Water is also raised up to the church from the spring in buckets by means of pulleys. The second church is reputed to have been built on the site of the house in which the Archangel Gabriel came and addressed the Blessed Mary, when he found her there alone at the appointed hour. This is information which we received from Arculf who stayed two days and nights in Nazareth. He was prevented from staying longer because he was with a Burgundian hermit named Peter. We were told that this soldier of Christ subsequently returned by a circuitous route to the hermitage where he had previously been living.

Some forty years later, about 720, an Englishman, while still a young man, visited the Holy Places. Palestine was in Arab hands, and ruled by the Ommayad dynasty from Damascus. Yet a few years before his visit, the Eastern Empire had been saved from complete Arab domination by Leo II who defeated the Arabs at Constantinople in 717-18. St Willibald, as he was later known, had royal connections in Wessex, and, through his mother, was a nephew of Wynfrith, better known as St Boniface, the Apostle of Germany. In the 720s Willibald set out with his father and his younger brother, Winebald, on a pilgrimage to Rome. The journey through France was hazardous. It is unclear whether they went before or after the Saracens had been stopped from further progress into Europe by their defeat by Duke Eudes beneath the walls of Toulouse. But the Arabs had already conquered much of Spain in 711-712, and the security situation for the traveller in both western and eastern Europe remained dangerous.

Willibald's father died at Lucca in Italy and was buried there. Winebald seems to have returned home after the visit to Rome. But Willibald decided to go on to see the Holy Places. The extract below is taken from an account of Willibald's visit which is part of a memoir which the saint himself dictated, when an old man, to Roswida, a nun of Heidenheim. By then St Willibald was a bishop. He had spent his life assisting his uncle, St Boniface, on the German mission where his work had been centred on Eichstadt. From here Willibald preached the Gospel to the roving tribes who hunted in the region. After acting as his uncle's chancellor for some years, he was made bishop of Eichstadt. When St Boniface was martyred by the pagan Frieslanders in 754, St Willibald began to play a leading role among the German bishops. He lived to be over eighty and is buried in his cathedral at Eichstadt.

St Willibald's journey from Italy to the Holy Places was by sea. He had with him a travelling companion, Tidbert. Beginning at Naples, their ship sailed to Reggio in Calabria, and then across to Sicily. They then crossed the Adriatic Sea to the west coast of Greece, then went on down the coast of Asia Minor calling in at some of the Greek islands. When the ship reached Cyprus, they remained there for Easter. The journey now became more difficult politically, for much of the area of the mainland on the land route to Jerusalem had been in Arab hands for about eighty years.

SAILING from Cyprus, they came to the city of Tharratae (Tartus) which is near the sea in the territory of the Saracens. From there they went on foot for about nine to twelve miles to a village called Arche (probably Husn el-Akrad). Here there was a bishop of the Greeks, and the pilgrims heard the Litany in the Greek rite. They walked on to Emesa (Homs) twelve miles further on, where there is a large church, which St Helena had built in honour of St

John the Baptist. For a long time St John's head, which is now in Syria, was there.

With Willibald there were seven of his fellow-countrymen—he made the eighth. When the Saracens heard that unknown strangers had arrived in the town, they arrested the company and held them in prison. Since the authorities were unaware of their nationality they assumed that they were spies. While prisoners, they were taken for interrogation to a wealthy elderly man whose role was to discover where they came from. He questioned them about their country of origin and their business. In their reply they gave a full account of their journey and its purpose.

The old man reached the following conclusion: "I have often seen men who are countrymen of these strangers and who have come from these foreign parts. They have no sinister intentions. They simply wish to fulfil their law." The prisoners then left him, and went to the administrative headquarters to ask the way to Jerusalem. But on arriving there, the governor still insisted that they were spies, and ordered them to be kept in prison until he could obtain instructions from the king of those parts about what should be done with them.

Yet as soon as they were back in prison they had an immediate experience of the marvellous providence of Almighty God. For He defends His own everywhere, when they are surrounded by weapons and instruments of war, or when they are among barbarians and soldiers, or in prison; he protects them and keeps them safe if they fall into the hands of their enemies. Now there happened to be a merchant in the town who resolved to purchase their release from prison. He regarded this as an act of charity and one which would benefit his own soul. His hope was that they might be set free and be able to go where they wished. However, when he was unable to achieve this straight away, he began sending them a main meal and supper every day. On Wednesday and Saturday he also sent his son to the prison to take them to the town bath, and to escort them back to prison. On Sunday he conducted them to church. He took them through the market, so that they could see what was for sale. And he purchased, at his own expense, anything which the prisoners had a mind to have. The citizens of the neighbouring towns, who were curious, used to come to stare at them, for they were young and handsome and very well dressed.

Later, while they were still in prison, a Spaniard came and talked to them, asking precise questions about who they were and where they came from. They gave him a coherent account of all their travels. Now this Spaniard had a brother who was a chamberlain to the king of the Saracens. During a visit which the governor made to the king's palace, the Spaniard, together with the captain of the ship which had brought them from Cyprus, presented themselves jointly to the king, Emir al-Mumanim, Commander of the Faithful.

There was some discussion of the pilgrims' case, and then the Spaniard informed his brother of all that they had told him when they were in prison. He entreated his brother to make this known to the king, and to plead for their release. He and the ship's captain and the governor then gave a complete and ordered account of their story. The king then asked where they came from. They replied, "From the shores of the West, where the sun sets. We know of no land beyond them. There is nothing but water after that."

In his reply the king said, "Why should we punish them? They have committed no offence against us. Let them have their liberty, and go on their way." Now other men detained in prison had to pay a three months' charge for their keep, but this was remitted in their case. The territory where the pilgrims were at this time is vast, and stretches away to the south and north, and to the east and the west. In the region there were the dioceses of twelve bishops. The Cypriots, who occupy territory lying between that of the Greeks and the Saracens, went unarmed at that time, since a treaty and a firm peace then existed between the Saracens and the

Greeks.

After the pilgrims had received the king's permit, they set out at once, travelling on a hundred miles to Damascus, where St Ananias is buried. They stayed a week in this city which is in the land of Syria. Two miles from the city is a church on the spot where Paul was first converted. Here the Lord said to him," Saul, Saul, why do you persecute Me? etc." And there they prayed.

Then they went on foot to Galilee where Gabriel first came to holy Mary and said, "Hail, Mary!" etc. There is a church there now, and the village in which the church stands is called Nazareth. Very often Christians have made common cause to fund the re-purchase of this church from the pagan Saracens when the latter wished to destroy it. The pilgrims commended themselves to the Lord there, and then continued their journey on foot to Cana, where our Lord changed water into wine. There is a large church there, and in it, at the altar, stands one of the six water pots which our Lord commanded to be filled with water, and which he then turned into the wine which was subsequently drunk by the wedding guests. They stayed there for a day, and then went on to Mount Tabor, where our Lord was transfigured. A monastery of monks is now on this site and a church dedicated to our Lord, and to Moses and Elias. The inhabitants call the place 'Age mons'. They had prayers there.

The next stop was a town called Tiberias. This lies on the shore of the Sea of Galilee. It is where our Lord walked on the water and kept his feet dry, and where Peter, while walking on the waves towards him, started to sink. The Jordan flows there through the midst of the sea of Galilee. There are many churches there, and also one synagogue of the Jews, even though here it is Sunday which is held in special honour. They stayed there for some days.

From this town they went round the shore of the lake, past Magdala, to Capernaum, where our Lord raised the ruler's daughter to life. There is a house there with a thick wall which is where, according to the local inhabitants, Zebedee lodged with his sons, James and John. The pilgrims then went on to Bethsaida, where Peter and Andrew came from. Here there is a church where their house formerly stood. They stayed one night there, and in the morning went on to Chorozain, where our Lord cured those possessed by demons, which he sent into a herd of pigs. There is a Christian church there where they prayed.

From here they went to a place where two fountains, the Jor and the Dan, gush forth out of the earth. As the two streams run down from the mountain above, their waters merge and form the Jordan. They spent the night there

between the two springs. Willibald remembers that some herdsmen gave them sour milk to drink. There were amazing cattle there, all of the same colour, with long backs,
short legs and huge horns. In summer the marshy edges around the springs become deep banks, and when the scorching sun begins to dry up the soil, the cattle go into the pools and submerge themselves in the water, except for their heads. After this overnight stay they went on to Caesarea, where there is a church and a large number of Christians. Here they rested for some time before continuing their journey to the Monastery of St John the Baptist (probably at Kusr el-Yehûd), where they stayed the night.

The next day they pressed on about a mile to the Jordan where our Lord was baptised. There is a church there now, raised up high on stone columns. Underneath the church is dry ground. On this very spot our Lord was baptised. They now baptise people here where a cross of wood stands in the middle in a little channel of water. A rope has been extended across the Jordan and is secured on either side. On the Feast of the Epiphany the sick and infirm come, and, holding on to the rope, are dipped into the water. Women who are barren also come here and receive the grace of the Lord, should they merit it. Willibald himself bathed in the Jordan on the one day they were there.

From there they went on a further five miles to Galgala. Here in the church, which is built of wood and is not large, there are the twelve huge stones which the children of Israel took out of the river and carried to Galgala, as testimony of their crossing the River Jordan. The pilgrims prayed there, and then went on to a point about seven miles from the Jordan. Here they found a spring at the foot of the mountain. It had been bitter and of no value to the inhabitants until Elisha came and blessed it. After this it flowed well, and all the people of that place channel its water through their fields and gardens, and everywhere else where water is required. All that the water irrigates grows strongly and remains healthy, thanks to the blessing of Elisha. The pilgrims went on from here to the monastery of Eustochius, which is situated in the middle of the plain between Jericho and Jerusalem.

At last they reached Jerusalem where the Holy Cross of our Lord was found. In that place, which was called the place of Calvary, there is now a church. The site was in the past outside the city of Jerusalem. But Helena, when she found the Cross, arranged that the place should be incorporated within the city. Outside the church, on the eastern wing by the wall, there now stand three crosses of wood, in memory of the Holy Cross of our Lord, and of those of the others who were crucified with Him. These are not now inside the church, but stand outside the church under the roof. Nearby is the site of that garden in which the

Sepulchre of our Saviour was.

The Sepulchre was cut out from the rock, and the rock stands above ground, and is square at the bottom and tapers towards the top. On the top of the Sepulchre there is now a cross, and over it there has been constructed a wonderful building. On the eastern side of the rock of the Sepulchre an entrance has been constructed through which people can enter to pray. There is a stone bench inside on which the body of our Lord was laid. Fifteen golden bowls, in which oil burns day and nigh, stand on this. This bench on which the body of our Lord was laid is on the north side, within the rock of the Sepulchre, and on a person's right as he enters the Sepulchre to pray. In front of the entrance to the Sepulchre lies a massive stone, squared so as to be like the former stone which the angel rolled back from the door of the Sepulchre.

Our bishop Willibald reached Jerusalem in time for the festival of St Martin (11 November). But on arrival he fell ill, and his sickness lingered on until a week before the Nativity of our Lord. When he was a little better and his resistance to its effects had increased, he rose from his bed and went to the church called Holy Sion. This stands in the midst of Jerusalem. After praying there, he went on to Solomon's porch where there is the pool beside which people who were ill used to lie, waiting for the moving of the water when the angel came. The first person who then went down into the water was healed. It was there that our Lord said to the man who was paralysed, "Rise, take up your bed and go home."

Willibald also told us that before the gate of the city there stood a high column. On the top of it a cross was set as a sign and a reminder of the place where the Jews wanted to carry off the body of holy Mary. The eleven Apostles had taken up her body and carried it to Jerusalem. But as soon as they reached the city gate the Jews wanted to seize it. But the moment they stretched out their arms towards the bier and attempted to grasp it, their arms became rigid and stuck to the bier. They were unable to move until, by the grace of God and the prayers of the Apostles, their grip was loosened, and they managed to detach themselves. Holy Mary left this world in that place in the middle of Jerusalem which is called Holy Sion. As I indicated, the eleven Apostles carried her there, and then angels came and took her from the hands of the Apostles, and bore her off into Paradise.

From Jerusalem Bishop Willibald went to the valley of Jehoshaphat, which is situated near the city of Jerusalem on the east side. The church of holy Mary, in which there is a sepulchral monument, is in the valley. Of course her body does not lie there, but it is her memorial. The pilgrims prayed there, then went on up to the Mount of Olives, which is near to the valley on the east side. The valley is between Jerusalem and the Mount of Olives. On the Mount there is now a church, where our Lord prayed before His Passion, and said to His disciples, "Watch and pray, that you may not enter into temptation." From there Willibald came to the church on the mount itself. From this place our Lord ascended into heaven. In the middle of the church there stands a square lantern made of brass; it is decorated and very beautiful, with glass on all four sides; within it there is a little glow-worm of a light. The lantern is covered in on all sides, so that it may burn continuously in rain and sunshine. For the church is open at the top and is without a roof. Within there are two columns which stand very close to the north and south walls. They are a commemoration and symbol of the two men who said, "You men of Galilee, why do you stand looking up into heaven?" Anyone who can squeeze himself between the wall and the columns gains a plenary indulgence from his sins.

From Jerusalem they went out to the place where the angel appeared to the shepherds, saying, "I bring you good news of great joy etc.," and then on to Bethlehem, where our Lord was born, a place which is seven miles from Jerusalem. The spot where Christ was born was once a cave below ground. It is now a square chamber cut out from the rock. The surrounding earth has been dug out and disposed of. Over it a church has been erected, and the main altar is set above the place where our Lord was born. There is another smaller altar, and this is used by those who wish to celebrate Mass in the cave itself. They carry it inside the cave for Mass, and afterwards take it out again. The church over the place where our Lord was born is a magnificent building, constructed in the form of a cross.

After praying at this church, they went on to a large town called Thecua, where the young children were massacred by Herod. There is a church there too where one of the prophets is buried. They then came to the Lavra valley where there is a large monastery. The abbot lives in the monastery, and so does the door-keeper of the church. But the other monks, who are numerous, live round about the valley in the recesses of the surrrounding mountain rocks. Here and there on the mountain side they have their cells, which have been carved out of the rock. The mountain circles the valley, and within the monastery is the tomb of St Sabas.

From here they passed on to where Philip baptised the eunuch. On this spot there is a little church set in the wide valley between Bethlehem and Gaza (Bethsura). Going on to Gaza, which is a holy place, they prayed there, then went on to St Matthias, which is a very fine church. However, while the sacred mysteries of the Mass were being celebrated there, our bishop, Willibald, while standing in the church, lost the sight of both his eyes. He was blind for two months. However, pressing on with their journey, they visited the church of St Zacharias, the prophet. This is not dedicated to Zacharias, the father of John the Baptist, but to another prophet. Their next stop was the village of Aframia where Abraham, Isaac and Jacob are buried with their wives.

On their return to Jerusalem, they entered the church where the Holy Cross of our Lord was found. It was here that Willibald's eyes were opened, and he received his sight again.

Willibald spent some more time in Jerusalem and made trips from there to Lydda, where St George is buried in the church, and to the church of St Peter the Apostle, where St Peter raised the widow Dorcas to life. He also made journeys to Tyre and Sidon, Mount Lebanon and Damascus. He wintered in Jerusalem, then set off to the furthest border of Syria where he fell ill again during Lent. His companions tried to get a permit from Emir al-Mumanim for more travel, but they could not contact him because he had fled from the plague which was rife in the region at that time. Eventually the governor, whom they had met before, gave them a letter, which enabled them to travel in twos. Travelling in larger numbers was not permitted because there was a food shortage. Eventually they managed to return to Jerusalem. Their last expedition was to Samaria, with its tomb of St John the Baptist, and where there is the well at which our Lord encountered the Samaritan woman.

The pilgrims now made their way to Tyre where they planned to pick up a ship for Constantinople. But before he left Jerusalem Willibald had carefully planned to smuggle some balsam (probably balm of Gilead, a very valuable substance in mediaeval medicine) back home with him. The account of this ruse, as told by Adamnan, is as follows.

While he was in Jerusalem Willibald bought some balsam, and filled a calabash with it. He then took a cane, which was hollow but blocked at one end and put some petroleum into it. He inserted the cane right into the calabash through its opening. He then cut off the top part of the cane so that it was level with the opening of the calabash. The top of the cane where it went into the calabash was now flush with the top surface of the calabash. Finally he corked the opening of the calabash.

When they arrived at Tyre, the inhabitants of the city seized and bound the pilgrims. They then examined all their baggage to see whether they had any contraband hidden. If they had found anything the pilgrims would have been summarily punished and made into martyrs. When the inhabitants had been through all the party's belongings they found nothing of note, except Willibald's calabash. They uncorked this and smelt what was inside. But because they got a whiff of petroleum, as this was in the cane set into the calabash, they failed to discover the precious substance. And so they released them. The pilgrims then spent a good many days waiting for their ship to be made ready. When at last they set sail it took the whole of the winter for them to reach Constantinople. Their journey had lasted from the Feast of St. Andrew (the 30th of November) until one week before Easter.

St Willibald spent two years at Constantinople before returning to Italy, and then ten years as a monk at Monte Cassino and another affiliated monastery nearby. At the request of the Pope he then accepted an invitation from his uncle, St Boniface, to join him on the German mission.

It is about three hundred and seventy-five years before our next pilgrim visits the Holy Places. He came in 1102 soon after the capture of Jerusalem by the Latin crusaders in 1099. Throughout this long period the whole of Palestine was under Arab rule. But for the population there, Christians, Jews and Muslims, the nature of the rule varied considerably. Until 750 the Omayyads ruled the territory from Damascus. Their outlook was strongly influenced by Byzantine culture: many Greeks were employed in the civil administration, and in architecture and the decorative arts.

The Omayyads were overthrown in 750 by the Abbasids who ruled Palestine from their capital in Bagdad. Omayyad supporters, who were ousted by the new rulers, fled to Arab Spain. The Abbasids were stricter Muslims, and their culture was more influenced by Persia and the Orient. To the extent that Christians were employed by them they tended to be Nestorians. However, the Caliph Harun al-Rashid (785-809) exchanged letters with Charlemagne in the West, and, as a result, the Franks were permitted to build a hostel for pilgrims in Jerusalem; Frankish nuns were allowed to serve in the Church of the Holy

Sepulchre, and Latin services were introduced in the Church of St Mary. This opening up to the West by the Abbasid dynasty was probably intended to counterbalance the political power of the Eastern Empire whose military fortunes had began to revive after the Arab defeat at Constantiople in 718.

But from 726 the Christian churches in the East entered a period of division which lasted over one hundred years. The quarrel was over the question of the use of images in religious art  and devotion. The Jewish religion and Islam, which had its roots in Judaism, took a strict view of the Mosaic commandment which forbad the worship of graven images. During this period many Christian bishops and rulers in the East took a similarly purist line, breaking with the earlier Christian tradition which had recognised images as an aid to devotion. The Second Council of Nicaea in 787 restored the veneration of icons, but the battle over this was not finally ended until 843.

The period also saw the sowing of the seeds of the schism between the eastern and western churches. In 794 the Council of Frankfurt added the 'filioque', meaning 'and the Son' to the Creed. This addition made more precise the way in which the Father, Son and Holy Spirit related to each other in the Blessed Trinity, by declaring that the Holy Spirit proceeded from the Father and the Son. But many in the eastern churches were unhappy with this change to the Creed, and, in 867, Photius, the Patriarch of Constantinople, wrote to the other eastern patriarchs denouncing the addition.

But as well as quarrelling among themselves, eastern and western Christians, who were not at this time directly subject to Muslim rule, were under threat from Arab attack throughout the Mediterranean regions. Sicily and Crete were lost to the Arabs in the early ninth century. The Arabs continued to make advances in Spain throughout the eighth and ninth centuries. In 846 St Peter's Church in Rome was pillaged by an Arab raiding army —there were nests of Arab pirates and brigands both in Italy and southern France. These were also active in the eastern Mediterranean.

People still made the pilgrimage to Jerusalem in the ninth century. But Bernard the Wise, who visited the Holy Places in 870, found that Charlemagne's pilgrim hostel, though still functioning, was empty, and beginning to decay. Nevertheless the tenth century witnessed a great change of fortune for Christians in both East and West, and a significant revival of pilgrimage. The practice of imposing a pilgrimage to a sacred shrine as a canonical penance for sin seems to have been growing. Christianity was also advancing northwards into eastern Europe. Prince Boris of the Bulgars was baptised in 864.

But the pace quickened in the tenth century with the baptism of Prince Mieskoy of Poland in 966, Duke Sezo of Hungary in 985 and Prince Valdimir of Russia in 988. These conversions eventually both helped to swell the number of pilgrims, and enabled new land routes to the Holy Land to be opened up. But even the sea routes were becoming safer, as the Byzantine navy began to regain control of the Mediterranean from the Arabs.

Yet this revival of Christian fortunes was not without its set backs in areas of Muslim rule. In 923-24 Muslim mobs destroyed the Christian churches in Ramleh, Askelon, Caesarea and Damascus, although the Arab ruler later helped the Christian communities rebuild them. The Abbasid rulers were beginning to lose control over their empire: local dynasties took power in Mosul, Aleppo and Egypt, and the Byzantine emperors took advantage of this. In 961 Crete was retaken. In 965 Niephorus Phocas reconquered Cilicia and Cyprus. In 969 both Antioch and Aleppo fell to the Byzantine army.

In the same year the Fatimid dynasty, which had originated in Morocco, seized power in Egypt, and followed this up with the conquest of Palestine in the following year. In 974 John Tsimisces, the successor of Nicephorus Phocas, swept down southwards to Damascus, Tiberias and Nazareth, and along the *coast to Caesarea. But he did not enter Jerusalem, and, when winter came, he returned to Constantinople where he died in 976. The Eastern Empire had been revived as a powerful force in the Near East, and northern Syria had returned to Christian rule.*

The beginning of the eleventh century, however, began unfavourably for Christians in the Holy Land. The Fatimid ruler, Caliph al-Hakim, although he had a Christian mother and had been largely brought up as a Christian, reacted against the formative influence of his early years. From 1004 to 1012 he carried out a systematic persecution of Christians in the Holy Land. He passed discriminatory laws against Christians, seized or pillaged church property, and ordered mosques to be built on church roofs.

In 1009 he ordered the Governor of Ramleh "to demolish the Church of the Resurrection and to remove its symbols, and to get rid of all traces and remembrance of it". This was not able to be completely accomplished, but the Martyrion was largely destroyed, never to be rebuilt. The roof of the Rotunda of the Church of the Holy Sepulchre was brought down, although a good deal of the walls survived. The archaeologist, Martin Biddle, believes that the rubble may have protected the lower parts of the edicule or little house over the rock-cut tomb.

30,000 churches were said to have been destroyed or plundered during these few years, and many Christians apostasized to Islam. But in 1013, as a result of a plea by the Byzantine emperor, Christians were permitted to emigrate to the Christian north. It is likely that they may also have been able to start restoring the Church of the Holy Sepulchre.

In 1016 a truly sensational event occurred. Caliph al-Hakim's divinity was proclaimed by Darazi, one of his supporters. This both shocked and angered Muslims. From then on al-Hakim favoured Christians and Jews: freedom of conscience was restored to them in 1017, restrictions on Christian dress abolished in 1020, and much church property restored from then onwards. But Muslims were further infuriated when al-Hakim's name was substituted for Allah at services in the mosques. In 1021 al-Hakim disappeared, perhaps murdered by his ambitious sister, and Darazi fled to the Lebanon, where he founded the Druze sect which continues to this day. The Druze still wait expectantly for al-Hakim's return. Palestine was temporarily ruled from Aleppo until the Fatimid rule was fully restored in 1029. Even before this, the Byzantine Emperor had obtained formal authorisation for the full restoration of the Church of the Holy Sepulchre, and work on this was probably completed by about 1040.

Despite these difficulties for Christians living in the Holy Land, pilgrimages continued. Travellers went to the sacred sites, even if the buildings associated with them were often in ruins or under restoration. But relations were worsening between the major Christian churches. Between 1045 and 1064 Christian Armenia was absorbed into the Eastern Greek Empire. It was partly a strategic military take-over to provide a bulwark against the Turks, who were now a growing force in Anatolia and the Near East. But there were difficulties because the Armenians and Greeks had theological differences.

In 1052 the Patriarch of Constantinople demanded that Latin churches in the city should adopt Greek practices in their services, which they refused. In 1054, while Pope Leo IX was a prisoner of the Normans, his envoy, Cardinal Humbert, on a mission from Rome about Greek and Latin liturgical usage, excommunicated Patriarch Cerularius, and denounced the omission of the 'filioque' in the Creed by the eastern churches. In 1056 western pilgrims were forbidden by the Arabs to enter the Church of the Holy Sepulchre, perhaps with the connivance of the Byzantine Emperor. Despite this, there was a great German pilgrimage in 1064. But the quarrelling among Christians was making it more difficult to achieve a co-ordinated response to the threat from the Turks, who took Jerusalem in 1070. In 1071 the Byzantine army was decisively defeated by them at the Battle of Manzikert. In 1073 the Turks launched a major invasion of Asia Minor.

In the same year, Hildebrand was elected pope in the west, and took the name of Gregory VII. Relations between the eastern and western churches did not improve greatly, although the pope began to take an interest in the situation in Asia Minor, and the difficulties which this created for pilgrims to the Holy Places. The

Papacy was already proclaiming the struggle of the Christians against the Muslim Arabs in Spain as a Holy War. Pope Gregory began to consider the possibility of a similar military expedition to help the Byzantine Empire in Asia Minor. But his ideas matured slowly, as he was preoccupied with his quarrels and wars with the German Emperor, Henry IV, and with stamping out the abuse whereby bishops and abbots were invested with their symbols of office by lay princes. Help for the Eastern Empire was made more unlikely when the Eastern Emperor showed himself sympathetic to Henry IV. This eventually led Gregory, in the year of his death in 1085, to excommunicate the Eastern Emperor.

But the idea of aiding the Christians in the East did not disappear in the West, and when Byzantine envoys attended the Council of Piacenza in 1095, the newly elected pope, Urban II, listened favourably to their request for help. Here, and later in the same year at Clermont, Urban preached the crusade. The extraordinary and immediate success of his call to retake the Holy Places, which by now the Eastern Empire was in no position to protect, surprised the pope. An ill-planned People's Crusade was wiped out by the Turks at Civetot near the Sea of Marmara in 1096. But within three years a coalition of leaders in the west was able to organise a stronger force. After many vicissitudes, Baldwin, the younger son of the Count of Boulogne, entered Jerusalem on 9 November 1099. All Muslims were slaugthered. A few weeks later, on Christmas Day, Baldwin paid homage to Daimbert, the Patriarch of Jerusalem, and was crowned King of Jerusalem.

Saewulf, a layman, made the pilgrimage three years after the Holy Places had come under Latin Christian rule. We know little about him, apart from what he tells us about himself in the account which follows.

I, SAEWULF, an unworthy sinner was on my way to Jerusalem to pray at our Lord's Sepulchre. I was originally with others who were going by the direct route. But, either because I was weighed down by my sins, or because the ship was poorly constructed, I found myself unable to cross by the open sea. So I have decided to note down the names of the islands which were on the route we took.

Saewulf then explains that he set out from Monopolis, about twenty miles from Bari in Southern Italy. His sea route took him to Brindisi, Corfu, Cephalonia, Patras, and Liva d'Osta. From there his party travelled by donkey to Thebes and Corinth; then by sea again to the islands of Petali, Andria, Tinos, Syra, Mykonos, Naxos, Carea, Omargon, Samos, Scio and Mytilene; then on to Patmos, Rhodes and Cyprus. Here is his description of the journey from Cyprus to Jaffa.

From the island of Cyprus we were on a changing course for seven days, and were tossed about by sea storms before we were able to reach a harbour. One night we were violently driven by a head wind and were being carried back to Cyprus. But by the mercy of God—who is near at hand to all who genuinely call on Him—we were stirred by much sorrow for our sins, and we returned again to the course we wanted. For seven nights we were so assailed by the storm and its dangers that we had almost lost all hope. But on the seventh morning, as the sun rose, the coast of the port of Jaffa appeared along with it before us. And just as the huge weight of our danger had cast us into the depths of despair, so this unexpected joy, which exceeded our hopes, multiplied our happiness a hundred times. So, after exactly thirteen weeks—for we embarked at Monopolis on a Sunday, and had always been either on the turbulent sea, or on islands in huts and empty hovels (for the Greeks are not hospitable)—we disembarked at the port of Jaffa on a Sunday, with great rejoicing and gratitude.

Now I beg all of you, my most dear friends, to raise your hands and clap them together, and sing joyfully in one voice a song of praise to God with me. For throughout my journey, He Who is mighty has continued to show me mercy. Blessed be His name now and forever! Listen, my dear friends, and hear how the loving-kindnesss of God was shown to me and my family when He had pity on me, although I am the least of His servants. For the very day we anchored, someone said to me— and I believe that God prompted him—"Sir, go on shore today, just in case tonight or early in the morning there is a storm, and you may not be able to land."

When I heard this, I was seized with a strong impulse to get ashore. I hired a boat, and landed with all my belongings. While I was coming ashore, the sea became rough, the surge of the waves grew, and a violent storm arose. But by the gracious favour of God, I reached the shore unharmed.

What happened next? When we had come ashore we went into the town to seek lodgings, for we were tired and exhausted from the efforts of our long journey. We had something to eat, and then had a night's rest.

But early in the morning, as we came out from church, we heard the loud roar of the sea and people shouting. Everyone was running about in groups, amazed by a noise which they had never heard before. In great fear we too ran along with the rest and came to the shore. As we arrived, we saw waves like mountains, and the pitiful sight of the bodies of countless men and women who had been drowned lying on the shore. We could see ships being dashed against each other and broken into small pieces. You could hear nothing but the roaring of the sea and the crashing of the ships together, since this was even louder than the cries of the people and the shouting of the crews.

Our own ship, since it was large and strongly built, and several others, laden with corn and other merchandise, and filled with pilgrims outward and homeward bound, were still held fast by their anchors and cables. But they were being violently tossed about by the high sea.

How terrified of impending disaster the passengers looked as their baggage was thrown overboard. Could anyone who

saw them be so unfeeling and stone-hearted as to hold back
their tears? Yet we had not been watching long when the
anchors gave way, and the cables were broken by the force
of the waves and the swell, and all hope was extinguished.
At one moment the ships were being lifted up on high,
then at the next they plunged down into the depths, and
very soon were either tossed on to the sand bank or on to
the rocks. There the ships were hurled from side to side,
and then were gradually broken up by the storm. Its violence made it impossible for the ships to return safely to the
sea, and the steepness of the beach did not allow them to
reach salvation there.

What is the point of recounting the despair of the sailors
and pilgrims when all hope was gone? They still hung on to
the ships, some to the masts, some to the spars, and some to
the cross-timbers. What more can I add? Some, petrified
with fright, were drowned. Others, still clinging on, were
decapitated by the timbers of their own ship. This may
seem unbelievable, but I saw it. Some were washed off the
decks and carried out to sea. Others who knew how to swim
decided to plunge into the waves: but a good many of them
were drowned. Only very few, who had not lost their nerve
and had stamina, managed to get safely to the shore.

Of thirty very large ships, some of which are called
Dromundi (light galleys of the Byzantine empire), some
Gulafri, and some Gatti (other types of galley), all of which
were laden with pilgrims and merchandise, only seven
remained unwrecked by the time I ceased my watch on the
shore. More than one thousand men and women died on
that day. No one ever witnessed a greater disaster on a single day. Yet by His grace our Lord delivered me from this.
To Him be honour and glory, world without end. Amen.

We then went up from Jaffa to the city of Jerusalem, a
journey of two days along a mountainous road, rocky and
very dangerous. The Saracens continually lay ambushes
there for Christians: they lie concealed in the mountain
passes and in caves, keeping a look-out day and night,

always watching for an opportunity to attack those who are in a small party, or have fallen behind the rest because they are exhausted. At one moment the Saracens can be seen all around everywhere, then, all at once, they vanish completely. Anyone who makes this journey can witness this. And what a large number of human corpses lie on the road and beside it, all savaged by wild animals! Some may be surprised that the bodies of Christians should remain unburied. But this is not surprising, for there is a very shallow depth of soil, and the rocky ground does not let you dig into it with a spade. But even if there was enough earth, who would be so foolish as to leave his party, and dig a grave for his companion on his own? If he did so, he would be making a grave for himself rather than just for his friend!

On that particular road it is not only the poor and the weak who are at risk, but also the rich and strong. Many are slaughtered by the Saracens, but more die from heat and thirst. An even greater number perish through drinking too much! Yet all our party arrived unharmed at the destination we were longing for. Blessed be the Lord, who has not rejected my prayer, nor turned away his mercy from me.

The entrance to the city of Jerusalem is to the west, under the tower of King David by the gate that is known as the Gate of David (the Jaffa gate). The Church of the Holy Sepulchre, which is also known as the Martyrion, is the first sight to see. This is not only because of its location on the street route, but because it is more prestigious than all the other churches. And this is right and proper, since everything which was foretold about our Lord Jesus Christ by the holy prophets throughout the world was truly fulfilled in that place. When our Lord's Cross was found, the Archbishop Maximus built the church, with the support of the Emperor Constantine and his mother, Helena, who endowed it with royal magnificence. In the middle of the church is our Lord's Sepulchre, surrounded by a very strong wall. It is covered over so that when it rains it cannot fall on the Holy Sepulchre itself, for the church above lies open without a roof. The church is situated on the slope of Mount Sion, as is the city itself. But this needs explaining.

The Roman rulers, Titus and Vespasian, completely destroyed the city of Jerusalem, an act which was the Lord's vengeance, and fulfilled His prophesy which He spoke when drawing near to the city. When He caught sight of it, He wept over it, saying, " Would that even today you knew the things that make for peace! But now they are hid from your eyes. For the days shall come upon you, when your enemies will cast up a bank about you, and surround you, and hem you in on every side, and dash you to the ground, you and your children within you, and they will not leave one stone upon another in you."

We know that our Lord suffered outside the gate of the city. But the Emperor Hadrian, who was also called Ælius, extended the city as far as the Tower of David, which had formerly been some distance from the city, when he rebuilt the city of Jerusalem and the Temple of the Lord. Anyone can see this from the Mount of Olives, where the extreme west walls of the city formerly were, and can work out by how much the city was afterwards extended. The Emperor renamed the city by his own name as Ælia, which means house of God. Some say that the city and the Temple of the Lord were restored, just as they are now, by the Emperor Justinian. But this is their own private opinion and not the truth. The Syrians, whose ancestors settled in that country from the time of the first persecution, say that from the time of our Lord's Passion the city has been captured and destroyed seven times, along with all the churches, but not actually levelled to the ground.

In the courtyard of the Church of the Holy Sepulchre you can visit some of the most holy places: first, the prison where our Lord Jesus Christ was confined after His betrayal. The Syrians bear witness to this fact. A little further on you can see the place where the Holy Cross and the other crosses were found. A great church was built there subsequently in honour of Queen Helena, but this was later destroyed by the pagans. Lower down, and not far from the prison, you can see a marble column of the praetorium. Our Lord Jesus Christ was bound to this, and then beaten with most cruel whips. Close by is the place where our Lord was stripped of His clothes by the soldiers. Then there is the place where He was dressed in the purple robe by the soldiers and crowned with the crown of thorns, and where they cast lots to share out His clothes.

After this you go up to Mount Calvary, where the Patriarch Abraham once built an altar, and, in response to God's command, was ready to sacrifice his own son to Him. In this same place, much later, the Son of God, whom Isaac prefigured, was sacrificed to God the Father as the victim for the redemption of the world. The rock of that very hill was a witness of our Lord's Passion. It was severely split close to the hole into which the Cross of our Lord was fixed, because it could not bear the killing of its Creator without splitting. As we read in the Passion: "And the rocks were split."

Underneath is the place called Golgotha, where Adam is said to have been raised from the dead by the stream of our Lord's blood which fell upon him. For we also read in our Lord's Passion: "And many bodies of the saints who had fallen asleep were raised." Yet in the *Sentences of St Augustine* we read that Adam was buried at Hebron, where afterwards the three patriarchs were buried with their wives: Abraham with Sarah, Isaac with Rebecca, Jacob with Leah, together with the bones of Joseph, which the children of Israel brought up with them from Egypt.

Hard by the place of Calvary is the Chapel of Holy Mary. This is on the site where our Lord's body was anointed after

being taken down from the Cross, before being buried with
sweet spices and wrapped in the linen cloth or winding-sheet.

Not far from the place of Calvary, at what you might call
the head of the Church of the Holy Sepulchre, and on its
outside wall, is a place called Compass. This is where our
Lord Jesus Christ himself, with His own hand, established
and marked out the middle of the world. As the Psalmist
testifies: "Yet God, my King is from old, working salvation
in the midst of the earth." Some also say that it was on this
spot that our Lord Jesus Christ first appeared to Mary
Magdalene as she was seeking Him and weeping, and, as
the Evangelist relates, thought that He was the gardener.

These most sacred places of prayer are in the courtyard of
our Lord's Sepulchre on the eastern side. Two very celebrated
chapels have been built on the sides of the church itself, one
on each side. They are to honour Holy Mary and St John,
because they played such a close part in our Lord's Passion,
with one standing on the right, and one on his left side.

On the outside of the west wall of the Chapel of Holy
Mary a picture of the Mother of God can be seen. Long ago
this was a wonderful consolation to Mary of Egypt. The
account of her life records how, with a heart full of remorse
and with the aid of the Holy Spirit, she addressed the
Mother of God, whom she saw portrayed in the picture,
and begged her assistance. On the other side of the Chapel
of St John is the very lovely monastery of the Holy Trinity.
There is a baptistery there, and attached to this is the
Chapel of St James the Apostle, who was griven the episcopal chair as the first bishop of Jerusalem. All these places
are so arranged and sited that anyone standing at the very
end of the church can clearly see into all five chapels
through their doorways.

Outside the entrance to the Church of the Holy
Sepulchre, and to the south, there is the Church of Holy
Mary. This is called the Latin Church, because services
there are always offered in Latin. The Syrians says that at
the crucifixion of her son, the Blessed Mother of God stood

at a spot where the church's altar now stands. Attached to this church is another one dedicated to Holy Mary, which is called Parva. Here some nuns serve her and her Son most devoutly. Nearby is also the hospital of the celebrated monastery dedicated to St John the Baptist (*headquarters of the Order of the Knights Hospitallers of St John founded in 1099*).

From our Lord's Sepulchre you go about twice a bow shot's distance to the Temple of the Lord, which is on the east side of the Church of the Holy Sepulchre. It has a courtyard of great length and breadth, and many gates. But the principal gate is that which faces the Temple. It is called the Beautiful Gate, because of the quality of the workmanship and the variety of its colours. It was here that Peter healed the cripple, when he and John went up to the Temple at 3 pm, the hour of prayer, as we read in the Acts of the Apostles. In ancient times the place where Solomon built the Temple of the Lord was called Bethel. It was to this place that Jacob, at the Lord's command, went on his journey. He rested there, and on this very spot saw the ladder with its top reaching the heavens, and the angels ascending and descending by it. And he said, as we read in Genesis, "Truly this place is holy." There he set up a stone as a sign, and built an altar, and poured oil on it. Afterwards, by divine inspiration, Solomon built the Temple of the Lord there. This was a magnificent building of incomparable workmanship and marvellously decorated, as you read in the Book of Kings...

Saewulf goes on to list a large number of references in the Old and New Testament to the events which took place in the Temple. His account continues in this way.

From the Temple of the Lord you go north to the Church of St Anne, the mother of Blessed Mary, at the place where she lived with her husband. It was here that she bore her most beloved daughter, Mary, the saviour of all the faithful.

Near there is the Sheep Pool, which has five porches, and is called Bethsaida in Hebrew. We read about this in the Gospel. A little higher up there is the place where the woman was healed by our Lord by touching the border of His garment, while He was being jostled by the crowd. This was the woman who had had a haemorrhage for twelve years, and was uable to be cured by her doctors.

From the Church of St Anne you go through a gate which leads into the valley of Jehoshaphat, where there is a church of Holy Mary. It was here, after her death, that she was carried in honour by the Apostles for burial. Her sepulchre is held in the highest honour by the fathful, as is right and proper. There are monks there who serve our Lord Jesus Christ and His Mother day and night. There too is the Kidron brook and Gethsemane. It was to this spot that our Lord went with His disciples from Mount Sion and across the Kidron brook. There is a kind of oratory there at the place where He left Peter and James and John, saying, "Remain here, and watch with me." And going forward, He fell upon His face and prayed, and came to His disciples, and found them sleeping. The separate places can still be seen where each of the disciples slept.

Gethsemane is at the foot of the Mount of Olives, and the Kidron brook is below, as a division between Mount Sion and the Mount of Olives. The level ground between the two hills is called the valley of Jehoshaphat.

A little higher up the Mount of Olives is an oratory at the spot where our Lord prayed, as we read in the Passion: "And He withdrew from them about a stone's throw... And being in an agony He prayed more earnestly; and His sweat became like great drops of blood falling upon the ground." From there you can see Acheldemach, the field that was bought with the money which was given for our Lord's betrayal. It is at the foot of the Mount of Olives, close to the valley. From Gethsemane it is about three or four bow shots to the south. There are a very large number of sites to be visited here. The field is near the tombs of the holy fathers, Simeon and Joseph, the step-father of our Lord. These tombs were built a long time ago in the form of towers and are carved out of the very base of the mountain. From there you go down past Acheldemach to the fountain, which is called the Pool of Siloem. It was in this that our Lord told a man who was blind from birth to wash his eyes. Before this our Lord had made a paste of clay with His own spittle and had anointed the man's eyes.

I mentioned above the Church of Holy Mary. From here you go up by a steep road to the east, almost to the top of the Mount of Olives. Here is the place from which our Lord ascended into heaven while his disciples were looking on. It has been marked off within a small tower, and has been respectfully maintained. Within, an altar has been built over the very spot, and the whole site is surrounded by walls on all sides. At the very point where the Apostles were standing with Blessed Mary His Mother when they were gazing in amazement at His Ascension, there is an altar of the Church of St Mary. It was here that the two men stood beside them in white robes and said, "Men of Galilee, why do you stand looking into heaven?" About a stone's throw away, according to what we were told by the Syrians, our Lord wrote down the Lord's Prayer in Hebrew, using His fingers to inscribe the words on the marble. A very beautiful church had been built there too, but this was afterwards completely destroyed by the pagans.

This is also the case with all the churches built outside the walls of the city, including the Church of the Holy Spirit, which was about a bow shot's distance to the south. Here the Apostles received the Holy Spirit on the day of Pentecost, as the Father had promised, and there they composed the Creed. In that church there is a chapel in the place where Blessed Mary died; and on the other side of it, a chapel on the site where our Lord Jesus Christ first appeared to the Apostles after His Resurrection. The chapel is called the Galilee, since here He Himself said to them, "But after I am raised up I will

go before you into Galilee." This place was also known as
Galilee because the Apostles who were Galileans used to
go there often.

Galilee itself is a great city near Mount Tabor, three days
journey from Jerusalem. On the other side of Mount Tabor is
a town called Tiberias. From there you come on to
Capernaum and Nazareth, near the Sea of Galilee and Sea of
Tiberias. It was here that Peter and the other Apostles
returned to their fishing after our Lord's Resurrection. Here
He afterwards showed Himself to them when they were on
the sea. Near Tiberias is the plain where the Lord Jesus
blessed the five loaves and three fishes and afterwards fed
four thousand men, as we read in the Gospel.

But let me return to where I was at Jerusalem. In the
Galilee on Mount Sion, where the Apostles were together
in hiding for fear of the Jews and had bolted the doors, Jesus
stood there in their midst. "Peace be to you," He said. He
showed Himself to them again there when Thomas put his
finger into His side, and into the place of the nails. There
He supped with His disciples before His Passion, and
washed their feet. There is still a marble table there on
which He ate the Supper. There are also relics there of St
Stephen, Nicodemus, Gamaliel, and the latter's son, Abibo.
They were placed there by the Patriarch St John, after they
had been discovered in 415 by Lucian, who is reported to
have found them at Caphagamala about twenty miles from
Jerusalem. The stoning of St Stephen took place outside
the wall on the north side, about two or three bow-shots
distant. A beautiful church was built there, but this too has
been entirely destroyed by the pagans.

The Church of the Holy Cross, which is about a mile from
Jerusalem on the western side, is in the place where the wood
of the Holy Cross was originally cut. The building was greatly
honoured and very beautiful. It was ransacked by the pagans,
yet not greatly damaged, apart from the buildings and cells
surrounding it. Outside the city, under its walls on the slope
of Mount Sion, there is the Church of St Peter, which is

called the Church of the Cockcrow. Here Peter hid himself
after his denial of our Lord in a very deep cave, which can
still be seen. There he wept very bitterly over his crime.

On the western side of the Church of the Holy Cross,
about three miles away, there is a very large and beautiful
monastery. This is in honour of St Sabas, who was one of
the seventy-two disciples of our Lord Jesus Christ. There
are now more than three hundred monks living there in
community, in service of God and the Saint. Yet the major-
ity of the brothers were killed by the Saracens. Some of
those remaining now live within the walls of the city near
the Tower of David in a monastery dedicated to the same
saint. Another monastery was entirely destroyed *(perhaps
the Monastery of St Euthymius)*.

The city of Bethlehem in Judaea is six miles from
Jerusalem. Only the great and celebrated monastery of the
Blessed Virgin Mary, mother of our Lord, remains there.
Everything else has been made uninhabitable by the
Saracens. In the monastery church there is a crypt under
the choir in the middle on the actual spot of our Lord's
Nativity. This is somewhat to the left. Near His birthplace,
a little lower down on the right, is the manger where the ox
and the ass stood when our Lord was laid before them. The
stone on which the Head of our Saviour was laid in the
Sepulchre was brought from Jerusalem by St Jerome the
priest, and can often be seen in the manger. St Jerome himself lies under the altar in the north of the Church.

The Innocents, who were killed by Herod as infants
instead of the Child Jesus, rest on the south side of the
Church under an altar. Two very holy women, Paula and
Eustochium, also lie there. There is also a marble table at
which the Blessed Virgin Mary ate with the three Wise
Men when they offered their gifts. There is a well too in
the Church, close to the cave, into which it is said that
the star fell. Another reputed item is the bath of the
Blessed Virigin Mary.

Bethany is about two miles from Jerusalem to the east,

and on the other side of the Mount of Olives. This is where Lazarus was raised from the dead by our Lord. The Church of St Lazarus is here. You can see his Sepulchre and those of many bishops of Jerusalem. The spot under the altar is where Mary Magdalene washed the feet of the Lord Jesus with her tears, wiped them with her hair, and kissed His feet and anointed them with ointment.

Bethphage, the place from which our Lord sent His disciples on before Him to the city, is on the Mount of Olives, but is hardly ever visible. About ten leagues from Jerusalem is Jericho, where Abraham came from. The land there provides good soil for trees: there are all kinds of palms, and every kind of fruit is available. The well of the Prophet Elisha is also here. Its water had been very bitter to drink and useless for growing plants. But when Elisha blessed it and added salt, the water became sweet. From this spot one can ascend a high mountain to the place where our Lord fasted for forty days. About three miles away He was tempted by Satan.

Four leagues to the east of Jericho is the River Jordan. Judea extends from that part of the Jordan region as far as the Adriatic sea (the Mediterranean), that is, to the port of Jaffa. On the far side of the Jordan is Arabia, a country particularly hostile to Christians and unfriendly to all who worship God. The mountain I mentioned is the one from which Elijah went up to heaven in a chariot of fire.

From the Jordan it is eighteen days' journey to Mount Sinai, where the Lord appeared to Moses in the fire of the burning bush. Afterwards he ascended the mountain at the Lord's command, and fasted forty days and nights. Here he received from the Lord the two tablets of stone on which the finger of God had written the law and commandments which were to be taught to the children of Israel.

Hebron is about four leagues to the south of Bethlehem. This is where the holy patriarchs Abraham, Isaac and Jacob are buried, each with his wife. Adam, the first man to be created, is also buried there. It was there that King David reigned for seven years before he acquired the city of Jerusalem from the family of King Saul.

The city of Hebron was once large and beautiful, but it has been laid waste by the Saracens. In the eastern part the tombs of the holy patriarchs, which were built in ancient times, are surrounded by very strong fortifications. Each of the tombs is like a large church. Within each are two sarcophagi, placed in a manner which gives them honour, one for the man and one for his wife. Even at the present time the smell of the balsam and precious spices with which the bodies were buried is sweetly fragrant, and fills the nostrils of those who enter there.

Lower down than the others, at the extreme edge of the fortifications, the bones of Joseph are buried, which the children of Israel brought away with them from Egypt as he requested. Not far from these fortification there is a holm oak which still bears leaves. According to the inhabitants it was under the shadow of this that Abraham stood and saw the three youths coming down the road.

Nazareth, the city of Galilee, is about four days' journey from Jerusalem. This is where the Blessed Virgin Mary received the greeting from the angel announcing our Lord's birth. The route there is through Shechem, a city of Samaria, which is now called Neapolis. Here St John the Baptist was sentenced to be beheaded by Herod. The well of Jacob is also there. The Gospel tells us that it was by this well that Jesus sat exhausted from His journeying. And when the Samaritan woman came to draw water He treated her with dignity by asking her for some to drink.

From Shechem it is equally a day's journey to Caesarea Palestina, and the same from Caesarea to Cayphas, and from Cayphas to Accaron. Nazareth is about eight miles east of Accaron. It has been entirely laid waste and flattened by the Saracens, but the famous monastery indicates the place of our Lord's Annunciation. The fountain near the city still bubbles forth most clearly and is still surrounded, as it used to be, with marble columns and slabs. It was from this fountain that the Child Jesus, together with other village boys, often used to draw water for His Mother.

About four miles from Nazareth to the east is Mount Tabor. Our Lord went up this mountain and was transfigured before Peter, James and John. It is very grassy and wooded there. The mountain rises up in the midst of a very level green plain, and is higher than all the mountains that can be seen around it. The three monasteries which were built in ancient times still exist: one is in honour of our Lord, another in honour of Moses, and the third, rather further away, is in honour of Elijah. This accords well with what Peter said, "Master, it is well that we are here; let us make three booths, one for you, and one for Moses and one for Elijah."

About six miles from Mount Tabor, to the north-east, is the Sea of Galilee or Tiberias. It is ten miles in length and five miles in breadth. The city of Tiberias is on the shore at one end. At the other end are Chorazin, and Bethsaida, Andrew and Peter's town. From the city of Tiberias the plain of Gennesareth stretches about four miles to the north. The Gospel records that it was here that our Lord showed Himself to His disciples as they were fishing. About two miles from Gennesareth to the east is the hill on which the Lord Jesus fed the five thousand with five loaves and two fish. The inhabitants call the hill the Table of the Lord. At the foot of the hill is the Church of St Peter, most beautiful, although deserted.

Cana, where our Lord changed water into wine at a marriage, is on a hill, about six miles to the north of Nazareth. There is nothing left there except the monastery, which is called the House of the Steward of the Feast. About halfway between Nazareth and Cana of Galilee is a village called Roma where all pilgrims going from Accaron to Tiberias are welcomed. Nazareth is then off to the right and Cana to the left.

Mount Hermon is a day's journey to the north. At its base the Jordan River begins from two streams, one of

which is known as the Jor, and the other, the Dan. The two
meet, and the river, now very fast flowing, is then called the
Jordan. It rises close to Caesarea, the city of Philip the
Tetrarch. As the Gospel records, it was when Jesus came
near here that he questioned his disciples with these words,
"Who do men say that the Son of Man is?" The Jordan,
which is very fast-flowing from its source, flows into the Sea
of Galilee at one end; then, with its powerful current, opens
up an outlet at the other end. It then travels the distance of
an eight day journey before flowing out into the Dead Sea.
The water of the Jordan is whiter and more like milk than
all other waters. In consequence the flow may be traced a
long way in the Dead Sea.

By now we had carefully examined every one of the
sacred sites of the city of Jerusalem and the surrounding
region that we were able to visit, and had offered our adoration. So, on the day of Pentecost, we boarded ship at Jaffa
to return home. Yet, our fear of the Saracens prevented us
from taking a course in the open sea of the Adriatic, as we
had done when we came, since we were now worried about
their fleet. So we passed alongside the cities on the coast.
The Franks hold some of these, and others are still held by
the Saracens. The names of the cities are: the city commonly known as Arsûph, but Azotus in Latin, is next to
Jaffa; then comes Caesarea Palestina, and after that Haifa.
Baldwin, the flower of kingship, has possession of these.
Then comes Acre, a very strong city, which is called
Accaron; then Sur and Saegaeta, which are better known
as Tyre and Sidon; then Jebeil (known as Byblus of old);
then Beirut, and so past Tartûs, which Duke Raymond
holds. After these we passed Gebelee, where are the mountains of Gelboe. We had also passed by Tripolis and Latakia.

On the Wednesday after Pentecost, while we were sailing
between Haifa and Acre, twenty-six Saracen ships belonging to the Admiral of the cities of Tyre and Sidon suddenly
came into sight. They were accompanying an army which
was going towards Babylon to provide assistance to the

Chaldaeans in their war against the King of Jerusalem. Two of the ships that came with us laden with pilgrims from Jaffa now left our ship behind, since they were the lighter craft. Using their oars they managed to escape to Caesarea.

The Saracens then sailed all around our ship, congratulating themselves on obtaining such a prize. Our men, however, were ready to die for Christ, and seized their arms. In the time available the castle of the ship was fortified with armed men. In our Dromund there were nearly two hundred men capable of defending it. After about an hour's delay, the leader of the enemy force, who had held a council of war, ordered one of his crew to go up the highest mast of his ship. Here he was to spy out exactly what we were all doing. But when the admiral learnt from the sailor the stoutness of our defence, he hoisted sail and made for the open sea. It was in this way that, by His grace, our Lord rescued us on that day from our enemies. Afterwards our people from Jaffa captured three of these same ships, and enriched themselves with their booty.

We sailed as close as we could along the coast of Syria and Palestine, and after eight days landed at the port of St Andrea on the Island of Cyprus.

CHAPTER THREE

THE VENETIAN PACKAGE TOUR

NEARLY *three hundred and eighty years elapses before our next pilgrimage. The existence of Latin kingdoms, founded by the Crusaders at Jerusalem and in other parts of the Near East, encouraged an increase in pilgrims to the Holy Places, particularly from the West. Many important visitors now had family connections in the region. Religious military orders, the Knights Templars, and the Knights Hospitallers, which became a military order in 1120, took as their prime function the defence of pilgrims and the Holy Places.*

However, although there were Latin Christian kingdoms in the region until the loss of Acre in 1291, the conditions experienced by pilgrims varied with the military and political situation. Jerusalem was lost to Saladin in 1187, reoccupied by the German and Sicilian emperor, Frederick II, in 1229 (at the time he was under excommunication from the Pope), and finally lost in 1244. The fortunes of the Latin kingdoms also depended very much on the military and political successes, or otherwise, of the Muslim rulers in the region. Relations between Latin Christians and indigenous eastern Christians were often strained, especially

when their practices or rights were interfered with. At the same time the Abbasid caliphate in Baghdad and the Fatimid caliphate in Egypt had different priorities, as well as strong disagreements about Islamic theology, and they were often in conflict. The Seldjuk Turks, whose incursions into Anatolia had provided a spur to the First Crusade, continued to undermine the Abassid and Fatimid caliphates.

In the middle of the thirteenth century the Mongols, whose empire had grown dramatically in Asia under Ghengis Khan, now threatened to overhwhelm both the Christian kingdoms of north-eastern Europe and the Islamic states of the Near East. King Bela was defeated by the Mongols at Mohi in Hungary in 1241. The Mongols sacked Baghdad in 1258, and Damascus fell to them in 1260. The Christians of the Near East had some reasons to believe that the Mongols were sympathetic to Christianity. Their communities had been deliberately spared the massacres which occured at the sack of Baghdad. The Mongols made clear that they had no intention of attacking the Latin kingdoms unless they were provoked. But the Mongol occupation was short-lived, and the Christian expectations of protection were quickly disappointed.

The death of the Great Khan Mongka at home in Asia led to a dynastic war, and the Mamluk Sultan of Egypt, Qutuz, managed to rally the Muslim forces. In 1260 he defeated the Mongols at Ain Jalud. Before the battle, the Mamluks had asked for assistance from the Latin kingdom of Acre: no troops were actually sent, but the Latins provided free passage and provisions to the Mamluk forces. Immediately after his triumph the Sultan Qutuz was murdered by his lieutenant, Baibars, who subseqently consolidated Mamluk rule in Palestine.This rule lasted until the time of our next account. After the end of the Latin kingdoms the remaining Christians in the region had to put up with humiliations and restrictions from their Muslim rulers, because their sympathies for the Mongol invasion were well known.

Elsewhere in Constantinople, and on the Greek mainland, indigenous eastern Christians had suffered grievously when the

Crusaders of the Fourth Crusade turned aside from their original purpose of aiding the Latin kingdoms of the Near East, and sacked Constantinople. The Pope, Innocent III, was appalled by their action and its barbarity. But the Crusaders were unmoved by his censure, and went on to found separate Latin kingdoms in Constantinople and mainland Greece. Eventually the Greek Byzantine Empire's fortunes revived, and the Latin Empire in the territory of the Greeks was brought to an end in 1261. But the legacy of this attack and occupation seriously scarred relations between Christians in the East and West.

In the first part of the thirteenth century St Francis established his band of friars at Assisi. He himself went on the fifth crusade to attempt to broker a peace. He managed to meet and preach to the Mamluk Sultan of Egypt who appears to have been impressed by his sincerity and holiness. A truce was subsequently agreed. But a proposal for a lasting peace was rejected by Pelagius, the Pope's legate, by the Patriarch of Jerusalem, and by the military religious orders. About this time the Franciscans had their first martyrs, when five brothers were tortured and executed after preaching in public in Morocco.

After the loss of Jerusalem by the Crusaders in 1187, the Latin clergy withdrew from the city, and the care of the Holy Places returned to Greek, Syrian and Armenian Christians. But when Frederick II retook Jerusalem, the newly founded Franciscans seem to have established a tenuous position in the city. It is a Franciscan tradition that some years after the fall of the Latin kingdom of Jerusalem, the Mamluk Sultan, whose predecessor had heard St Francis preach, granted the Franciscans the right to live in the Holy Sepulchre. They also took up residence on Mount Sion at this time.

In 1300 Franciscan rights were formalised. Rupert, king of Apulia, a nephew of St Louis, made an agreement with the Sultan of Egypt whereby the Franciscans were granted the Church of the Cenacle on Mount Sion, the Virgin's chapel in the Holy Sepulchre, and the cave of the Nativity at Bethlehem for the sum of 32,000 ducats. In 1422 the Franciscans lost the Church of the Cenacle when the Muslims decided that part of it was sacred to *the Jewish king David, whom they also revered.*

The beginning of the thirteenth century also saw the establishment of a second band of friars, the Order of Preachers, founded by St Dominic. At first this was associated with the Church's struggle to re-establish its authority in Southern France. This Albigensian crusade against the Cathars lasted from 1209-29. But the Dominicans then turned their attention to the intellectual defence of the Catholic Church in the universities of Paris and Bologna. One of their most distinguished friars, St Thomas Aquinas, brought out his definitive work, the 'Summa Theologiae' from 1266-73.

In the fourteenth century a French pope, Clement V, moved the papal court to Avignon in 1305. One of the crusading military orders, the Knights Templar, whose main role had ceased with the loss of the Latin kingdoms of the Near East, was suppressed in 1312. The Black Death (1347-53) produced an upsurge of popular religion, with much emphasis on repentance and public penance for sins. The western church was much weakened by its great schism (1378-1417) when there were rival popes in Rome and France. Wycliffe in England, and John Hus in Bohemia questioned aspects of church doctrine and practice.

The fifeenth century saw some improvement in the fortunes of the Church in the West. The great schism finally ended in 1417 with the election of Martin I as sole pope. Lay movements, such as the beguines for women, and the brethren of Gerhard Groote, testified to the continued fervour of the laity, although the authorities were rather wary of movements which did not have a codified rule approved by the Church. An end to the schism between the Orthodox Greeks and the Catholic West at the Council of Florence in 1438-9 was widely welcomed in the West. But the Orthodox negotiators were subsequently unable to gain acceptance for the agreement when they returned to their constituent churches.

In 1453, after the Eastern Emperor had failed to obtain adequate military assistance from the West—he had hoped for this as a reward for the reunion of the eastern and western churches—Constantinople fell to the Turks. Poignantly, the last Christian service in the great Church of St Sophia was a united one of Orthodox and Catholic Christians. After receiving Holy Communion the last Emperor of Byzantium went out of the church and died fighting on the walls of the city. There was some consolation for western Christians later in the century when King Ferdinand and Isabella of Spain finally defeated the emirate of Granada, the last outpost of Islam in Western Europe.

In the 1480s a brother of the Order of Preachers of St Dominic, Felix Fabri, who was a member of the Convent at Ulm in Upper Bavaria, went twice to the Holy Places. In the preface to the account of his visits he describes his many years of longing to go on the pilgrimage. He confesses that before he went he hardly ever had any other subject on his mind whether awake or asleep.

But he was careful to take advice before he decided to go. He consulted Prince Count Eberhard, an elder statesman of Wurtemburg, who had been made a knight of the Holy Sepulchre in Jerusalem when a young man. Brother Felix explained that although he was keen to make the journey, he was terrified of the sea, which he had never seen.

The elderly knight's advice to Brother Felix was as follows: "There are three acts in a man's life which no one ought to advise another either to do, or not to do. The first is to contract a marriage, the second is to go to the wars, and the third is to visit the Holy Sepulchre. All three acts are good in themselves, but they may easily turn out badly, and when this happens the person who gave the advice is blamed as if he were the cause of the unhappy outcome." Yet the elderly Prince added that to go on the pilgrimage was "virtuous, holy, praiseworthy, and exceedingly useful, provided those who undertook it did so to praise God, and not out of frivolity, curiosity, or from love of the pomps of this world, which are empty and transitory vanities."

Brother Felix also consulted a nun of exceptional holiness. She gave him this straightforward advice: "Leave immediately on the journey you are intent on! On no account stay here any longer! And may God be your companion on your way."

His first visit in 1480 was very rushed. When it was generally known that he was going on the pilgrimage, Apollinaris von

Stein, the Governor of Upper Austria, asked him to be a companion to his son, Master George von Stein. As someone bound by religious obedience Brother Felix took the precaution of getting a licence to make the pilgrimage from Pope Sextus IV and the General of his order in Italy. He did this before he laid his wishes before the local Provincial of his Order and the Prior of his own convent, to seek their approval.

He set out on his first visit on Friday the 14th of April 1480, travelling first to Memmingen to collect Master George from his father. The subsequent journey by sea was dangerous because of the possibility of attack by Turkish ships, even though they were on a Venetian ship, and a treaty was currently in force between the Turks and the Venetians. During the journey, forty pilgrims, who were alarmed by the risks, abandoned the pilgrimage at Corcyra and returned to Venice. Here they gave out that those who had continued on the pilgrimage would certainly be captured by the Turks and killed.

When Brother Felix returned home he learned that requiem masses had been said for his dead soul in Swabia. In fact, the pilgrim party had favourable winds, eluded the Turks, and arrived in Jaffa sooner than they expected. They spent an unpleasant seven days on their galley waiting for their guides to come up from Jerusalem. But they had to spend only one night in the caverns on shore where pilgrims were traditionally lodged on arrival. In the event they spent nine days in the Holy Land, and it was clearly a very perfunctory pilgrimage, such as happens sometimes today.

On the other hand, an important objective was fulfilled. George was made a Knight of the Holy Sepulchre, and completed his grand tour in Nicosia by being made a Knight of the Order of the Kings of Cyprus by the Queen of Cyprus herself. This required George to defend the island of Cyprus against any future attack of the Saracens, Turks or Tartars. During the rest of the journey back to Venice the party were dogged by appalling weather and contrary winds, and almost everyone went down with dysentery. They called in at Rhodes just after it had repulsed a Turkish attack, but they were not particularly welcome—they were travelling on a Venetian ship, and the Venetians had signed a treaty with the Turks. Later, when the pilgrims eventually arrived at Crete, everyone got very drunk on the strong local wine. By the time he reached Venice Brother Felix was too ill to continue travelling, so George went home to his father at Memmingen with some other companions.

Brother Felix later concluded that his first pilgrimage was one hundred times more disagreeable and dangerous than his second one. It had been particularly spoilt by rows between disorderly pilgrims. The French bishop of Orlean's party came in for much criticism. There were continuous rows between the French and German pilgrims. In the Introduction to the account of his second pilgrimage Brother Felix describes his feelings on his return to Ulm:

I CAME back to Ulm sound in body, and seemed superficially happy and cheerful. But in my heart and soul I was gloomy and troubled, because of the worry I knew that I should have over the possibility of a further pilgrimage, and a return to the Holy Land and Jerusalem. For when I left the Holy Land I had made up my mind to return, but I had not communicated my decision to anyone else.

I was by no means satisfied with my first pilgrimage. It was exceedingly short and hurried. We ran around the Holy Places without any understanding and feeling for what we were seeing. Moreover, both within and outside Jerusalem, we were not allowed to visit some of the Holy Places. Only once were we permitted to walk over the Mount of Olives and its holy sites. Our only visits to Bethlehem and Bethany were at night! And so, once I had returned to Ulm and had begun to reflect on the most Holy Sepulchre of our Lord, and the manger where He had lain, and the Holy City of Jerusalem, and the mountains around about it, and the other holy places—their appearance, shape, and the way they were arranged, I found that everything eluded me. Indeed the Holy Land, and Jerusalem and its sacred places, appeared to me as shrouded in a dark mist, as though I had seen them only in a dream.

In my view I seemed to know *less* about them than I did *before* I visited them. And when I happened to be questioned about any of them I could give no precise answers. Nor was I able to write down a clear description of my journey. I was exceedingly disatisfied that I had undergone such suffering, difficulties and dangers, and had spent such sums of money and time, without receiving any lasting fruit, consolation or knowledge. Often when I thought to comfort myself by turning my thoughts to Jerusalem and its holy places, I was only able to conjure up a vague picture of them. I then said to myself angrily, "Just stop thinking about these places, for you have only been there in your imagination!" And so I conceived a burning desire to return and prove the reality of my visit. But this thought only made me gloomier, for I could see no way of going back there. Indeed I believed that a return visit was impossible.

But Brother Felix was clearly a resourceful young man. Since no study or writing gave him any pleasure except the stories of the Bible which mentioned Jerusalem, he began to make a collection of the accounts of pilgrimages of the Crusaders, of memoirs written by pilgrims, and of any descriptions of the Holy Land. But the more he read the sadder he became. He realised how imperfect, superficial, irregular, and confused his own pilgrimage had been.

After a year's study he managed to meet the Master of the Dominican Order when they were both on ecclesiastical business in Colmar, and persuaded him to agree to allow him to go on a further pilgrimage. He then persuaded a Friar Minor, who had recently been made a suffragan bishop and was going to Rome for his consecration, to obtain the Pope's permission for a further pilgrimage. When these licences were obtained, he then had to find a way of funding his journey. In due course, with the help of the local representative of the Holy Roman Empire in Ulm, he managed to obtain a position as chaplain to a party of pious German noblemen who were going to the Holy Land in some style. Perhaps understandably, the Prior of his convent in Ulm was not particularly pleased at the idea of this second pilgrimage.

*But he was unable to object when he learned of the approval of
the Pope and the Master of their Order.*

*The party to which Brother Felix belonged consisted of twelve
pilgrims. He describes them as follows:*

The Lord John Wernher, Baron von Cymbern, a handsome and wise man, remarkable for the grace of his manners, and his learning in Latin;

The Lord Henry von Stoefel, Baron of the Holy Roman
Empire, a physically powerful and active man, of virile
character as a true Swabian nobleman should be;

The Lord John Truchsee von Waldpurg, a nobleman of
tall stature, of a respectable and elevated character, serious,
and deeply concerned about the salvation of his soul;

The Lord Ber (Ursus) von Rechberg, a noble of the
Hohenrechberg family. He was the youngest of the party
and the tallest, as well as the liveliest, bravest, most cheerful, kind and generous of them all;

With the four nobles there were the following attendants:

Balthazar Büchler, a sensible man of great experience; all
their lordships were guided and governed by his advice,
whom they regarded as their father;

Artus, their lordship's barber, a man who could play so
sweetly and so well on musical instruments, that one cannot believe that anyone could be found to match him;

John Schmidhans, a man-at-arms who had fought in
many wars, and who came on the pilgrimage as their lordships' servant;

Conrad Beck, a respectable and sensible man, a citizen of
Merengen, who was their lordships' steward who purchased
the provisions;

Peter of Waldsee, a good simple fellow, patient when
faced with hardships, who was the cook for their lordships
and the entire company;

Ulric von Rafensburg, who had once been to sea as a galley slave, and had suffered a great deal; he was by profession

a trader, and acted as their lordship's interpreter;

John of Babenhausen, a man of peace, who was a schoolmaster, and eager to serve their lordships;

Brother Felix, priest of the Order of Preaching Friars at Ulm, a pilgrim for the second time to the Holy Land, chaplain to their lordships and to the whole company.

The rendez-vous for the party was at Innsbruch, the seat of the Duke of Austria. From there they were to proceed to Venice where they were to board the pilgrim ship for Jaffa, the port for the Holy Land. Brother Felix describes his preparations for the pilgrimage as follows:

From the day I received approval for my pilgrimage I let my beard grow. I adorned both my cap and scapular with red crosses. They were sewn on my clothes for me by virgins dedicated to God and spouses of Him who had been crucified. I also assumed all the other outward signs of that holy pilgrimage, as I had a right to do.

There are five outward marks of a pilgrim. The first is a red cross on a long grey gown, with the monk's cowl sewn to the tunic—unless the pilgrim belongs to some order which does not permit him to wear a grey gown. The second is a grey or black hat, also marked in the front with a red cross. The third is a long beard growing from a face which is serious and pale because of his future efforts and dangers. For in every land even the heathens themselves when travelling let their beards and hair grow long until they return home. They say that this was first done by Osiris, a very ancient king of Egypt, who was reputed to be a god, and who travelled throughout the whole world. The fourth mark is the scrip or knapsack on the shoulders, which holds his few provisions, together with a bottle—sufficient not for luxury, but for the bare necessities of life. The fifth mark is one which he takes on when in the Holy Land. This is an ass, with a Saracen driver, instead of his staff.

Brother Felix describes his departure from Ulm as follows:

On the 14th of April, which is the feast of Ss Tiburtius and Valerianus, after hearing Mass and breakfasting, I called together all the brethren, and said to them that I now wished to leave. I asked for a pilgrim's blessing from our Reverend Father, Master Ludwig (Brother Felix's special friend and counsellor). He led me into the choir. The whole convent community accompanied me. Then, kneeling in the middle of the choir in the presence of the Holy Sacrament, I received a blessing from the altar. The prior of the convent and my fellow brothers were all sobbing bitterly. When I had received my blessing, my own sobbing and tears made it impossible to frame words to bid a farewell, but my tears, sad face and sobs spoke for me. I embraced and kissed each one of my brothers, and begged to be remembered in their prayers. I was scarcely able to persuade Father Ludwig to stay quietly at home. He wanted to see me safely to Memmingen, as he had done on my earlier pilgrimage. But I absolutely forbade him to do this, so that we both should avoid fresh grieving when we parted there.

Although I set out on the pilgrimage with a joyful spirit and cheerful heart, yet I was leaving behind this father, my most faithful friend, and my much loved brothers, who were all so sorrowful and downcast that I could not prevent myself from crying a great deal myself.

But at last, having got the baggage together that I was intending to take with me, I set it on a horse which I had purchased, and mounted. I was just about to ride off in company with the Count's servant; but as soon as I got on my horse, all the brothers flocked around me and eagerly begged me to take a careful note of all the Holy Places that I saw, and to write an account of them and bring it back to them. This was so that they might too enjoy the pleasure of visiting the Holy Places, in mind, if not in body. I promised my brothers that I would do this. Then with the Count's servant I rode out of the convent and we stealthily passed out of the city, as though we were hiding ourselves. We crossed the river Danube by the gate which leads to the sheep bridge.

In the Introduction to the account of his second pilgrimage, no doubt remembering his earlier failure to keep records, Brother Felix wrote the following:

... I never passed one single day while I was on my travels without writing some notes—not even when I was at sea, in storms, or in the Holy Land. I have frequently written in the desert as I sat on an ass or a camel; or at night, while the others were asleep, I would sit and put into writing whatever I had seen.

After riding for thirteen days and staying at various monasteries and inns he and his companions reached Mestre near Venice on the 27th of April. They had crossed the Brenner Pass in the Alps and met the other pilgrims of their party at Stertzing. The lords and their party had set off from Innsbruch a day earlier than they had planned because they had become bored with life at the Duke of Austria's court. Lord John von Cymbern, who had gone on ahead to Venice in advance, had arranged for them to be given a meal at an inn on the mainland at Mestre, and had organised their forward transport on to Venice. Brother Felix gives the following account of their journey to Venice:

He (the German agent of Lord John von Cymbern) took us into the garden of the house, and showed us a large boat on the river, which at that point runs down from the mountains to the sea. The boat had been sent over to Mestre from Venice by the Lord Baron. We were very cheered by this, and sat down and ate and drank what had been made ready for us. Then we carried all their lordships' baggage on board the vessel. All of us then got aboard, which loaded it pretty fully, for there were many of us and the baggage of their lordships and their servants was not inconsiderable. And so we said goodbye to the land and entrusted ourselves to the waters.

Once we were aboard we sailed down the river for about a mile towards the sea. When we reached the place where the river glides into the jaws of the Mediterranean and were on the perimeter of that sea, and were sailing into the bitter salt water, we began to sing the pilgrims' hymn with a loud and cheerful voice. This is customarily sung by those travelling to the Sepulchre of our Lord: "In Gottes Namen fahren wir; Seiner Genaden begehrn wir: Nu helf uns die Gottliche Kraft, and das heylige Grab; Kyrie eleison," ("In God's name we are sailing; His grace we need: may His power shield us and the Holy Sepulchre protect us: Lord have mercy.")

By now we had reached the castle of Malghera, and were passing the tower called the Torre di Malghera. Here we met a boat in which some tough young men were rowing very wildly towards Margerum. Their boat ran into ours, and the two craft crashed together. Ours was driven to one side by the impact and struck a post which was standing in the water. We were in serious danger of capsizing. In fact the boat very nearly did roll over with the passengers and baggage in it, and we were all frightened out of our wits. The sailors of both boats began to abuse each other. But in the end we went our separate ways.

A little later we met another boat with passengers aboard. One of them asked us the name of the inn in which we were proposing to stay at Venice. When we said the St George, where Lord John von Cymbern had booked rooms for us, the fellow began to criticise that particular inn and its landlord. Then he stood up on the prow of his boat and tried to prevent us from going on our way, while pointing in the direction of some other inn at which he said that we should lodge. But as he stood there loudly shouting in an effort to convince us, he suddenly lost his balance and fell from the prow of the boat into the water. His comrades then had a lot of difficulty in dragging him out of the water and saving his life. He was dressed in new silk clothes, and these were baptised with him! All this caused a great deal of laughter aboard our boat.

As we sailed on a little further, we caught sight of that famous, powerful, rich and noble city of Venice, the mistress of the Mediterranean. It was standing there in an amazing fashion in the middle of the water, with its lofty towers, great churches, and splendid houses and palaces. We were astonished to see such massive tall buildings with their foundations in water! A little later we found ourselves sailing into the city, then travelling down the Grand Canal as far as the Rialto.

On each side we saw buildings of amazing height and beauty. Below the Rialto we turned off the Grand Canal into another canal. On the right bank of this is the Fondaco de' Tedeschi. We proceeded along this, passing a number of houses, till we arrived at the door of our inn. In German the St George is known as "Zu der Fleuten." Here we disembarked, then walked up some sixty stone steps from the water to the rooms which had been prepared for us. Then we carried all our belongings up to them.

Master John, the landlord, and Mistress Margaret, the landlady, received us with great good humour. They greeted me with particular friendliness, since I was the only one they knew. I had been their guest for many days during my former pilgrimage. The rest of the household were also introduced to us and made us welcome, showing their keenness to be of service. The entire household, landlord, landlady, and the men and women servants, were all German and spoke German. No word of Italian was heard in the house. This was a great relief to us, since it is most exhausting to live with people and be unable to converse with them.

The last to greet us when we entered was the big black dog which guards the house. To show how pleased he was he wagged his tail and jumped up at us as dogs are inclined to do with those they know. The dog receives all Germans from whatever part of Germany they come with similar warmth. But when Italians, Lombards, Gauls, Frenchmen, Slavonians, Greeks, or men of any other country except Germans come into the house, he becomes so angry that you would think that he had gone mad. He rushes at them, barking loudly, and leaps up at them in fury. He will not cease worrying them until someone from the house quietens him down.

He has not even grown accustomed to the Italians who live in the house next door, but barks furiously at them as though they were complete strangers, and treats them as implacable enemies. Nor does he allow their dogs to enter the house. Yet he takes no exception to German dogs. Even when German beggars come to the house looking for alms, he does not attack them. Yet he falls on poor Italians who come to beg for charity, and sees them off. I have often rescued a poor man from being bitten.

Some Germans say that since the dog is an implacable enemy of the Italians, this is a proof that German *men* can never become bosom friends with Italians, nor Italians with us, because each has the dislike rooted in his very nature. The animal, being irrational and governed only by its passions, quarrels with the Italians since its nature urges it to do so. But human beings restrain their feelings through reason, and keep down the feelings of animosity although it is engrained in their nature.

We found many noblemen from various parts of Germany at the inn, and some from Hungary. They were all bound by the same vow as ourselves, and intended to make the sea crossing to the most Holy Sepulchre of our Lord Jesus at Jerusalem. There were more Germans in other inns, where they had formed themselves into companies, some large, and some small.

Brother Felix, in view of his religious vows and status as a priest, had some scruples about living completely with lay people, as he now explains.

Our twelve were inseparable, and lived at the common expense of the four lords in our party. The lords summoned the landlord and made arrangements with him for lodging, meals and all the other facilities of the inn which

they wished to make use of. When these arrangements had been made in front of all of us, I thought privately of another arrangement for myself. Without informing the lords what I was up to I went by boat to the convent of St Dominic, and asked the prior of the house to take me in as a guest until the pilgrims' galley left port. After much importunity on my part I prevailed on him to agree. It was disagreeable for me, and very distracting to my thoughts, to live entirely among secular lay people.

So I returned to my inn and packed up my belongings. Then I arranged a meeting with my lords and told them of my intentions. But this proposal did not please them at all! Indeed it annoyed them very much. They were quite unwilling to agree to my living apart from them. And so, to persuade me to agree to stay with them, they made special arrangements with the landlord for me to have a private room, where I could be quite alone. There I would be able to sleep, pray, read and write, and escape from all the vice of the inn as if I were back in my own cell at Ulm. And so I remained with the party all the time we were in Venice. But often, in fact almost once every day, I used to visit the convent of the brothers of my Order.

Brother Felix and his party spent five weeks in Venice before their ship sailed. Their time was spent in inspecting the choice of possible pilgrimage ships, seeing the sights, going to venerate important religious relics, and attending the splendid church and civic ceremonies which Venice offered.

The galley they finally settled on for their voyage was owned and captained by Master Peter de Lando. It was a new galley, lengthy, broad and clean. They made a trip out to view it early on in their stay in Venice, and examined the passengers' berths in the huge dormitory cabin in the hold. The other ship that they looked over was the one which Brother Felix had been on during his first visit. Although Brother Felix rather liked the captain of this ship, who was called Master Augustine Contarini, the vessel was much older and less clean, and the nobles favoured the other.

They then followed the current arrangements for what was in fact a kind of early package tour. The party signed a formal agreement with their chosen captain at the Doge's Palace in front of the protonotaries of Venice. The names of all those in the party were entered in a large book at the Palace, then the pilgims went off to the vessel to reserve their births, and have them marked with chalk. Each berth was a place for one man, extending from his head to his feet. The berth was assigned to him for sleeping, sitting and living, whether the pilgrim was well or ill. The articles of the party's agreement were as follows:

Article 1.—That the captain shall take us pilgrims from Venice to Jaffa, a port of the Holy Land, and shall bring us back again to Venice. He shall be ready to leave within twenty-six days, and shall sail as soon after this as there is a fair wind.

Article 2.—That he shall well and properly provide a galley with experienced seamen who understand the art of sailing with whatever wind may blow, and shall have on board sufficient armament for the defence of the galley from attacks of pirates and enemies if need be.

Article 3.— That the captain beware of putting into strange ports on his way, but that he shall stop only at those where he usually obtains provision for his galley; as far as possible he shall avoid putting in to harbours, but continue on his way. We specially wish him to avoid the Kingdom of Cyprus, and not to put in there; but if he has to, he shall not remain there more than three days because we have a traditional belief that the Cypriot air is unhealthy for Germans. But if any of our company should wish to pay his respects to the Queen of Cyprus, and wait on her at Nicosia, and receive from her the decorations of her Order, the captain shall be bound to wait for his return, since this is an ancient custom among noblemen from the time there has been a king in that kingdom.

Article 4.—The captain shall give the pilgrims two meals of food and drink a day without fail. If for any reason any of us shall not wish to attend the captain's table or come to supper in the evening, or if all of us choose to stay in our berths, the captain shall nevertheless be bound to send food and drink to us without argument.

Artiicle 5.—That the captain shall be bound to provide for the pilgrims, during their voyage from Venice to the Holy Land and from there back to Venice, an adequate allowance of good bread and biscuit, good wine and sweet water freshly put on board, with meat, eggs, and other food of the same sort.

Article 6.—That every morning before we eat our food

he shall give us a beaker or small glass of Malvoisie wine, as is the custom on shipboard.

Article 7.—If the pilgrims ask to be put ashore near where the galley happens to be, but where the captain does not wish to land for any reasonable purpose, such as to obtain water, medicines or other necessities, the captain shall be bound to provide us with a boat and crew to carry us to port.

Article 8.—If the captain shall call in at any uninhabited harbour where the pilgrims shall not be able to obtain necessities for themselves, he shall be bound to supply them with food, just as if they were not in harbour; on the other hand, if he shall put into a good port, then they shall be bound to provide for their own meals.

Article 9.— The captain shall be bound to protect the pilgrims, both in the galley and out of it, from being attacked or ill-used by the galley-crew, or from being thrown off the galley-rowers benches, should the pilgrims wish to sit with the galley-rowers. He shall be bound to prevent the galley-rowers from molesting them on land, as far as he can, and he shall not place any article on the pilgrims' berths.

Article 10.—The captain shall let the pilgrims remain in the Holy Land for the proper length of time, and shall not hurry them through it too fast, and shall lead them to the usual places and go with them in person. We especially wish him to raise no objections to leading them to the Jordan River, which pilgrims always have difficulty in doing, and he shall save them from all troubles with the infidels.

Article 11.—All dues, all money for safe-conducts, and for asses and other expenses, in whatever names they may be charged, or in whatever place they have to be paid, shall be paid in full by the captain alone on behalf of all the pilgrims without their being charged anything, and he shall likewise pay the great fees; the smaller fees we shall see to ourselves.

Article 12.—In return for these expenses to be incurred and things to be done by the captain, each pilgrim shall be bound to pay him forty-five ducats of the kind called *de Zecha*, that is, newly minted coins, on condition that the pilgrims shall pay one half of this sum in Venice and the remainder at Jaffa.

Article 13.—Should any pilgrim happen to die, the captain shall in no way interfere with the goods which he bequeaths, but shall leave them untouched in the possession of the person or persons to whom the deceased left them in his will.

Article 14.—Should any pilgrim die before reaching the Holy Land, the captain shall be bound to restore one half of the money previously received, to be dealt with by the executors according to the instructions of the deceased.

Article 15.—Should any pilgrim die on board, the captain shall not immediately order his body to be cast overboard, but shall cause it to be taken ashore and buried in some graveyard. If, however, the galley be at a distance from the land, then the body of the deceased may be kept on board until some port is reached, or the comrades of the deceased pilgrim agree to have it cast into the sea.

Article 16.—If any pilgrim wishes to go to St Catherine's monastery at Mount Sinai, the captain shall be bound to hand over to each person expressing such a wish ten ducats of the money previously paid to him.

Article 17.—That the captain before leaving Jerusalem with the pilgrims shall loyally help those pilgrims who are setting out to St Catherine's, and shall draw up a friendly agreement between them and their guide.

Article 18.—That the captain shall assign to the pilgrims some convenient place on board the galley for keeping chickens or other fowls, and that his cooks shall permit the pilgrims' cook to use their fire for cooking for the pilgrims at their pleasure.

Article 19.—Should any pilgrim on board the galley happen to become so ill as to be unable to remain in the stench of the cabin, the captain shall be bound to give such a person some place to rest in on the upper deck, either in the castle, the poop, or on one of the rowers' benches.

Article 20.—That if in this instrument of contract anything has been left out or inadequately expressed or provided for, which, nevertheless, by law and custom it is the captain's duty to perform, then it shall be held to have been
expressed in this instrument, and shall be held to have been
written down therein.

WHAT THE PILGRIMS DID IN VENICE

On the first day of the lovely and joyful month of May
we are offered for our devotion the Holy Apostles, St Philip
and St. James. And so, very early in the morning, when the
lords and the rest of the company had risen and were making themselves ready for Mass, they asked me where we
should hear it today.

I then spoke to them along these lines: "My lords, we
have set out on our pilgrimage in the name of God. It would
not be right for pilgrims to sit around idling. We now have
to remain in
this city for a
whole month
longer than
we thought.
Since we are
surrounded by
water on all
sides, we can-
not cheer our-
selves up by
passing the

time in visiting flower gardens and the pleasant countryside—shady woods, green meadows, and charming land-
scapes filled with trees and wild roses, lilies and other native
flowers. Nor can we pass the time in hunting; nor would it
be appropriate for us to go to tournaments and dances. My
advice then is that while we are here we should make a pilgrimage every day to some church, and visit the bodies and

relics of some of the saints, of which there are a great number in this city. In this way, throughout the month of May,
we will be plucking spiritual flowers—the roses and lilies of
virtues, graces and indulgences."

This suggestion went down well, and it was unanimously
agreed that we should either row or walk to a church each
day. And if every one did not go to church every day, some
should do so, so that afterwards they should be able to tell
the others what they had seen.

And so on the 1st of May we hired a boat and went to
the Church of the holy Apostles St Philip and St James and
attended a service there. At the end of this we went up to
the altar and kissed the holy head of St Philip, which is
kept there, and the holy arm of St James. There was a great
crush of people to see and kiss these sacred relics. So we
waited until we could have a better view of them without
being jostled. This opportunity came after the service had
ended and the people had left.

Our objective was to touch the relics with our jewellery.
Pilgrims to the Holy Land usually carry with them to the
holy places choice rings of gold or silver, beads of precious
stones for 'Paternosters' or rosaries, or the actual rosaries,
little gold or silver crosses, or any other similar precious and
easily portable trinkets. They are entrusted to them by their
parents or friends; or else they buy them in Venice or overseas to give as presents to those who are dear to them on
their return. So, whenever pilgrims come across relics, or
arrive at any holy place, they take these pieces of jewellery
and touch the relics or the holy place with them. They do
this in the hope that they may obtain some sanctity from
the touch. Eventually they are returned to the friends of the
pilgrims as pieces dearer and more valuable than before!

I was the least important and poorest member of all our
company. Yet I had with me many precious jewels which
had been lent me by my friends, patrons and patronesses, so
that I might touch with them the relics and holy places
that I visited. I was to return the trinkets later and receive

recompense for doing this. Among others, Master John Echinger, the worshipful Mayor of Ulm at that time, had entrusted me with his most prized ring. His father, James Echinger, had drawn this from his thumb during his last moments in this world and given it to Master John, just as his father had received the ring from his father before him. I am sure that it was already of more value to him than 100 ducats. I know that he now values it at more than 200 ducats!

It was my duty, at holy places, or where relics were kept, to take all the jewels belonging to the lay pilgrims in my hands and touch the sacred objects with each item, and then give them back to their owners. In fact, some of the nobles left their jewels in my keeping throughout the pilgrimage.

...On the 8th of May, which was the feast of our Lord's Ascension, we went up to the Church of St Mark to attend the service there and see the grand display. Countless people flock there on that day. When everyone has gathered there, a procession moves off from St Mark's to the sea. The Patriarch of Venice, with his clergy and the religious of all the convents, together with the Doge and the Senate, as well as the leaders of the guilds in order of precedence and wearing their special badges, all walk together, accompanied by banners, torches, reliquaries and crosses. Then they go aboard ships specially prepared for them.

The Patriarch, with the Doge and the Senate, embark on the Bucintoro (in Latin, Bucephalus, the name of Alexander the Great's horse). This great ship is built in the form of a tabernacle. It is painted, covered in gilding, and draped with silk hangings. The embarkation is accompanied by magnificent ceremonial. All the bells in the city are rung, trumpets sound, and the clergy sing various hymns. As the Bucintoro moves off from the shore, powered by three hundred oarsmen, it is accompanied by over five thousand other sea craft. They sail as far as the castles which form the entrance to the harbour of Venice, and then beyond the harbour into the sea. Here the Patriarch blesses the sea, just as it is customary in many places to bless the waters on that day.

When the ceremony of blessing is over, the Doge takes a gold ring from his finger and throws it into the sea. In this way he marries the sea to Venice. After the ceremony many strip off and dive to the bottom to search for the ring. He who finds it keeps it for his own, but he also lives for a whole year in the city free from all taxes and charges which are borne by the rest of the Venetian citizens.

While this is going on all the other ships crowd around the Bucintoro making a great maelstrom. They create a tremendous racket, firing off cannons, sounding trumpets, banging drums, shouting and singing, so that they seem to be shaking the sea itself. We managed to witness all this from our hired boat. After the blessing of the sea and the marriage ceremony, the ships all row towards the monastery of St Nicholas on the Lido. When they reach the shore they disembark from the ships and all try to enter the church. But though it is a massive church, not a hundredth part of the crowd are able to get in. Yet in all the crowd there is not one single woman. The whole ceremony is performed by men alone.

As the Patriarch, dressed in his pontifical robes, and the Doge, accompanied by all his retinue, are walking towards the church, the Abbot of the monastery, wearing his mitre, and all his monks in their ecclesiastical robes, come out to meet the crowd. The Abbot takes the Patriarch and the Doge by the hand and leads them into the choir of the church, where they hold the service for the day with great solemnity. After this they return to their ships, and everyone goes back to his own home for dinner.

On the 29th of May, which was the feast of the most holy Corpus Christi (the Body of our Lord), we again went up to St Mark's and attended the solemn procession. Never had we seen such magnificence as we saw on that day at Venice. The procession was wonderful. There was a great mass of priests and the religious of all congregations, everyone wearing their sacred vestments and carrying most precious reliquaries of every kind. They walked in an orderly way around the great square of St Mark. The whole circuit of the route along which the procession moved from one great door to the other was draped with linen hangings.

The Patriarch bore the Sacred Host, and beside him walked the Doge, wearing his precious ducal cap. After them came the Abbots, wearing their mitres, and the entire Venetian Senate. The ecclesiatical robes displayed were magnificent. But it was also very interesting to see the solemn demeanour of the lords senators in their very impressive robes. After them came the many guilds, and the ordinary people. The religious, both those in religious orders and secular priests, walked first. There was singing and the playing of every kind of musical instrument, and displays and pageants of all sorts. In this particular procession no college, no monastery and no guild was represented which did not also put on some pageant of its own to arouse admiration and entertain the spectators.

The Dominicans of St John and St Paul added lustre to the whole procession by their amusing yet splendid pageants. We saw so much gold and silver, and so many precious stones and expensive clothes, that no one could hazardous a guess at their total value. The whole scene was of a teeming, hurrying and pushing mass of humanity.

After dinner we went by water to the convent of Corpus Christi. Here live the rich and noble Venetian ladies who are nuns of the Order of St Dominic. Almost the whole city came across the water to their church. There was a great crush of a crowd to see the procession. The preaching friars from the three monasteries of St John and St Paul, St Dominic and St Peter Martyr, all came and made a superb procession with the Corpus Christi. The column was long, and wound its way right along the Grand Canal. There were many little pageant scenes.

Yet among these holy solemnities I was struck by how much vanity there was to be seen among the vast crowd that gathers together for this occasion There was a good deal of extravagant dressing among the women, and of dissolute behaviour by laymen, as well as disorderly conduct both by the clergy in religious orders and secular priests. Whether the honour shown to the most holy and divine Sacrament is acceptable when it is offered in such a profane way, God, who knows all things, is alone able tell! When everything was over we went back home to our inn for supper.

...On the first day of June we began our sea-voyage. It was the first Sunday after the Feast of the Blessed Trinity. We rose very early before sunrise on that morning and carried all our belongings to a large boat that we had hired. It was moored at the door of our inn. Then, after saying good-bye to everyone in the house, we embarked. We went down the Grand Canal beyond the city, then over to the church of St Nicholas on the Lido. Here we left one of our party to guard our luggage in the boat, while the rest of us went into the church. It is a vast building, with a monastery of Benedictine monks next door. I asked to see the sacristan, then requested the wafer bread which he had promised. I also asked him to supply us with a bottle of good wine in addition to the sacramental wine, and I set this on the altar as well. I then put on my sacred vestments and went to the altar. Then, in the presence of the pilgrims, I said the Mass appointed for this Sunday.

After Mass I also blessed the wine which had been brought to me in the bottle. I used the special blessing of St John the Evangelist. Then I gave the wine to my lords the pilgrims to drink for the love of St John, so that our journey might be happy and successful. After this had been done very devoutly, we got back again into our boat, and sailed out of the harbour between the two castles that guard the entrance to the port. Our galley lay out at sea about a mile beyond the harbour.

As we proceeded a dreadful wind got up. This hindered our course so seriously that it was with difficulty that we reached the galley in the space of two hours. Eventually we arrived and went up the ladders into the ship. We found her already full of people. Our companions, whom we had sent on as an advance party four days earlier, were all in a sorry state. The ship, as she lay at anchor, had been tossed about in various directions by the force of the wind and this had made them sick. They cheered up when they saw us and began to feel better. But they filled their lordships in with details of all the unpleasant hardships of life at sea of which they had had a small taste.

During the day one knight begged me to return to the city by boat with him. He wanted to fetch a long chest that he had had specially made to fit into his berth. It was designed for him to sleep on, for he was too proud to lie directly on the floor. His berth was located where he would just be able to squeeze the chest in.

So we both got back into the boat and proceeded to Venice. When we had collected the chest we brought it back to the galley. But our return trip was equally difficult because the wind remained against us. So it was late evening when we succeeded in bringing the chest down into the cabin. The knight put it into his berth with great satisfaction in the hope that he would sleep well on it. But, had he known the future, he would have been alarmed rather than comforted by his acquisition. For it was on this very chest that the knight later died a cruel and horrible death. He was a knight of a different company to mine.

We now arranged our berths and beds to sleep in. This resulted in a great deal of confusion, effort and argument, because we were not used to doing this. When it was dark and all the lights were out and everyone was quiet, a violent wind sprang up. This tossed the ship about, and caused alarm and concern. As we were lying silent and worrying, or were asleep in the darkness, suddenly a nobleman, terrified by a dreadful dream, began to scream horribly at the top of his voice. It was as if he had been run through with a sword. At his shouts everyone on board awoke. Since we were all half-asleep and it was dark, there was total chaos, with people thinking that the knight must have been stabbed by some thief. The nobles arose and tried to find their swords in the dark. Others attempted to make their escape, fearing some terrorist act against the pilgrims. As a result, a dangerous *melée* ensued throughout the galley's main cabin. Eventually the man who had been lying next to the noble who had screamed, realised what had happened, and shouted out his explanation as loudly as he could. In the end this persuaded everyone to lie down again in his own berth. Thus passed this rather disturbed night. The captain had not yet come aboard the galley.

On the 2nd of June the captain arrived before sunrise with his servants and all his household. He brought with him some pilgrims who had been accepted as passengers at the last minute. Among these were a Fleming and his wife. When this woman came on board many were annoyed, because she was the only woman among the passengers. Master Augustine, the captain of the other pilgrim galley had collected together all the rest of the women on board his ship.

There was nobody on our galley who was not irritated at the fact that this old woman had come aboard. People were alarmed at the idea of one woman having to live alongside so many noblemen. The feeling was aggravated when we first saw her, because she seemed to be restless and inquisitive, as indeed she proved to be. In fact the seven elderly women with whom I had made my earlier voyage made far less noise and were less in evidence than this old beldame. She ran here and there all over the ship; she was full of curiosity, and wanted to hear and see everything. In this she made herself thoroughly unpopular. Her husband seemed a decent chap, and many said nothing for his sake. But if he had not been with her, she would have had a hard time, for the woman was a thorn in everyone's side.

Now that we were all on board and it was light, some sailors were ordered to dress the galley. Seven large silken banners were hung from the castle on the poop and from the top, which was also surrounded with a piece of tapestry. The first and largest banner was that of the lord pilgrims to the Holy Sepulchre. It was white, with a red cross running from one end of it to the other. The second was the banner of the Lords of Venice, the banner of St Mark; it was also white, with a red lion—beneath its fore-feet was the sea and beneath its hind-feet the land. The third banner was that of our Lord Pope Sixtus IV; it was the colour of the sky, with a green oak-tree bearing golden acorns, and two Apostolic keys. The fourth was that of the captain; this was of very many beautiful colours. The fifth showed the arms of Venice and those of the captain together. There were two other banners, both alike, white with black lions.

When the galley had been dressed they began to get her ready to set sail, since we had a fair wind which was blowing the banners aloft. The crew, who were making a lot of noise, began to weigh up the anchors and take them on board, to hoist the yard aloft with the mainsail furled on it, and to drag up the galley's boats out of the water.

All this was done with loud shouts and a great deal of effort, till at last the galley was loosed from her moorings. The sails spread and filled with the wind, and with great rejoicing we sailed away from the coast. The trumpeters blew their trumpets just as if we were going into battle; the galley rowers shouted, and all the pilgrims began to sing together, 'In Gottes Nahmen fahren wir.'

The galley ploughed powerfully through the sea, and we soon left Venice behind, the port where our journey proper had begun. We were as happy to leave it as if we had been released from prison, for all our longing was for Jerusalem. The ship was driven along so fast by the force of a fair wind, than within the space of three hours we were unable to see any mountains, or any part of the earth or shore, or

anything on dry land. All that we could see was the sky and the water. In this short time we had gone so far out to sea that we had risen above and higher than the highest Alps, and were unable to see them. They were now, as it were, low down, with the sea's curvature interposed between them and us. Once we were out of sight of this world, the crew took down all the ornamental dressing of our ship and gave it the everyday look as they made it ready for work.

Brother Felix gives some information below about galleys and the way they were organised, including the system of justice and religious services aboard, ordinary aspects of life on the ship, including how people passed their time, shipboard meals and sleeping arrangements. He concludes with some warnings and advice about the various dangers and inconveniences of life on a galley and in the ports on the way.

A galley is an oblong vessel propelled both by sails and oars. All galleys resemble each other, and are very nearly alike in shape, but differ in size. Some galleys are large and are called triremes, some small, which are called biremes. There is a further difference in that some galleys are ships of war, and others carry cargo. On my first pilgrimage I crossed the sea in a bireme, but on my second I went on a trireme. A bireme is one which is rowed by pairs of men and pairs of oars; a trireme is rowed by three men and three oars; on each bench there are three oars and as many rowers.

The galley on which I made my second pilgrimage had

sixty cross-benches, and on each bench there were three rowers with their oars. If a ship is equipped as a war-galley it has an archer with his bow on every bench alongside the rowers. The length of the ship was thirty-three cubits. A cubit is the distance of a man's reach with his arms outstretched. The length is the measurement from the prow to the stern. The width of the ship is seven cubits, when measured across the ship just before the mast. But if we were to measure the entire width which it has when the oars are extended on either side then it will be thirteen cubits in width. The height of the ship, measuring from the well to the keba, which is on top of the mast and in the round top, is more than eighteen cubits.

Now all galleys of the same size are so much alike in every respect that a man who goes from his own galley on board another, would hardly know the difference, except from the fact that the officers and crew are different. Venetian galleys are as alike as swallows' nests. They are built of very tough timber, and fastened together with many bolts and chains, and with ironwork.

The first and foremost part of the galley is called the prow. It is sharp where it meets the water, and has a strong beak, made rather like a dragon's head, with an open mouth, entirely fashioned out of iron. With this it can strike any ship that it may meet. On either side of the beak are two holes, which a man can put his head into. Through these the cables of the anchors pass, and through them the anchors are hauled up. Only in a great storm is the sea able to come in through these holes. The beak of the prow reaches high up, and from it the ship's belly begins to swell out against the sea.

The prow has a sail of its own called the *dalum*—commonly called the *trinketum*. Beneath this is a small cabin, where ropes and sails are stored. There the captain of the prow sleeps. He has a detachment of crew of his own who live there too. They do not work anywhere else but carry out any work that is needed in that part of the ship. This is also where any poor wretches whom the crew of the prow pick up from the sea are put. On either side of the prow hang the great iron anchors, which are let down at the appropriate time.

The stern, which is at the other end, that is at the back part of the galley, is not sharp where it meets the water like the prow, nor does it have a beak. It is wide and curves from above downwards to the water. It is much higher than the prow, and on it there is a structure which they call the castle. From the castle the rudder, or rudder post, hangs down into the sea. Above this, in a latticed cabin, is the helmsman, who holds the tiller with both hands.

The castle has three storeys. The top storey houses the helmsman and the compass, together with the man who tells the helmsman where the compass is pointing, and others who watch the stars, note the winds, and point out the sea route. The middle storey has the cabin of the Lord captain of the galley, and of his noble comrades and messmates. The lowest storey is the place where any noble ladies are lodged at night, and where the captain's treasure is stored. This cabin has no natural light except from the hatchway in the floor above.

On either side of the poop hang the boats, one large, and one small. When you are in a harbour they are lowered into the water and used for landing passengers. On the right hand side are the ladders by which you go down to the boats at sea, or climb up from them. The poop also has its own sail, which is bigger than the sail at the prow. They call this the *mezvala*, that is the middle sail. Its Latin name is *epidromus*. There is always a flag on the poop to show the way the wind is blowing.

Two benches away from the three storey structure on the poop is the kitchen. It is not roofed over. Below this is the cellar, and next to this is the stable of the animals for slaughter. Here sheep, goats, calves, oxen, cows and pigs are all stalled together. Further on, on the same side, are the benches with their oars, which go all the way to the prow.

On the left hand side there are also rowers' benches all the way from the poop to the prow. Every bench has three row-ers and an archer. On the edge of the ship, in a position between two benches, hangs a cannon in a moveable iron swivel, and on either side there is a caterpault, from which, in time of necessity, stones are fired.

In the middle of the ship stands the mast. It is a tall, thick strong tree made of many beams fastened together. This supports the yard with the *accaton* or mainsail. On the top of the mast is the chamber, which the Germans call the basket. The Italians call it the *keba*, the Latins *carceria*. On deck beside the mast there is an open space where men assemble to talk, just as in a market-place. It is known as the galley's market place.

The mainsail is fifty-three cloths wide, and each cloth measures more than an ell. But to cope with different kinds of weather different sails are hoisted, which are not as large as the mainsail. During storms they set a square sail of tough canvas called a *papafigo*.

On this upper deck of the galley live the officers and the sailors, each man on his own bench, which is where they sleep, eat and work. Between each bench, along both sides of the galley, there is a rather wide space. Here stand great chests full of merchandise. Above these there is a walkway from the stern to the prow. The officers run up and down this when the oars are being used.

Close to the mast is the main hatchway. Seven steps take you down to the cabin, which is where the pilgrims live, or where the cargo is put in trading ships. The length of the cabin reaches from the cellar in the stern to the small cabin in the prow. Its width is from one side of the ship to the other. It is like a vast and spacious chamber. It receives no natural light except that which comes from the four hatch-ways by which it can be entered.

In this cabin each pilgrim has his own berth or sleeping-place. Pilgrims' berths are so arranged that all along the ship, or rather the cabin, one berth meets the next without any space between them. One pilgrim lies side by side another along both sides of the vessel. They have their heads towards the side of the galley and their feet stretching out towards each other.

Since the cabin is wide, along the middle of it, between the berths, stand the chests and pilgrims' trunks. These stretch from the cellar to the chamber in the prow. In them the pilgrims keep their private property. The feet of the sleeping pilgrims stretch out as far as their trunks.

Beneath the pilgrims is a large space which reaches deep down to the bottom of the galley. This is called the belly of the galley, since a galley is not flat-bottomed like other ships, but is sharp from the bows to the stern. The galley terminates in such a sharp foot below that when it is not in the water it cannot stand upright but has to lie on its side. This sharply pointed hold is filled with sand right up to the decking on which the pilgrims lie. Pilgrims lift up the decking and bury in the sand the bottles in which they keep their wine, eggs, and other things which need to be kept cool.

Down below, in the place where the pilgrims are housed, is the well for the bilge water which is very near the middle mast. The well does not contain human faeces. Yet all the water which comes into the galley, either visibly or which surreptitiously filters down, collects here. The stench from this is more disgusting than the smell from any human latrine. Each day the well has to be pumped out, but in rough weather the water has to be pumped out continuously. The lavatories themselves are placed all along the outer sides of the galley.

The whole galley, within and without, is covered with the blackest pitch, as are the ropes, planks and everything else, so that they may not easily be rotted by the water. The ropes for working the sails take up a large amount of galley space. There are a great many of them, long, thick, and of many different kinds. It is marvellous to see the vast number of ropes and their knots and twists all about the ship.

A galley can be compared to a monastery. The place of

prayer is on the upper deck beside the mast where is also the market-place. The middle of the poop is the common refectory. The benches of the crew and the berths of the pilgrims are the dormitory. The chapter house is over against the kitchen. The prisons are beneath the deck of the prow and the poop. The cellar, kitchen and stables are all open to the sky on the upper deck. Here you have a portrait of a galley, with many things omitted.

...No one is appointed captain of a galley, especially one which transports pilgrim knights, unless he is noble, powerful, rich, wise and honourable. When he is appointed he takes with him some prudent and trusted friends from whom he receives advice, and to whom he confides his inner thoughts. He also chooses and engages a brave military man, experienced in naval warfare, and appoints him chief of the armament, or, what they call master-at-arms. This soldier provides the galley with cannons, catapults, bows, spears, clubs, swords, corslets and shields. The captain also has a steward who provides everything connected with the supply of food. They call him the *Schalk*. He manages the cellar and the kitchen, and sees to the bread, wine and animals for slaughter. Every day he gives orders to the cooks and the cellarer to make the necessary arrangements for food and drink. If food and drink fail it is no one's fault but his, and he alone gets the blame. *Schalks* are therefore generally disliked on board ship.

The captain has another powerful officer, whom they call the *Caliph*. He runs the entire work of the galley everywhere. He is always on the look-out to see whether anything is amiss or broken, or is hindering the galley's sailing. He trims the cargo, refits and repairs damage, and looks after the galley from her well to her mast-head, from her prow to her poop.

One other important ship's officer is called the *Pirate*. We Germans suppose that by this is meant the pilot. He knows the safest and shortest routes across the sea. The ship's course is directed on the basis of his orders and advice. If he enters a part of the sea which he does not know he is required to put into the nearest port. Here he surrenders his position, and the captain engages another pilot who knows the sea routes. The fear is that through ignorance the ship might meet with a Bythalassium, a Syrtis or a Charybdis!

In the pilot's team are some men skilled in understanding the stars and making forecasts; they watch the constellations of the stars, study the sky, decide what winds will blow, and then give their advice to the pilot himself. These men are all equally skilled in their profession; by examining the sky they can predict storms or periods of calm. They can also interpret the colour of the sea, the shoaling and swimming patterns of dolphins and flying fish, the pattern of smoke from the fire, the smell of the bilge water, the glittering of the ropes and cables at night, and the flashing of the oars as they dip into the sea. At night they can tell the hour by looking at the stars.

They have one compass by the mast and another in the top cabin of the castle. A lamp always burns by this at night. They never turn their eyes from it when sailing at night. One of them always gazes at the compass and chants a sort of sweet song, which indicates that all is going well. In the same tone he sings to the person who holds the tiller of the rudder, indicating the quarter towards which the rudder should be turned. The helmsman never dares to move the tiller anywhere except when ordered to do so by the person in charge of the compass, for the latter can see whether the ship is going straight, crooked, or sideways.

They also have other equipment from which they learn the position of the stars, the force of the wind, and the sea routes. For example they have a chart an ell long and an ell wide on which all the sea is marked with thousands and thousands of lines. Countries are marked out with dots and miles by figures. From this chart they plot and note where they are, even when they are unable to see land, and when the stars are hidden by clouds. They discover their position from the chart by drawing, with amazing care, a curve from one line to another and from one point to another. They have also many other instruments with which they find their way across the sea, and they sit together every day conferring about these matters.

In addition to these experts, there is the chief officer of the galley who does the actual work. He first receives the orders from the navigators. He is called the *Cometa*, being, as it were, the galley's mate. His place is below the castle between the rowers benches on the upper deck. It is to him that the captain confides his orders. The mate then sets the whole crew in motion. Hanging around his neck he wears a silver whistle, and with this he gives the signal for whatever nautical task is to be done. Whenever by day or night his whistle is heard, all the men immediately come running, making a whistling noise in response.

This officer gives them the orders to put into or out of harbour, to let down or weigh the anchors, to set or furl the sails, to work at the oars, or cease from doing so, to heave the lead, to plant mooring posts ashore, or to release the moorings. All those under him fear him as they would fear the devil, because he strikes them with rods, and punishes anyone he wishes with his fists or with the end of a rope. No one dares murmur against him, since everyone would rise up and attack the murmurer if the signal were given. I have seen the most inhuman cruelty perpetrated by these mates on poor crew members.

Next below him in rank there is another officer called the *baron*, or boatswain of the galley. He carries out the mate's orders, and always has his quarters in the middle of the galley near the mast. He also wears a whistle hanging round his neck to alert the crew to orders. Wherever the mate cannot be, the boatswain runs, whistling, shouting and encouraging the men to get to work. His special responsibility is the ropes, sails and anchor. He must ensure that they are in good order and ready for use at all times. Because of this he has special rights and privileges on board the vessel.

Under the mate is the *sub parono*, who receives the mate's orders, and passes them on to others. Below him are about nine men called *compani*, or comrades, although some are superior to others in rank. These are crew members who know how to run about the ropes like cats. They climb the awnings very quickly up to the cap, run along the yard and stand upright even in the fiercest storms. It is they who weigh the anchors, and dive into deep water to free them if they get stuck, and who do all the most dangerous work on board. They are usually very energetic young men, who are quite reckless of their own lives. In the galley they have a fearless and powerful image as the baron's armed followers.

Below these are others known as mariners, who sing when their work is being done, because work at sea is particularly hard. Tasks are carried out in concert, with one chanting out the orders and the mariners singing in response. The 'comrades' stand near those who are working, and sing to them, encouraging them and threatening to hurry them on with a beating. In this way huge weights are dragged about. These mariners are usually old men of good character.

The lowest class of all are the galley rowers of the first and second class. In Latin we call these *remiges*. They sit on the cross-benches to work at the oars. There are a great many of them, and they are all big men. Their work is only really fit for asses. Shouts, blows and curses are used to encourage them to work. As when horses are drawing loaded carts up a steep road, the harder they pull, the more they are urged on, so these wretched men, when they are pulling with their utmost strength, are still beaten to make them pull the harder. It makes me sad to write about this, and I shudder when I recall the torments and punishments which these men face. I have never seen beasts of burden so cruelly beaten as they are. They are frequently forced to let their tunics and shirts hang down from their belts, and work with bare backs, that they may be within reach of the whips and scourges.

For the most part the rowers have been hired by the captain; they are men of the lowest standing, prisoners, or escapees, or people who have run away from their own countries or been sent into exile. Some have had the misfortune of being unable to live or find employment ashore.

Whenever there is a concern about them jumping ship, they are tethered to their benches with chains. They are usually Macedonians, Albanians, or men from Achaia, Illyria and Sclavonia. Sometimes they are Turks or Saracens who conceal their religion. I never saw a German rower, because no German could survive such a miserable existence! They are so inured to their unhappy life that they work dispiritedly and aimlessly unless someone stands over them and beats them like asses and curses them. They are poorly fed and always sleep on the boards of their rowing benches. Day and night they are always in the open air ready for work. In stormy weather they stand in the middle of the waves which break on the deck.

They are usually thieves, and do not return anything that they come across. For such crimes they are often most severly tortured. When they are not at work they sit and play cards, and dice for gold and silver, with terrible oaths and blasphemies. I never heard such terrible swearing as I did on board these galleys. They do nothing, either in fun or in earnest, without using the foulest blasphemies of God and the Saints. Yet there are sometimes among them respectable merchants, who subject themselves to this very harsh regime so that they may trade in the ports. There are also some craftsmen, such as tailors or shoemakers. When they are not working, they make shoes, tunics or shirts on board. There are also some who are washermen who charge for washing others' shirts.

Indeed, all the crew are alike, for they all ply some sort of trade. Everyone has something to sell under his bench. He offers goods for sale when in port, indeed trade with one another goes on every day. In general they all know at least three languages, Sclavonian, Greek and Italian; a lot know Turkish as well. Even among the rowers there are ranks and degrees. Some are put in authority over others. Those who are trusted are stationed as guards round about the gangways of the galley, and are called guardians. Some are in charge of the prow, some on the right-hand and some on the left-hand side. Those who serve in the stern are the best treated. On board most galleys there are also three or four strong youths who are learning to run about on the ropes. They also practice other tasks that need courage.

Alongside the rowers there are some who fire the cannons. Then there are the trumpeters who sound their trumpets in the morning and in the evening each day before and after dinner, and in all ports. Others are employed in cleaning and decorating the galley. There are at least two barbers on board, who are also the ship's physicians and surgeons.

There are also some who have the task of torturing those who break the rules. Like 'lictors' ashore their job is to inflict this on the orders of the captain. Another powerful officer on the galley is that of the scribe or clerk. He has the names of all the passengers aboard the galley written down in a book. He takes down their name as they come aboard and leave the ship at each port; he also settles all arguments about berths, makes men pay their passage money, and has many other duties. He is usually disliked by everyone!

CRIME AND THE SETTLEMENT OF DISPUTES ABOARD

A place is set aside aboard for justice, so that there may be peace among such a large number of people. Justice is strictly applied on a galley, and there are judges aboard. Every day, as the occasion arises, they sit in their court, hear both sides, and decide cases. The procedure is very strict.

When there is a dispute about anything aboard a galley, the matter has to be settled by a judgement of the naval court; neither side is allowed to plead against the other in any court not held at sea. No one is obliged to honour a contract made with another after he has left the vessel. Nor will

a judge ashore interfere with agreements made
man lends ten ducats at sea, and then, after the\
ashore, the other says that he never received the\
will compel him to repay, and no witnesses will
hearing against the presumed lender...Thieves are punished
comparatively lightly. No one is condemned to death. The
harshest sentence on board is that anyone who has committed a grave offence is tied to the awnings and flogged. Then,
after this punishment, he is rowed to the nearest land and
abandoned there, and the ship sails on its way. I once saw
them also deal with a homicide in this way.

RELIGIOUS OBSERVANCE ABOARD

We must not fail to mention the way that those who go to
sea conduct themselves towards God during their work
aboard. For they should not forget God amid all the risks and
dangers. God is worshipped three times a day aboard ship.
First, in the early morning at sunrise, one of the servants of
the captain stands aloft on the top of the castle, calls for
silence with his whistle, then lifts up a wooden board. On
this is painted the Blessed Virgin, holding her child in her
arms. When they see this, everyone kneels and says the *Ave
Maria*, and other prayers if they choose. As soon as the picture has been taken away the trumpeters begin to sound
their trumpets. Then everyone goes to his usual task.

About the eighth hour aboard, before mid-day, the signal
for prayer is again given. A chest which stands on the upper
deck near the mast is covered with a fine cloth, and two
candlesticks are set on it. Between the candlesticks a crucifix is set up and a missal made ready. It is just as if Mass is
about to be celebrated. All the pilgrims come on deck and
stand around the mast.

Then the priest comes there wearing a stole around his
neck. He begins the *Confiteor* and goes on to read the service which follows. But he leaves out the canon of the
Mass, since he does not consecrate. Thus he performs Mass
without the sacrifice, and ends with the Fourth Gospel "In

the beginning was the word..." These Masses are termed 'dry' or 'torrid.'

I cannot recall having read whether this way of saying Mass is based on canon law. Yet I know that some learned men are unhappy with it. They say that to read the part of the service which is publicly performed by the choir is unobjectionable. But to read that part wearing a stole, with all the observances and priestly solemnities of the Mass itself, is a sham. On feast days they chant masses of this kind, but the Sacrifice of the Mass is never consummated on board ship.

Before I had carefully considered the matter I was surprised at this. I attributed it to a lack of concern on the part of our church authorities. They seemed to me to have less concern for the salvation of the children of the Church than was right and proper. I was supported in this opinion when I read that, in the days of St Gregory, masses *were* celebrated on board ship. This can be seen from his *Third Dialogue*, where we read that some who were once in danger in the Adriatic Sea partook of the Lord's Body and Blood. Another example occurs in a story of St Louis, King of France. Indeed it seemed to me a serious piece of negligence on the part of the present day Church, since not long ago it *had* provided for the Sacrament to be given to men who were in the middle of great dangers, and particularly to pilgrims who are enduring these dangers for the love and honour of God.

But after I had carefully weighed up and considered the matter, I realised why our wise and holy mother Church does not want the most holy Sacrament of the Eucharist to be consecrated, or preserved aboard ship. First, because this sacrament is not a sacrament of necessity. It is sufficient for a man's salvation if he has the intention of partaking of it at a suitable time and place. Now on shipboard there is no fitting place, as can be seen later. And even if there be occasion for it, yet the time is at every moment unsuitable. Secondly, on board ship there is no proper priest whose special duty it is to celebrate Mass, as the law directs. For no one knows to what parish a ship belongs.

Thirdly, the Host cannot be well preserved there. Large, solid, well-baked loaves of bread do not last long on board ship, but in a few days become damp and mouldy. Bread of the thinnest kind and lightly baked would survive for even fewer days. In wet weather the Host could not last three hours without turning into liquid paste. This happens to wafers ashore in damp weather, which become quite unfit for use.

Fourthly, the Sacred Body ought to be preserved in a church, and in a holy place. Now a ship is not a church, nor is it a consecrated place, hence it is not a suitable place for the Sacred Body to be kept. Fifthly, a light should always burn near the Blessed Sacrament. This cannot happen on a galley. The force of the wind and the waves often means that the whole galley is covered in water. No light could be kept continually burning, either in lanterns or lamps.

Sixthly, Mass should not be consummated nor the Host kept on board because of the uncertainty of the dangers which ships face. Storms arise suddenly, in the twinkling of an eye, and the ship is violently tossed about. If a priest were to be standing at the altar, he would not be able to stay on his feet, and the chalice or the crucifix or the altar table would be unable to stay in its place. In an instant everything would be upset. Seventhly, because of the force of the winds, the altar candles would not stay alight, and the corporals and other altar cloths would be swept off the altar. Eighthly, the motion of the sea is unpredictable; it can toss about all over the place, even when there is little wind. Then, when no one is expecting it, waves splash up over the galley and wash over everything in their path.

Ninthly, there is nowhere on board where due reverence can be guaranteed; everywhere is subject at times to an irreverent rush of activity. The crew when running about as their tasks require could not show respect for the priests in the act of celebrating, or to the Sacrament itself. They would overturn everything, priest, altar and the Sacrament together. Work at sea has to be done quickly, as it were with lightning speed; it is pressing and cannot be delayed. Moreover, in every part of a galley men sleep, eat, drink, gossip, lie and perjure themselves. And this is destructive of the respect due to the Sacrament.

Tenthly, Mass ought not to be consummated on board because of the presence of unsuitable persons. For on board these ships there are frequently Jews, Turks, Saracens, schismatics, heretics, men banished by law and judge, and those who have been excommunicated. Even if there is not an example of each aboard, yet some of them are always aboard in whose presence Mass should not be celebrated.

Eleventhly, a bar is the major sins which are committed on board. Men daily play at dice and cards, horribly blapheme God and the Saints, perjure themselves, lie, sneak and steal, overindulge in food, and get drunk. I have often heard, and I pray God that it may not be true, that the eastern rowers commit the most unspeakable sin of sodomy on board galleys. As a result the place where such vices are practised is unworthy of the performance of so great a sacrifice.

Twelfthly, the foul stench and dirtiness of both the galley and the men aboard make her unsuitable. Thirteenthly, Mass ought not to be celebrated because of the derision of unbelievers, and the scandal of their presence. For if they heard that God was present on board in the Sacrament, as we believe according to our religion, yet they saw us living sinfully, or being beset by troubles, this would cause grave scandal. And they would hold the most Holy Sacrament in contempt.

Fourteenthly, because of the foolishness of bad Christians. For if the Sacrament were on board a galley, and a storm arose at sea, and the ship was in danger, and relief or assistance did not come immediately, those foolish Christians would at once use this as a criticism of the Holy Sacrament and would say in their hearts, "Are you not the

Christ? Save yourself and us." I have seen an example of this with my own eyes. Once when a storm had lasted a long time and was growing fiercer, I and other priests and persons in holy orders turned to the Lord and sang litanies, and invoked the help of the saints, since the storm was dangerous. Yet when the storm was at its height, a nobleman who had received knighthood at Jerusalem (but was still without faith), said that we must cease praying. He believed that as a result of our prayers the storm was raging all the more. When they had stopped us singing psalms and litanies, they said, "If your prayers had found any favour with God, we should have been saved from this danger long ago."

So it is doubtless correct that if Holy Communion were to be celebrated on board ship, the same thing would happen. Ignorant and unbelieving secular people would imagine that when the Sacrament was present among them no evil would befall them. But if anything did happen to them, it would be blamed on its presence. In the same way the children of Israel, when they took the Ark of the Lord into battle with them, thought that they could suffer no harm at the hands of their enemies. But in spite of this they were defeated, and the Ark of God was taken, as is explained in the Fourth Chapter of the First Book of Kings. For an unworthy and irreverent handling and carrying about of holy things provokes the displeasure of God more than a humble and reverent surrender of them. In the same way some peasants require their curates to carry the Sacrament through their fields so as to prevent their crops being destroyed by hail. If the crops do well, they are ungrateful; but if they fail, they are scandalised and murmur against God.

The last reason why the Eucharist is not distributed on shipboard is because of the ease and suddenness with which men vomit there. If a storm should blow up immediately after the priest had celebrated Mass, he could be compelled by a powerful natural instinct to spew out the Sacrament, without being able to hold it down—something which is too horrible to speak about. In summary it is therefore out of reverent piety that this Sacrament is withheld from those at sea.

The third time when men praise God on board is at sunset. Then they all assemble about the main mast—the meeting place on the galley. Here they kneel and sing the *Salve Regina*, prefacing it with litanies when they are in great difficulties. After the *Salve*, the captain's chamberlain blows a note on his whistle. Then, standing aloft on the poop, he wishes everyone good night on behalf of the captain, then, as in the morning, he shows the picture of the Blessed Virgin. On seeing this they all say the *Ave Maria* three times, as is customarily done on shore at the sound of the angelus bell.

Once this is over the pilgrims go down into the cabin to their births. Then, after the pilgrims have left, the clerk of the galley stands on the castle and begins a long chant in ordinary Italian, and adds a litany. At this all the crew and officers of the ship respond on their bended knees. They use a lot of words, and the prayers last about a quarter of an hour. I have often been present for these prayers. At the end, the clerk asks everyone to say one *Pater Noster* and one *Ave Maria* for the souls of the parents of St Julian. They do this every night and never omit it.

Since this prayer is offered every night I enquired why it should be made for the parents of St Julian. I received two answers to my question. Some told me that the prayer was offered in praise of Simon, the leper, who was called Julian at first, and who hospitably received our Lord. The prayer is said so that, by his intercession, mariners may reach a good port and be hospitably received. I replied that the prayer is not made in praise of the saint, but for the soul of his parents. If they wanted to say a prayer that they might meet with hospitality why, I asked did they not pray to St Martha, who received our Lord with particular hospitality.

They were unable to answer my point. Others said that they said this prayer for the parents of St Julian because of what we read in the *Speculum Naturae* of Vincentius (Part ii, Book 10, chapter 115). Julian, when a young man, killed his father and mother in their bed without realising who they were. He thought that his mother was his own wife, and that his father was in the act of adultery with her, as the story relates. But how this custom was established here on board no one knows.

I have set out above the order of divine services in use at sea. In addition pilgrims say many additional prayers by day and night. As soon as they arrive at any port they all rush off to hear Mass. Yet at sea the celebration of Sundays and saints' days is well known for being badly done. I am sure that the devil makes a special effort to put obstacles in the way of keeping feast days holy. I have often noticed that on solemn feast days there is always a greater disturbance on board ship than at other times. Sometime we have lain three or four days in some port, but as soon as Saturday evening comes we make ready to set out. Then, when we have started, we sail the whole night so that on Sunday no Mass can be held. This happened so often on board the ship on which I sailed, it was as if it were done deliberately. Indeed the holier the day, the harder is the work done at sea.

On holy days it was my custom to preach a homily. I will tell you briefly what happened to me in this religious task. During my first pilgrimage, while I was preaching, a certain son of Belial frequently interrupted the Word of God by his laughter. Neither entreaties nor nudges could keep him quiet. He only laughed all the more. In the end I gave up, and after that would not preach the Word of God any more, although many begged me to do so. For the wise man says in Ecclesiasticus xxxii, 4: "Do not display your cleverness out of season." And our Lord says in St Matthew vii. 6: "Do not give dogs what is holy; and do not throw your pearls before swine."

Yet in my second pilgrimage there were a greater proportion of nobles and respectable people on board who were very pleasant companions. They used to invite me to preach the Word of God to them, which I did on all holy days. Yet my preaching made me disliked by many noblemen. They believed that I targeted them and used them in my homilies as examples of certain vices. As flattery gains friends, so truth breeds hatred!

The burial of the dead is also a part of divine service. It is conducted aboard as follows. When anyone falls ill, he confesses to any priest he pleases. This practice seems covered by the rule which allows any priest to give absolution in case of need. When someone draws near to death his comrades take care of him, watching over and waiting on him.

As I have said there is no Eucharist on board, nor is there any provision made for extreme unction. Yet it seems to me that this rite might be used, since it is not the oil itself, but the use made of it which constitutes the Sacrament. Yet the sick man only has confession before he dies. When he is dead and rolled up in his shroud they put him into the boat and row him to the nearest shore, provided they are near land. If there is a church there, they bury him in its cemetery. If not, they commit him to the earth somewhere else.

If they are near land, but it is in the hands of infidels, they do not take him ashore, but cast his body into the sea. If they are a good distance from land they take the shroud, bring up sand from the hold, lay the corpse on the sand, roll it all up, and tie a bag of stone to the feet. Then, in the presence of the whole ship's company, with the priests chanting *Libera me, Domine*, the crew take up the body, and let it fall into the sea in the name of the Lord. The body, weighed down with the stones, immediately sinks into the deep, and the soul climbs to heaven. I have often seen this ritual.

But I have never seen the other method of burial which some say they have witnessed. The body is wound about with its shroud, then bound to a plank, and thrown with the plank into the sea. However, it is fact that when a dead man has any friends they do what they please with his body, and can put it into the sea, with or without stones, or with a plank.

When the body has been laid out, the clerk of the galley makes a written list of all the property left by the deceased, and gives it to the captain; then the clerk pays his debts if he has no friends. If he has friends these do this for him, and they have him buried when they land at the next port. Unless the pilgrim has previously made an agreement with the captain, as we did, the captain acquires the bed and bedding and the clothes of the deceased.

There are many who believe that burial at sea is best for a person of distinction, and preferable to his being crushed by the weight of earth. At the present time the Aethiopians throw their dead into the Nile, as we are told by Diodorus. They take the view that the river is the best of all sepulchres. For whether the body is eaten by animals or rots there, it does not pollute the atmosphere or the soil. However, if one of the Venetian grandees dies at sea, they bury his corpse in the sand within the galley, and then bring him to Venice.

HOW MEN PASS THEIR TIME
ON BOARD A GALLEY

The pilgrims' way of life on a galley varies with their different temperaments. In order to pass the time when afloat they take up various occupations. Unless a man knows how to occupy his time, he will find the hours aboard very long and tedious. Some of them, as soon as they get up from the meal table, go around the galley asking where the best wine is being sold. Then they sit down and spend the whole day over their wine. This is usually done by Saxons and Flemings, and other men of low standing. Others gamble: some with board and dice, and others just with dice; some with cards, and others with chess-boards. One may say that the greatest number gamble.

But some sing songs, and spend time with their lutes, bagpipes, clavichords, zithers or other musical instruments. Others discuss world affairs, read books or pray with their beads. Some sit still and meditate, others shout a lot because they are full of the joys of life; some laugh and some whistle. Others work wih their hands, while some just sleep because they are lazy. Indeed there are some who spend their whole time asleep in their berths! But others run up and jump across the rigging, or show off their strength by lifting heavy weights or carrying out other physical feats. These men have others who troop around with them as spectators, looking first at one, and then another.

Some just sit and look at the sea and land as they pass by it. Then they write about what they see and produce travel books. This was my daily task, outside the religious services I have mentioned. Busy men are never tired of life, even on board ship. St Jerome, when he was on board a ship returning from Rome to Jerusalem, wrote a very beautiful letter to Asella about false friends.

Finally I should mention that there is one occupation common to all seafarers, which, although disgusting, is a daily task, and most necessary. This is the hunting and catching of lice and vermin. Unless a man spends several hours each day on this task when he is on a pilgrimage he will have very disturbed nights!

...All these occupations are pursued more or less according to the state of the weather. Men's inclinations vary remarkably at sea, more so than on land. Aboard they are influenced by the heavenly bodies, the atmosphere, and the motion of the sea. I have often witnessed days when we were all happy, contented, and good comrades; when no one slept, but all were in the best of spirits. But I also recall days of deep silence and stillness, when no man's voice could be heard, and everyone was either dozing or sitting about miserably.

I have often seen pilgrims united together in great peace and concord as though they were all brothers and children of one mother. Yet on occasion I have seen so many quarrels and disputes arise over the most trivial matters, that the galley has become very much like hell with pilgrims' curses and blasphemies. I have observed it for a fact that all human emotions are more violent on water than elsewhere.

HOW PILGRIMS EAT ON BOARD A GALLEY

When it is nearly time for dinner or supper four trumpeters stand aloft and sound the call to meals with their trumpets. As soon as they hear this, everyone who usually dines at the captain's table runs very quickly to the poop. They hurry so that they can get a comfortable seat, for anyone who arrives late gets a poor one. Three tables are set out on the poop and they are nicely laid and prepared. Those who are able to sit at these tables are well off. But anyone who arrives late has to sit outside the poop on the rowers' benches, where it is uncomfortable, and in the sun, rain or wind.

There are no reserved seats at the tables. He who comes first sits where he likes. Poor men do not make way for the rich, the peasant for the noble, the working man for the priest, the laymen for the learned doctor, or the man of the world for the monk. The only reason for any courtesy is friendship. The reason for this lack of precedence and respect is that everyone, great and lowly alike, has paid the same fare to the captain.

I am sure that if people of high rank paid sixty ducats, and ordinary people twenty, or if the captain charged people according to their rank, then honour and respect would be shown to the more important by the less important. It is for this reason that noblemen with their own servants always eat on deck near the mast, or in their berths below, where they have lights, even at mid-day, since the cabin is dark. Before every meal everyone is served with malvoisie wine.

For everyone the meal that follows is prepared in the Italian way. First there is a lettuce salad dressed with oil, if fresh vegetables are available. For dinner there is mutton and a pudding, or a broth of crushed wheat or barley, or bread soup and some thin cheese. On fast days when meat is not eaten, little fish called *zebilini* are served salted, with oil and vinegar, or a cake made with eggs, and a pudding. Fresh loaves are served when the ship is near a port, for bread will not keep fresh on board a galley after the fifth day. When there are no fresh loaves, they serve twice baked cakes, which they call biscuits. They are hard as stones but immediately soften if water or wine is poured on them.

One has as much wine as one can drink. Sometimes this is good, and sometimes it is thin. It is always well mixed and diluted with water. The pilgrims' dinner is quickly served; everything is brought to them in a rush, then, when their meal is at an end, the trumpeters again blow their trumpets. When the tablecloths have been removed, the tables are carefully laid again for the captain and his council. His table is more frugal than that for the pilgrims, but the food is brought to him on silver dishes. His drink is always tasted before it is presented to him, as is done for princes in our own country.

Women pilgrims do not come to the common table, but remain in their berths where they both eat and sleep. My lords had their own cook and their own eating-place. The rowers eat in messes of three on their rowing-benches, and prepare their own food. I have often seen them eat meat which is still red with blood.

If pilgrims want anything special from the kitchen they have to tip the cooks. There are three or four of these, all very bad-tempered, and they cannot be got around unless they receive cash. They are not interested in providing credit. Yet it is not surprising that they are so bad tempered, since the kitchen is narrow, there are many pots and different things to cook, and only a small fire. Outside the kitchen there is always a great deal of shouting going on, with many asking for things to be done. Anyway a cook's job always has my sympathy!

Lords and knights always loathe the food provided by the captain. They give the cooks great sums of money to have separate meals of their own food. They pass on the captain's food to the crew. The meat provided by the captain is particularly disgusting, since they slaughter those animals which they see cannot live longer, and any sheep with disease. When they see a sick animal that will soon die of its own accord they slaughter that. No wine is served from the captain's cellar except at dinner, but the crew sell excellent wine, which the pilgrims buy from them. In stormy weather eating and vomiting take place at the same time!

SLEEPING ABOARD THE GALLEY AND OTHER DIFFICULTIES

After supper the pilgrims sit around and talk with each other on the upper deck near the main mast. They never go to bed until they need lights to descend. When they do go off to their berths there is a frightful rumpus while they make their beds. Dust is stirred up, and serious rows break out between those who sleep next to each other. This happens particularly in the early days before they all become used to the ritual. Someone criticises his neighbour for allowing his bed to encroach on the other's berth. The neighbour denies it. The other persists with his criticism. Each calls on his companions for support. Sometimes whole companies of pilgrims quarrel with each other, During these rows I have seen pilgrims fall on each other with naked swords and daggers, and shout, and create an awful riot.

It is the clerk's job to divide berths equally. But if he were to intervene during one of these quarrels he would be torn to pieces! Even when such a quarrel has come to an end, or even if one does not occur, some pilgrims still come down to bed late and make themselves a nuisance to others with their lights and long protracted talking. I have seen hot-tempered pilgrims throw their chamber pots at burning lights to put them out, which leads once again to massive arguments.

Even after all lights are put out, some people then begin to settle world affairs in discussion with their neighbours, and go on talking, sometimes right up to midnight. If anyone criticises them, and asks them to shut up, they talk all the more loudly, and a new argument begins. If there were not some good and well respected men to settle disputes, the night would never pass peacefully, especially when there are drunken Flemings around!

There are other things which stop one getting a good night's rest besides these. Monks are used to sleeping alone in their cells. They find it hard to sleep aboard a ship because of the restlessness and snoring of their neighbours. On many nights I never closed my eyes. Because the space for your bed is narrow, and your pillows are hard, you become restless. A pilgrim can hardly move without touching his neighbour. The cabin itself is enclosed, exceedingly hot, and full of foul smells. This means that you sweat all night, which greatly restricts your sleep. During the night fleas and lice swarm in very large numbers, and there are also mice and rats.

Often, I might say almost every night, I have got up quietly and gone out into the open air. I then felt as if I had been released from a filthy gaol... I once spent time in a berth on a galley where the horses and mules stood directly above us. Day and night they kept up a continuous shuffling with their hooves on the planks above us. Added to this there is the sound of the crew running about above you, and the noise of the sea, and many other disturbances, all of which take away a pilgrim's rest!

On deck there is the heat of the sun, and in the cabin, darkness, overcrowding, foul heat and tainted air. Although the blowing of the wind is essential for those who sail aboard a ship, yet it is very unpleasant. When the ship is tossed about by it, the pilgrims are made to feel dizzy and sick. All their innards are so shaken about that they vomit up everything in their stomachs, and their bowels are completely upset. It is impossible to stay on deck because of the strength of the wind, and the waves which it casts up over the ship, and the activity of the crew who are running hither and thither. If the mainsail is hanging over that part of the ship where your berth is, you cannot even stay there in it; you must then cross to the other side of the cabin. Sometimes too you need to shift your bed so as to put your foot where your head normally is, since the power of the sails makes the ship lean over on one side.

Smoke from the kitchen is blown back into the ship too when there is a wind, and this can trouble pilgrims a good deal. During a storm healthy men become feeble, and sick men grow weaker still. The continuous pumping out of the bilge water is also a nuisance for pilgrims. First, there is the stench arising from it. Secondly, while the pumping is going on, they are not allowed either to go up on deck, or to come down to the cabin....

Over time mice and rats breed in a ship in great numbers, and they run about all night long, nibbling at men's private food stores, gnawing their way into them, and befouling the food. They also make a mess on pillows and shoes, and drop on to men's faces while they sleep. But they are seasonal, and they do not always come on board. When certain winds blow, all living creatures on board perish and disappear: fleas, flies, mice and the like, so that not one can be located. But when the wind or air changes they breed again. If it is their season, gnats annoy pilgrims very much by their buzzing and bites.

The damp on board encourages fat white worms, which crawl everywhere. They stealthily attach themselves to men's legs and faces. When you become aware of one, and put your finger on it thinking that it's a fly, it bursts, and besmirches with your blood the place where it was hanging. However, although there are many disgusting creatures on a galley, yet nothing poisonous can breed or live aboard. There are no scorpions, vipers, toads, poisonous snakes or spiders. For the sea-water drives away poison, heals the stings of scorpions, cures the bites of vipers and snakes, and is the enemy of poisons of all kinds. Unless Divine Providence had ordered things in this way, no one could live on board large old ships.

A further nuisance for pilgrims is having to make their beds at night and pack them away in the morning. Every morning each man rolls up his bed and ties it with a rope, together with his sheets, pillows and blankets. He hangs this bundle on a nail driven into the side of the ship above his head. The point of this is to ensure that there is free passage through the cabin during the day. In the evening he has to take it down again, unroll it and make up his bed. This is all very exhausting.

Finally, as I have said, pilgrims are troubled by the untrustworthiness and thieving of the crew. You cannot be sure of anything, for crew members steal whatever they can lay their hands on. This is why they are forbidden to go below to the pilgrims' berths, and none dare do this. Even when pilgrims call out for them, they are frightened of going below.

HINTS FOR PROSPECTIVE PILGRIMS

A pilgrim to the Holy Land needs to be on his guard. He needs to avoid sinful thoughts which will endanger his soul, and carelessness, which could lead to bodily injury and loss of life. Here I intend to put down some advice which I hope will be helpful for a pilgrim making the sea crossing. I am not here giving advice which a doctor should give, but the counsel of a friend, based on what I have learned from experience.

In general doctors advise pilgrims to beware of fruit, of drinking-water, of sea air, and of fish. They give advice for the heat, and other advice for the cold. They prescribe many different remedies for thirst, constipation, diarrhoea, and sea-sickness, and medicines which encourage the appetite and counteract poison. They also give those going to sea remedies for many other illnesses, and much other advice. All this is certainly valuable and good, and it is only reasonable to follow the directions of doctors in these matters.

Yet here I confide to you what I myself have seen. I have known pilgrims who were so careful and precise in following their doctor's orders that they did not dare swallow anything or do anything unless it had been recommended to them. Yet, nevertheless, they became sick and weak during their pilgrimage, and some of them died.

On the other hand I have seen men who ate, drank and did whatever they pleased, both at sea and on land, who kept no rule of diet, and often ate to excess, yet with all this they never took to their beds, and were always cheerful and happy. I am not writing this to hint that the former died because of their carefulness in taking medicine, and that the latter lived because of their intemperance, but rather to show the uncertainty of fortune. Let a pilgrim first commit himself to the care of God, and next follow the advice of his doctors in a moderate degree.

In other ways let him be guided by the following advice. A pilgrim should beware of plunging into the sea to bathe. There are a lot of dangers around, even for those who know how to swim very well. When on board ship he should be very wary as he moves from one cross bench to another in case he falls. Falling over anywhere on board is dangerous. He should always use due deliberation when going up and down through the hatches to the place where the berths and sleeping places are. I have had two falls down these steps myself. It is a wonder that I was not badly hurt. After these accidents I always went down with concentration and caution. I have seen men fall down these and nearly kill themselves. Above all a pilgrim needs to be particularly careful when going to the lavatory, since the way to this is dangerous. When walking along the ship's side he should not trust any ropes without testing them with his hands to prove that they are firmly stretched. For if the rope goes slack when he tries to hang on to it, he will fall into the sea.

Pilgrims should beware of insulting or angering the poor crew members. It may happen that they may be of great value to him, or, again, they may do him very great harm or injury. As to the rest of the ship's company, he should act in a way that does not arouse others' dislike. It is damaging for a man to have enemies on board ship. I once saw a stuck-up pilgrim who insulted and angered many people. He ran out of money, and then was forced to beg help from those whom he had insulted. Even though some of the more pious performed acts of charity towards him, he nonetheless suspected that they despised him, for he knew that he deserved to be disliked for his conduct.

A pilgrim should avoid occupying a place either on deck or below which belongs to another, except with that person's full consent. By day he has a place to stand near the mast, which is common to all. But by night he has no right to be anywhere except in his own berth. If anyone goes anywhere other than his own at night, those who don't know him assume that he is a thief. But if for any reason he cannot remain quiet in his berth let him go up on deck and sit himself on the wood at the side of the galley and dangle his feet down towards the sea, while hanging on to the rigging shroud which supports the mast.

Experience will teach a man about these sorts of things. He will hardly credit them when he is first told about them. A pilgrim should be careful, when sitting on the deck, not to rest on any ropes. The wind may change suddenly, and the ropes may cast him overboard or injure him. On no account should he touch with his hand any rope when the crew are pulling it, for his hand or fingers may be forcibly torn off, as often happens. The crew pull with great violence and move enormous weights.

He should also take care not to sit in any place where there are pulleys hanging above him. This can lead to him being grievously injured or killed in the time taken for an arrow's flight. This happened to a steersman on board. He should also beware of getting in the way of the galley crew when they are running about their work. However noble you are, even if you're a bishop, they will push against you, knock you down and trample on you. Work at sea needs to be done with lightning speed, and allows no delay. A pilgrim should also avoid giving a hand in the crew's work, for this annoys them. Above all, he should not stay on deck with them at night during a storm.

He should also be cautious where he sits down, in case he sticks to his seat, since everything is coated in pitch and becomes soft in the heat of the sun. Anyone who sits down then goes off with dirty clothes. A pilgrim should also be careful not to hold anything in his hand which he values, and then let it fall into the sea when he is sitting resting on the side of the galley. A nobleman who was once sitting there with me let go a rosary of precious stones. He valued it very much and would not have parted with it for many ducats. But it was hopelessly lost.

In the same way I myself was sitting reading the service of vigil for the dead, when the book fell from my hand and was lost overboard! Many things slip from careless people's hands in this way! Hats blow off from people's heads when there is a strong wind!

Pilgrims should beware of carrying a light on the deck at night. It is odd, but sailors dislike this very much. They cannot bear lights when they are at work. In storms they carefully extinguish all lights, or cover them with bushells, even when down in the cabin. A pilgrim needs to watch any property of his own carefully, not even leaving it unguarded when among his own friends. For no sooner does he turn away his gaze than it is gone. Nor should he leave his money in a box in his berth, but he should carry it at all times about his person. He should trust it neither to his servants or comrades. For men are peculiarly ready to take to thieving on board ship, even though they may dislike thieving when not at sea.

This is particularly the case with small items, handkerchiefs, belts, shirts and the like, which comrades will steal from one another. For a man often wants things on board ship, and since he is unable to do without them, he uses any means, right or wrong, to supply himself with them. For example, if, when you are writing, you lay your pen down and turn your face away, your pen will disappear, even though you are among men whom you know. And if you lose a pen you will have a great deal of trouble in getting another. This is the case with other items too.

…When in ports the pilgrim should be wary of leaving his galley and wandering hither and thither, especially in unfrequented places by the seashore. All of a sudden he might be captured by pirates and made into a slave and live in the most miserable circumstances for the rest of his days. This often happens to people. I knew of a knight who was attacked when he was on his own by the sea beneath the walls of a city. His assailants then robbed him of his money and valuables. A pilgrim should also take particular care not to enter any house when a woman beckons him in. There is a great risk in doing this, not only for one's virtue and possessions, but also for one's life!

Indeed, anyone who wants to be upright and honest, and keep his holy pilgrimage unblemished, should only walk around during the day when in port. As evening draws on, he should return to his galley and sleep securely there in his berth. For inns on the islands are all brothels. Keepers of houses of ill-fame, (who are for the most part Germans!), are the only ones ready to accept German pilgrims. The landlords live there with their prostitutes, but send them away when pilgrims arrive at their premises. A good and godly pilgrim, if he follows my advice, can spend the day with his companions at such an inn, but should by no means sleep there. Experience will teach a man many other things to be wary of and avoid.

Brother Felix then continues with his account of their sea-voyage. The galley's route took them down the Adriatic coast of Dalmatia. They called in at Rovigno, Zara in Dalmatia, Corfu (where they did not stay long, because of the plague), Metona (where they met the other pilgrim ship from Venice), Crete, Rhodes and the Salines (near modern Larnaca) in Cyprus. While they were anchored off the Salines the ship's captain went off to Nicosia to see his wife who happened to be a lady of the bedchamber of Queen Catherine of Cyprus, now a puppet ruler of the island under the control of Venice. Here Brother Felix persuaded some of his companions to make a little pilgrimage ashore.

When the captain had left us, we pilgrims stood on the deck staring at the shore. While I was standing with them

I mentioned to those near me how uninteresting the port was, and explained the nature of the surrounding country. For I had spent many days there during my earlier pilgrimage. I also indicated the places on the shore which I knew.

Among these I pointed out the Mount of the Holy Cross. On its summit is a church, where hangs the cross of the thief who was crucified at the right hand of Christ. I told their lordships the whole story of that cross. While my lords and the others were thinking about this and gazing in the direction of the mountain, which was five German miles away, I said to them, "Look, my dear brothers, our captain has gone to Nicosia. At the earliest he will be back by tomorrow evening. We cannot set sail until he returns. Tomorrow we shall have a long and boring day. Anyone who would like to go with me to the Holy Mount should come to the stern of the galley, and we will visit that blessed cross. We will return in good time tomorrow."

I then went to the stern. Many noblemen followed me there, thinking that what I had said and done was a practical joke. But while on the poop I had hired a servant who knew the way to the Holy Cross. I promised him that he would be given a mark from each of my companions. I also hired a boatman to take us ashore. However, when the noblemen saw that I was serious, all except one went off again and left me! Six others, however, joined the party, including a priest and two knights. The eight of us then went down from the galley into the boat. When we were set ashore we began to discuss the arrangements for our pilgrimage.

The hour was late, the sun had set, and it was growing dark. Our guide and servant led us in the gloom to a village called Ornyca, a mile distant from the sea. There he roused a countryman whom he knew. This fellow produced wine, bread and cheese, which we ate and drank.

We then hired eight mules in the village, mounted, and set out in a happy mood. Meanwhile the moon had risen, and this too lifted our spirits as her light drove away the dark from our select band of eight, who were all comrades. The weather was fine, the countryside beautiful, and the road good. All the bushes along the way gave off a very sweet aroma, since almost all of the plants on the island are culinary herbs of various kinds; and the scent is by far the sweetest at night when they are moist with dew.

We continued on our way until the rising of Lucifer, the morning star, which precedes the rising of the sun. Then we came to the village which is called St Cross, where we tied up our animals and lit a fire. My comrades drank, but I abstained since I intended to celebrate Mass on the Holy Mount. We then lay down to rest for a little while, and slept on until it was bright day, lying on the ground beside our animals.

It was the 26th of June, which is the Feast of the Holy Martyrs John and Paul, when we arose. We had camped in front of the house of a Greek. So we asked him to prepare a good meal for us, since it was our intention to return to him from the mountain without breaking our fast. Then we mounted our mules and set off.

We were alarmed by the size of the Holy Mount looming up before our eyes. But at its foot we came to a delightful valley through which ran a clear stream of running water. The banks were covered in the most beautiful wild flowers, whose names we did not know, and sweet-scented shrubs. There were also many trees laden with carob beans, popularly known as St John's bread. We made our way through the valley and up the mountain in very chilly shade since the sun's rays, although they were warming up the peaks round about, could not yet reach us in the valley.

Soon we reached the steepest part of the mountain. From here we were unable to ride our mules, so we tied them up to trees and climbed on foot. The task was very laborious and we sweated a good deal because of the gradient and the distance we had to climb. It is said to be exactly like Mount Tabor in the Holy Land where our

Lord was transfigured. I have heard this from someone who had climbed both.

When we reached the top, we knelt in prayer in front of the church. Before going in we sat down in the open air to recover our breath, wipe off the sweat which was all over us, and cool ourselves off from the heat.

After we had done this I got ready first, as was appropriate, and entered the church. I tolled the bell so that the sacristan might hear this and come. A priest arrived immediately. Although he did not know Latin, he brought out some very ancient Latin service books and other things needed for Mass. After the bell had been rung again I read the Mass for the Holy Cross, with the collects for the Holy Martyrs John and Paul, and one for travellers.

After celebrating Mass I turned around to my brothers and comrades and gave them a homily. I told them that they should show a fitting and worthy reverence to this cross. I explained how the cross we were about to see differed from that of our Saviour. I warned them not to be over-inquisitive when they viewed it. They should not wish to witness a miracle. When we came to the most Holy Sepulchre of our Lord at Jerusalem we should see no miracle, how much the less should we look for one here. I made this point because we had heard strange and peculiar stories about the cross which was to be seen here.

After this I took a lighted candle in my hands and went to the place where the cross was. My fellow pilgrims followed me and the sacristan accompanied us. When we reached the place the sacristan opened it up, so that we had the holy cross plainly before our eyes. I myself went up to it first and kissed it, and examined it carefully both at the front and the back. My companions came forward and honoured it after me, and then carefully examined it, one after another. It is quite a large cross. In the front it is covered with plates of silver, which have been gilded. On the back facing the wall it is without any covering. It is made of fine sound wood, resembling cypress wood.

They say that this is the cross of Dysmas, the thief who was crucified on the right hand side of Christ, to whom our Lord promised paradise on the Cross. The Blessed Helena found three crosses beneath Mount Calvary. She threw away the one belonging to Gesmas, the unrepentant thief on the left hand side. The second cross of Dysmas she kept.The third, which was the Cross of Christ, she openly showed to all the world, that it might be duly honoured.

She then brought her own complete cross, which had been that of Dysmas, from Jerusalem to this mountain, and here she had constructed a great convent for monks, and a church in which she placed the cross.

Here it stands to this day having never been moved, even though the monastery itself was raised to the ground long ago by the Turks and the Saracens. The monks of the Order of St Benedict, who once lived here, have now been dispersed.

The position and setting of this cross is wonderful. It stands in a blind window. Both the cross' arms have been let into holes made in the wall, and its foot has been let into a hole in the floor. Yet the holes that contain its arms are much larger than the wood, and the cross nowhere touches the wall; it is free and clear of contact with the wall on every side.

The miracle which is talked of in connection with this cross is that it hangs in the air without any fastening, and yet remains as firm as if it were fixed with very strong nails, or built into the wall. All three holes are very large so that a man can put his hand into them and feel by touch that there are neither fastenings there, nor at the back nor at the head of the cross.

I could have examined this phenomenon more carefully than I did, but I feared God and had no right to do what I had forbidden others to do. I climbed the mountain to show honour to the cross, not to test whether there was a miracle or not, nor to tempt God. To make the cross even more worthy of reverence they have attached to it a piece of the True Cross of Christ.

There is a bell hanging in the chapel, which we rang both before and after Mass. I told my companions that we should hear no more bells until we returned to Christendom. This was true, for from now on I did not hear any bell for four months, apart from this one, which we believe to have been placed here by St Helena, who also deposited the cross here.

When we had finished at the church and gone out, we went into the sacristan's house. We hoped to find some refreshment there, but the house had no provisions at all, not so much as a biscuit or cold water. The fellow was unable to talk to us because he was a pure Greek. Latin was completely foreign to him. To him Italian was Arabic and German Tartar!

So we left unrefreshed, and went for a stroll around the brow of the mountain. Here we found some thick ancient walls, the ruins of a temple of Venus. Whichever way we looked, whether along or across the island, we could see the sea. But the heat haze made the air rather misty and cloudy so we were unable to see the Holy Land. Nor could we see the mountains of Armenia, Cappadocia, Syria or Galilee, all of which we should have been able to see if the air had been clear.

After our walk we again entered the church, venerated and kissed the holy cross, then hurried down the mountain to where our mules had been left standing. When we had ridden down to the village of St Cross we found the meal that we had long been waiting for was ready, and we ate this with much gratitude. We found it impossible to leave straightaway because it was exceedingly hot. The sun burnt like a fire, so we went into the church of the Greeks, which stood near the inn, to pray and have a little rest out of the heat.

But while we were sitting in the church a priest in holy orders came and spoke to us in Latin. "What are you doing here in the Greek church? Here, close by, is the

Latin church of your own rite; it is there that you should pray and rest yourselves." So we got up and went with him to the Latin church. Here he brought out for us from the treasury the arm of St Anne, the mother of the Blessed Virgin, which was honoured by being enclosed in silver. He also produced a nail, likewise covered in silver. He said that this was one of the nails of Christ with which he had been nailed to the Cross. We kissed these relics and touched them with our jewels in the way I have previously described.

I discovered that this priest was a monk, although I could not discern this from his dress, because he was covered with a plush cloak. He was the priest in charge of both churches, the Greek and the Latin one, and he conformed to the separate rites for each! On Sundays he first celebrated Mass in the Latin church, and consecrated in the western manner with unleavened bread; when he had finished this service he crossed over to the Greek church, and consecrated in the eastern fashion with leavened bread.

I was very unhappy about this, and took the view that the priest was a heretic of a very unsatisfactory kind, since he was leading the people all over the place. The two rites are not rightly able to be celebrated by one and the same person. They should hardly be allowed in the same city because they disagreed in many key rubrics. It is true that in the past the Roman Church used to tolerate the Greek rite, yet even then it did not allow a person to be a Greek and a Latin at the same time!

The situation is worse now that the Church condemns the Greeks as schismatics and heretics, and the Greeks denounce us in their services. Every Sunday Greek clergy tell their congregations that the Roman Church is excommunicate, and that they dislike those of us who are of the Latin rite and wish that we were all dead. How then is it possible for an honest man who is a good Catholic to be a Latin and Greek priest at the same time? No one could act in this way unless he had financial motives, or was a liturgical pleasure seeker. For priests like that simply adopt whatever they find pleasant in either ritual, and give up that which is more demanding and difficult to cope with, whether they are using one rite or the other. Many Latin priests do transfer to the Greek rite so as to be able to marry: yet at the same time they wish to enjoy the privileges of priests of the Latin rite which they have foregone!

In the afternoon, as the heat of the sun began to abate, we mounted our animals and went down to the sea as far as the church of St Lazarus. This is on the shore, and our galley was anchored opposite it a long way out to sea. Here we returned our mules to their owners.

There was a great market by the shore, and a large crowd had assembled, attracted by our galley. Our sailors had brought over their wares and were selling them to the Cypriots. This happened whenever we went into a port. After we had had a look over the market we returned to the galley and our lords and comrades.

We found them gloomy and bad-tempered because the captain had not yet returned, and they had spent a very boring day. All the pilgrims then crowded around us to hear what we had seen. When they heard our tale they said we had been lucky and that they were sorry that they had not gone with us.

On the 27th of June we found that the captain had further delayed his return. So some of the pilgrims, myself included, were put ashore to spend the day there. Most of the pilgrims, however, again stayed on board because they were nervous of the Cypriot climate, which is generally regarded as harmful to Germans, unless they are robust and have a sound bodily constitution. Noblemen who are worried about their health do not land in Cyprus!

On shore we went to the place where the salt works are. Here we could see the ruins of what once was a town of not inconsiderable size. All around it are dunes. Sometimes when the water rises, the area within becomes a lagoon, then, when the sea ebbs away, all the water left behind evaporates with the heat of the sun and is turned into the finest, whitest and most valuable salt. It is then transported to many countries for sale, and the Queen of Cyprus receives a lot of income from the salt dealers for it.

During my first pilgrimage I saw many men working here to separate the salt from the water, which had not yet dried up. There were numerous tall piles of salt standing like hillocks. But there was not a single man there now, and where the piles of salt had previously stood there was fairly deep water. About the time for vespers we returned on board the galley. We were very displeased with the captain.

During the evening a boat arrived with the woman whom I mentioned earlier who had been left behind at Rhodes. There was little joy at her return. Yet I was now sorry for the poor creature because of the difficulties she had had to face when the galley had set sail without her.

On the 28th of June, before sunrise, the captain arrived from Nicosia. He was accompanied by some Cypriots who wanted to visit the Holy Places in Jerusalem. Among these was a pious lady of the Queen's court who intended to end her days in Jerusalem near the Holy Places. After weighing anchor, we sailed very slowly out of the harbour because the wind was light.

The galley taking Brother Felix and the other pilgrims took four days to travel from the Salines to the coast of Palestine. At one point they were driven back by a contrary wind and had to anchor in Cyprus again near Limassol. We resume his account on the fifth morning after their departure from the island.

It was on the 1st of July, the month of pilgrims' joy, that the most hallowed of all lands was sighted by the pilgrims whose adventures are recorded in this book. The previous day we had sailed with speed and good fortune through the sea off the coasts of Pamphilia, to those of Syria and Phoenicia. Then, being driven on from there towards the south, we came during the night into the sea off Palestine, which we were all longing for.

Soon, as the dawn rose, the Holy Land, the land of Cannan, the land whose name is above every other, shone forth brighter than the sun! As soon as the look-out in the maintop sighted it, he let out a sudden shout, "My lord pilgrims, rouse yourselves and come on deck! Look over there, the land that you are waiting to see is in sight! When we heard this shouting, everyone—men and women, old and young, sick and healthy—hurried from every corner of the galley and went aloft. Their one object was to catch sight of the land for which they had quit their native country, and exposed themselves to so many hardships and risks to their life.

Yet, because it was still a long way off, we could not see anything but the sea! The crew maintained that they could see the land, for they are used to the sea, and can make out ships or land when they are still far away. After an hour had passed, as we drew nearer and nearer, we too began to catch a glimpse of the peaks and mountains rising as if from the sea.

Our pilots were still in doubt about which land it might be. Some said that it was Cappadocia, some that it was Cilicia, and some that it was Syria Phoenicia. Most maintained that we had had Cappadocia on our left, and had already passed beyond it, so that now we were off Antioch. The land then appearing on our left was Syria Phoenicia, and that beyond, a great way off, was Philistia in Palestine, which is adjacent to the Holy Land. And so it proved to be.

When there was at last no further doubt that we were looking at the Holy Land, and that the mountains of Israel were before our eyes, the captain ordered everyone to be silent. Then with the voice of a herald he verified to us that this was indeed that blessed land where Jesus Christ, the Son of God, our Lord, was conceived, born, lived, was crucified, died, and was buried; and then rose again from His Sepulchre on the third day, as we all declare that we firmly believe. He then said that it was fitting and right that we should give thanks to our Redeemer, and sing a hymn of joy with our loudest voice.

And so two pilgrims who were priests and monks and had good voices passed along the rowing benches as far as the mast. Here in the place where Mass at sea is usually said, they began to sing together in a loud voice the *Te deum laudamus*, the hymn of Ambrose and Augustine. This was taken up by all the other clergy present as it is sung in church, with each man singing according to the harmony of his own choir at home.

I have never heard such a sweet and joyful song, for there was a mass of voices, and the different parts made, as it were, sweet music and harmony. Everyone sang the same words, but the notes were different, yet they beautfully harmonised together. It filled me with joy to hear so many priests singing the same hymn together with gladness of heart. There were many Latin priests, also Sclavonians, Italians, Lombards, Gauls, Franks, Germans, Englishmen, Irishmen, Hungarians, Scots, Dacians, Bohemians and Spaniards.

There were many who spoke the same language but came from different dioceses and belonged to different religious congregations. All of them sang the glorious *Te Deum*, and even the lay pilgrims and the crew of the galley joined in, singing away loudly and happily at our good fortune. Our trumpeters on board blew their trumpets loudly, and sounded their shawms. A jester called Borgadellus played on a drum and sackbut, while others blew flutes and bagpipes.

Meanwhile some prostrated themselves on the deck on their faces and prayed, looking up in the direction of the Holy Land. Others were weeping for joy as they sang. And then everyone burst into a new song before the throne of God, and the world and the sea rang with their voices.

It seemed to us that while we sang like this the galley bounded along beneath us and sailed faster, ploughing into the waves more freely; and that the wind billowed the sail out more fully, and that the water, stirred up by the breeze, pushed us along more speedily. When we had finished our hymns of praise, the trumpets sounded the call to dinner, and every man, with joy in his heart, got himself ready to sit down at the table.

Now there was a serious, respectable priest, well on in years, who had his berth next to mine. After the singing, he was hurrying down to his berth when his foot slipped on the top step of the ladder, which was polished with the constant traffic. Down he plunged with terrific momentum into the cabin and lay there as if dead. We all ran down to help him. He had cracked his head and bruised his limbs, so we carried him to his berth where he lay like a corpse. Some hours later, however, he came too, and was bandaged up and treated by the doctor; and several days later he was on the way to recovery!

Brother Felix spent the rest of the afternoon on deck pointing out the sights on the shore and giving some historical and religious background to the pilgrims. His account of their arrival at Jaffa follows.

Meanwhile we were drawing near the Holy Land, and coming to the port of Jaffa. Here we found that Master Augustine's galley with his pilgrims had not yet landed. We were very pleased at this because if they had landed we should not have had proper attention. When we were not far from Master Augustine's galley, we took soundings, and finding the bottom, let down our anchors.

The galley was moored outside Andromeda's Rocks, which guard the port. We could not risk going closer to the shore in case we angered the Saracens, for we had no safe conduct from them. We lowered our mainyard, furled our main sail, and put on no display. We acted in this way so that the Saracens in the towers guarding the port of Jaffa should realise that we came in peace.

Normally when we went into other harbours, we hoisted banners, fired cannons, lowered a boat to proceed ashore, dressed the galley and sounded trumpets, shawms and horns. And so, like timid, humble tributaries of the Lord

Sultan, needing his safe-conduct, like captives and slaves of the Moors and Saracens, we lay off the towers of Jaffa awaiting their good pleasure!

Before we had arrived, Master Augustine, the captain of the other galley, had sent a messenger to the men ashore in the towers to discuss with them a safe-conduct for his galley alone. But when the Saracens realised that another galley with pilgrims was also on its way, they would not listen to Master Augustine, but sent him away. He was made to go back aboard his galley until the other galley arrived. This was exactly the opposite of what the two captains had had in mind. For each of them had intended to show his own group of pilgrims around the Holy Places separately, because of the rivalry between them.

But the Saracens went along with the wishes of the pilgrims, rather than that of the two quarrelsome captains. The pilgrims were united in their view that they should be taken to see the Holy Places together. And so ended the first day of July. We slept that night on board the galley as we were forced to do.

Brother Felix now revealed to his noblemen that he wished to go on to Mount Sinai and St Catherine's monastery after their tour of the Holy Places. This meant leaving the party without a chaplain on their return voyage, for he would return from the port of Alexandria in Egypt on another ship. After an hour's tense deliberation among themselves the lords agreed to this, and passed round the hat to help pay brother Felix's expenses for the trip. He was extremely grateful, and then tried to drum up enthusiasm among the pilgrims for this extra journey. He even made a boat trip to Master Augustine's galley to look for additional enthusiasts. He was pleased with the support he received there, but, on his return to his own galley, his captain, who had been conferring with a Mamluk from Jaffa, tried to put him off.

The two claimed that the Arabs had recently laid waste St Catherine's Monastery and killed all the monks, so that there could be no pilgrimage to Mount Sinai that year. Brother Felix suspected that this was a ploy, because the captain did not wish to reimburse pilgrims who wanted to go on to Mount Sinai (and hence would not be returning to Venice on his galley) the twelve ducats specified in the tourists' contract. Brother Felix later discovered that the captain's story was indeed false. Nor was he impressed when the captain's Mamluk friend, who was supposed to be a devout Muslim and so refrain from alcohol, got roaring drunk and had to stay the night on board.

The galley captains' contacts with the Saracens at Jaffa meant that messages were sent to the Governor of Jerusalem, the Governor of the neighbouring towns of Gazara and Ramleh, and to the Franciscan Father Guardian at Mount Sion in Jerusalem, informing them of the pilgrims' arrival. They spent five days waiting offshore, and while they remained on board the Saracens came in large mounted armed bands and set up camp on the shore. At last the day when the pilgrims were allowed to go ashore arrived.

...After the captains had conferred with the governors they agreed to bring us ashore from our galleys. The venerable Father Paul, the Provisor of the Latin Church in the East, and the Guardian of Mount Sion, rowed over to us, accompanied by his brothers in religion. With them was an important Saracen, Calinus, who was Master of the hospice for pilgrims at Jerusalem. They sat themselves down in the poop with our captain. Then, when we had all assembled, the Father Guardian, who was a distinguished-looking and learned man with a long beard, greeted us politely and elaborately with a speech in Latin. He bade us welcome, and urged us to be devout, patient and exemplary in our behaviour. He promised that at Ramleh he would provide us with the rules which we would need to observe during our stay with the Saracens in the Holy Land.

Calinus, our guide, also greeted us respectfully. He said that the carrying of weapons was forbidden. This meant that we could not take any sword or bow from the ship. We were to go unarmed as was fitting for pilgrims. After this, the

Father Guardian and his brothers and Calinus got into the boat, after telling us to hurry and get ready to follow them.

It was by now time for our meal, so we all ate and drank in haste so as to get to the Holy Land as soon as possible. During the meal all the officers on board came to each one of us, one after another, carrying silver cups, and asking for tips, which we call drink money. They made their requests very aggressively. If anyone refused, they said that they would not let him go ashore in the boat! There was a great deal of trouble aboard because of their shameless and importunate begging.

When this problem had been sorted out and we had paid our tips, we prepared to leave the ship. We took with us a couple of jars of wine, and hid these in sacks in case the Saracens should see them. They will not allow wine to be carried about openly. If they see this, they smash the jars if they can. We also took in our sacks some cheese and smoked meat, our water bottles, and all our pilgrims' gear. Then we came up from our cabin to the poop, and went down into the boats.

As we began to row towards the Holy Land we sang loudly with great joy, "In Gottes Nahmen fahren wir," etc. The song could not be heard by the Saracens ashore because the Andromeda Rocks were between us and the shore, and the sea breaks on to them with a mighty roar. We sailed close to these rocks, and as we passed we were splashed and soaked through. But our little boat managed to avoid being hurled against the reefs as had been our fear.

And so we reached the shore and landed. As soon as we felt the Holy Land beneath our feet, we threw ourselves down on our faces and kissed the sacred earth with great devotion. Just by touching the Holy Land we received a plenary indulgence for the remission of our sins.

...When we had finished our thanksgiving we went up from the shore on to higher ground, mounting some rocks which are on the edge of the bay. Above us stood the Father Guardian of Mount Sion and his brothers, together

with the governors of the land, the elders of the Saracens
and the Moors, and a secretary. They were in two lines with
a narrow path between.

Each pilgrim had to pass between them. Two pilgrims
were not permitted to go up together but only one after
another. We were not allowed to pass in a continuous
stream, but they took hold of each man, looked at him
thoroughly, and asked his name and that of his father. The
secretary then wrote both names down in his document.

My name Felix causes an inordinate amount of difficulty
in their language! On my former pilgrimage, and on this
one, I had to repeat it several times. Even then they could
neither pronounce it nor write it without putting an out-
landish dipthong at the beginning. They gurgled its sylla-
bles in their throats so that they did not say 'Felix,' but
some word which I cannot pronounce....As soon as the
name of a man and his father had been written down, some
Saracens appointed for the task seized each pilgrim and
dragged him to the entrance of a dark and foul dwelling-
place beneath a crumbling vault. Each pilgrim was shoved
in, as men push a sheep into a stable to be milked. If a pilgrim enters into this cavern with a devout spirit he obtains
a seven year indulgence.

The caverns are called St Peter's Cellars. So as to be
prepared to gain these and other indulgences many of the
pilgrims had confessed to me previously aboard the galley;
some others did so as we stood on the sea shore. When we
got inside these caverns we discovered that where we were
to stay was full of disgusting litter, and fouled with human
excrement. Every man then had to clean up a space to
stretch out.

The pilgrims moved all the filth into the middle of the cavern with their feet so that in the centre a great pile of rubbish
and excrement mounted up. We set ourselves up all round
along the walls on the bare, damp ground next to one another,
just as we had done in the galley. What a wretched inn, what
poor hospitality, and what a filthy place to be!

Brother Felix then raises the point that pious pilgrims accustomed to talking with God might think that this was a peculiar way for the Almighty to allow pilgrims to be greeted on their arrival. But he reminds his readers that our Lord was born in a foul stable, had no room to lay his head during much of his preaching life, and had no final resting place but the shameful cross and a borrowed tomb. Almost immediately after they arrived at the caverns help was at hand, as he explains.

...Certain poor Saracens called on us: they had collected together rushes and branches of trees which they sold on to us. We covered the damp earth with these and made them into mattresses. Then merchants from Ramleh and Jerusalem entered our cavern carrying sweet-scented goods, and established a little market there. They brought rose water from Damascus in glass bottles, very precious, which they sold for one Venetian penny a bottle. Some had balsam, some musk, some soap, some precious stones, some rolls of the whitest muslin, some mitres. Many other valuable and sweet-scented things were brought in to us.

All the merchants and Saracens were themselves anointed with aromatic lotions and distilled perfumes, and their scent wafted all around them. They too were unable to bear the smell and filth of our lodgings so they burned frankincence and Arabian gum. So this place of disgusting smells became like a perfumery!

Moreover those who had undoubtedly been responsible in the past for some of the mess in the cavern, now helped clean it up by walking some of the filth away on their feet as they passed! Quite soon, with their tramping in and out, the place, previously so foul, became quite pleasant and fit for human beings. Indeed, if weak and sick men had come in, they would have been strengthened by smelling the pleasant odours there! A little earlier, even animals would have shied away from entering!

We had arrived feeling very downcast and with bitter feelings, but within an hour we were rested and comfortable. Then came some Saracens who cooked eggs with oil in a frying pan. Some brought loaves of bread, some cool water, some fruit, some salads, and some hot cakes made of eggs, which they sold to us. When we had made our purchases and eaten, we settled down to sleep because it was late.

But just as each of us had got to the place where he intended to pass the night, a tough Saracen, armed with a club in his hands, came in. He demanded a Venetian penny from each pilgrim. I had not previously seen this happen before. But to avoid any trouble we each paid this amount for our lodging.

When it was dark we hired two Saracens to keep guard at the entrance of the cavern during the night so that no one might come in and molest us. There was a great crowd of people of all sorts outside. I have since realised that the extortionate Saracen with the club was probably the owner and lord of the caverns, and that this encouraged him to levy the charge on us as was his lawful right.

The pilgrims remained in St Peter's Cellars for eight days. The main reason for the delay was the inability of the two captains to agree on a joint tour of the Holy Places which was what the governors and the pilgrims all wanted. There were further exactions from the Saracen with the club, and Brother Felix's attempt to hold a service in the cavern on Sunday was thwarted because yet another group of merchants arrived and set up their market.

Eventually the pilgrims were allowed out of the cave on to the seashore, but there were a lot of arguments with the young Saracens who congregated outside the cave. A large flask of Malvoisie wine was confiscated.

One attractive young pilgrim without a beard was so badly teased by the Saracens, who made sexual remarks about him, that he complained to the Saracen guide in charge of the pilgrims. The guide said that there was nothing he could do about this, which put the poor young man right off the pilgrimage. So he returned to the galley and remained on board until the other pilgrims had come back from Jerusalem. Yet when one of the merchants defrauded a pilgrim in a trading deal, the Governor of Ramleh did intervene, and restored the pilgrim's money, and had the merchant beaten.

At last all arrangements were made, and on the ninth day a Saracen woke them up before dawn, and escorted them out of the cave and down to the shore where mules were waiting. The pilgrims were again all checked by their own and their father's name against the earlier list. Then there was a great scrum in which each mule driver tried to force a pilgrim to mount his mule, and not that of another driver. Brother Felix, who knew the ropes from his first pilgrimage, actually managed to find the driver whom he had engaged during his earlier pilgrimage. He takes up his story:

…A pilgrim keeps the driver whom he engages at Jaffa throughout the whole of his journey in the Holy Land, and he never rides a mule belonging to anyone else. Whenever a pilgrim has to set off again after a halt he has to run among a crowd of mules and look for his driver, loudly calling out his driver's name. So, on this my second pilgrimage, when I had come down from the place where the governors were standing, I wanted to find my old mule driver.

Before I reached the herd of mules I shouted out, 'Galela-cassa', the name of my driver. When the other drivers heard this, none of them pulled me over to his mule since I had a driver whom I knew. While I was shouting, a king-like Saracen noble, whom I did not recognise, rode up to me on his horse, and touched me gently with the staff in his hand.

The lord was in fact responsible for Cassa my old mule driver. He signalled to me to keep silent and and stand quietly at his side. The running hither and thither of pilgrims and mule drivers is very chaotic. Everyone is in a hurry to make a good deal for himself. While I stood waiting, others were running to and fro or were being dragged over to the mules. I began to feel uneasy in case the Saracen lord had forgotten me. So I tried to move away from him. But when he saw this he spoke to me in Chaldean which I did not understand. I have since guessed that he must have said, "Stay here by my side. I am Galela and my servant Cassa will presently come to me and provide you with an animal."

Eventually Cassa came up to his master. As soon as he saw me he recognised me, and I him. He ran over to kiss me in the Saracen fashion, and welcomed me with the most delighted look on his face, quite amazed at my return. He laughed and said a lot which I did not understand. I had brought with me two iron stirrups from Ulm, which I now presented to him. He received these with much gratitude, and then led me to where his mules were standing among the herd, and introduced me to his best animal.

My lords and the other pilgrims were surprised to see the Saracens treat me with such friendliness. For pilgrims often have a great deal of trouble with their mule drivers. Sometimes they are struck by them, thrown off their mules, and have their property stolen. I was free from all these problems.

This man served me most faithfully, as on my former pilgrimage, and obeyed all my requests as though I had been a prince. He often changed my mule so that I might have one which pleased me better. He supported me when my mule was going up hill; and when we were going down a steep

and rough path he held on to me so that I would not come
off. He also gave me drink from his water-skin, and shared
his biscuits with me. He would climb over the stone walls of
gardens and bring me figs, grapes and other fruits. He even
let me have use of the goad which he used on his mule,
even though other drivers would not allow *their* pilgrims to
have charge of the goads for their mules.

Because of his great services to me the nobles and all my
companions assumed that I had given him a great deal of
money on the quiet. But this was not true, for I gave him
nothing other than what was required.

I have often imagined that he supposed me to be some
great lord, and that this was why he served me so sollici-
tously. Yet it is a fact that during both my pilgrimages I was
never ill-treated in any way by a Saracen, Arab, Midianite
or Mamluk with whom I had dealings. I can report to you
that I never received blows or insults, even though I often
saw other pilgrims insulted and beaten. I always had good
animals on both my pilgrimages, and all the time remained
strong and healthy, praise be to God!

...When everyone was eventually provided with an animal we mounted by the shore and sat there for a time until
the Moorish lords were ready. Some pilgrims, for reasons of
religious devotion, refused to mount their mules; they wanted to run along at the back of our company. The Saracens
allowed them to do this. They were quite content, as long
as pilgrims could run as fast as the mules could manage in a
day's journey, and could keep up with the party and not lag
behind. But when we went at speed they could not in practice keep up with us, partly because of our travelling speed,
and partly because of the sandy roads along which we were
travelling. And so these pilgrims were eventually obliged to
get back on their mules.

It is not true, as we are so often told at home in our country, that the Saracens force us to ride to Jerusalem and travel
through the Holy Land on the backs of mules because they
believe us unworthy to touch the earth with our feet. They

do not care whether a pilgrim walks on foot or rides a mule, as long as the contract made between them and the captain is kept, and that anyone who walks on foot does not lag behind and make them wait for him.

The reason why we are made to take mules is so that we can all keep together, and arrive at Jerusalem without falling ill. If pilgrims had to walk on foot all the way from the sea to Jerusalem, and cross the Holy Land in such torrid weather over roads which are sandy on the plains and rough in the mountains, few would remain alive. The heat, the thirst, and the effort required in such an odd climate, would get the better of them. If we were forced to walk on foot through the Holy Land how could we escape from the Bedouin and peasants in the villages, or stand up to them when they attack us? So it is for our benefit that animals are provided for us, not out of contempt for us, as some ignorant people allege.

When all was ready, the captains and the governors, mounted on their horses and leading the way, took a route away from the shore. We followed behind riding our mules, with our drivers accompanying us. The servants of the Moorish lords rode at the back of the pilgrims. In this formation our caravan left the sea behind very rapidly.

...The Bedouin, who during this historical period were scattered over many parts of the Holy Land, came three times to confront us. But when they saw that we were well-protected by armed defenders, they avoided violence, and did not throw stones or threaten us with cold steel. Instead they sidled up alongside our escort, who was next to the pilgrims, and tried to make off with any knapsacks, clothes or similar items.

They knew that *we* were unarmed, and therefore circled round us and snatched up anything which the pilgrims let fall, or did not guard carefully. If we had not been travelling in such a large force, they would have fallen on us and attacked us with stones, sticks and staves. This often happens to pilgrims between Jaffa and Ramleh. When the

Bedouin are not in the area, the villagers themselves band together and attack pilgrims on their journey, causing them a lot of harm. So the journey from Jaffa to Ramleh is particularly dangerous because of the ambushes and insulting behaviour of the infidels.

As we continued our journey we caught sight of the city of Ramleh on a low hill in most beautiful country. When we were within a furlong of it we were forced to dismount from our mules and walk on foot, each of us carrying his baggage on his shoulders. We handed over our mules to our drivers, and hurried along in great discomfort because it was very hot. The dust flew about, and there was a huge crowd and much jostling. The infidels will not permit Christians to enter their cities and towns when riding animals, except if they arrive in the dark: during daylight hours they are not allowed to do so. The city of Ramleh is considered to be of greater dignity than others since the Thadi, the equivalent of their bishop, has his residence there. His presence means that they keep a look out for Christians entering the city other than on foot.

When we had entered the city and were no great distance from the gate we came to a house with a low narrow door. Here the governors stood and counted us one by one, just as they had done when we left the sea. They then asked us to go in through the little door. Inside there was a large and beautiful courtyard, off which were many chambers and vaulted rooms of various kinds, and there was a fountain full of good and wholesome water.

The house had been acquired long ago by Philip, Duke of Burgundy, of blessed memory, for the use of pilgrims. It was entrusted by him to the

care of the brothers of Mount Sion, and was called the pilgrims' hospice. The brothers let it to an eastern Christian
who lives there. I have heard that before this house was
acquired as a lodging, pilgrims used to have to stay in the
city's public inn near the market place. This was a miserable
and contemptible place, and pilgrims were greatly mistreated
there by the Saracens—the Saracens and Moors of Ramleh
have a special hatred of Christians and treat them badly.

We now divided ourselves up among the various rooms,
with each company in its own group. My lords and their
followers had a spacious chamber. We purchased mats to
cover the floor so that we did not have to sit, lie or sleep on
the bare stones. Our lodging consisted of nothing more
than a vaulted chamber with walls and a paved floor. There
was no furniture except that which we brought in ourselves.
It was about nine in the morning when we entered the city.

The Father Guardian arranged for an altar to be set up in
the inner garden of the building where the captain's lodgings were. It was placed against the trunk of a great palm
tree which stood there laden with dates. He then summoned all the pilgrims into the garden. When the gates had
been barred so that the infidels should not interrupt us, one
of the brothers celebrated Mass.

When this was over the Father Guardian preached a
beautiful homily in Latin—he was an Italian and knew no
German. Since he had no one with him who could speak
fluent German to interpret what he was saying to our
German party, he asked me to stand beside him and translate his exhortations for the benefit of the German pilgrims.
I was happy to do this, so I stood at his side. As he uttered a
sentence in Latin, I immediately repeated what he had said
in colloquial German.

During his homily he laid before the pilgrims certain articles which covered the rules and procedures which they
needed to follow while they lived among the Saracens and
infidels in the Holy Land. He was concerned that they
might run into danger through ignorance.

"Article 1. Any pilgrim who had come there without the express permission of the Pope, and had thereby incurred the Pope's sentence of excommunication, should present himself to the Father Guardian after Mass. He would then absolve him from his transgression by virtue of the Apostolic authority granted to him. The Pope takes note of anyone who goes on a pilgrimage to the Holy Land without obtaining his leave to do so.

The reason for this excommunication is that after the Christians were driven out of the Holy Land some disloyal Christians, even some of the Latin Church, remained behind; they allied themselves to the Saracens and swore allegiance to them. Other Christians, who had left the Holy Land, later returned and became subjects of the Saracens. These subsequently sailed to Christian countries and returned with ironwork and arms which the rulers in the East needed.

When the Pope saw what was going on, he excommunicated both those who had stayed behind with the Saracens in the Holy Land, and those who made common cause with them. He also excommunicated those who transported arms and other supplies to them. Indeed he excommunicated the land itself, so that anyone who entered it without his permission should be *anathema,* since no one could possibly take up residence there without collaborating with infidels and heretics.

Members of religious congregations who visit the Holy Land are exempt from this excommunication. A similar exemption is available to any man who has a friend who is being held prisoner by the Saracens. He may enter that country to bargain for his friend's freedom without the Pope's leave. I read all this in a book by a pilgrim who visited the Holy Land one hundred and fifty years ago. No Dominican friar is given leave by the General Master of the Dominicans unless he has also first received the Pope's permission.

Article 2. No person should wander about the Holy Places alone without a Saracen guide because it is dangerous and unsafe to do so. I, Brother Felix Fabri, did not observe this article strictly, as will be apparent later!

Article 3. The pilgrim should beware of stepping over a Saracen's grave. They get very angry when they see this done, and pelt anyone who does so with stones. They believe that when we do this the dead are disturbed and tormented.

Article 4. If any pilgrim is struck by a Saracen, however unjustly, he should not return the blow, but he should make a complaint about his assailant to the Father Guardian or the guide, or to Calinus, the Master of the pilgrims' hostel. They will put the matter right if they can. Yet if they are not able to deal with the offence satisfactorily, since young men are sometimes ill-mannered and proud, the pilgrims should patiently submit to the injury for the glory of God and for their own greater merit.

Article 5. Pilgrims should refrain from chipping fragments from the Holy Sepulchre and from buildings at other places, and from damaging any of the hewn building stones. This is forbidden under pain of excommunication.

Article 6. Pilgrims of noble birth should not deface walls by drawing their coats of arms or writing their names on them; nor should they fasten on them pieces of paper on which their arms have been painted; nor should they scratch columns or marble slabs, or bore holes in these with iron tools to leave marks indicating that they have visited these places. Such conduct is gravely offensive to the Saracens, and they think that those who do such things are fools.

Article 7. Pilgrims should make their visits to the Holy Places in an orderly manner, without jostling or arguing. No one should try to outrun another, because there is a great deal of crowding within these places, and people's devotion is hindered by this.

Article 8. Pilgrims should avoid laughing to one another as they walk about Jerusalem; they should be serious and devout. They should act in this way because of the Holy

Places themselves, and to set a good example to the infidels. It is also wise not to give them any suspicion that we are laughing at them, which annoys them very much. They are always suspicious of laughter and foolery among pilgrims.

Article 9. Pilgrims should be careful not to make jokes about or laugh at any Saracen boys or men whom they meet. However well meant this kind of thing may be, a good deal of trouble can arise from it. If boys do something ridiculous, the pilgrim should turn away and keep a serious expression, so that there is no risk to peace.

Article 10. Pilgrims should be careful not to stare at any woman whom they meet. All Saracens are exceedingly jealous, and a pilgrim may find himself in the dangerous situation of facing the anger of a jealous husband.

Article 11. If any woman beckons a pilgrim, or invites him by sign language to enter a house, he should on no account follow her. The woman will be doing this as a ruse at the instigation of some man. The object will be to rob the Christian, or perhaps kill him.

Article 12. Every pilgrim should avoid giving wine to a Saracen who asks for drink, whether on the road or elsewhere. As soon as he has had one drink he goes mad, and the first person he attacks is the pilgrim who gave him the drink.

Article 13. Let every pilgrim hold on to the mule which he first received from his driver; he should not change it or exchange it with another, except with the consent of the driver. Otherwise there are ructions.

Article 14. Pilgrims of noble birth should beware of revealing their nobility when Saracens are present. There are many reasons why this is imprudent.

Article 15. When Saracens are present, no pilgrim should put a white turban on his head, nor wind white cloths or napkins around his head, since they believe that they alone are privileged to do this, and it is a sign which distinguishes them from those of other nations. They cannot bear seeing Christians in white garments.

Article 16. No pilgrim should wear knives or any similar

items slung about him since they are likely to be torn off. Nor should a pilgrim carry any weapon.

Article 17. If a pilgrim forms a friendship with a Saracen he must be careful not to trust him too much, since they are capable of betraying one's trust. He should be particularly wary of touching his beard or turban, even with a light touch, or in fun. They take this as an insult, and all joking is forgotten, and they become angry. (I, Brother Felix, have had personal experience of this.)

Article 18. Every pilgrim should carefully look after his own property and never leave it lying about where Saracens are. Otherwise, whatever it may be, it will immediately disappear.

Article 19. If a pilgrim has a bottle of wine and wishes to drink, he should hide the bottle and drink secretly if Saracens are present. He should ask a friend to stand in front of him, or cover himself with his cloak so that he may drink without being seen. Since the Saracens are forbidden to drink wine, they envy us when they see us drinking, and, if they can, they persecute those who drink.

Article 20. No Christian should have financial dealings with a Saracen except in transactions where he knows that he cannot be cheated. The Saracens strive to cheat us, and believe that they are serving God by deceiving and defrauding us. Pilgrims should also beware of German Jews, and be on their guard against them, since their object in life is to profiteer and take our money from us. They should also be wary in their dealings with eastern Christians, since they have no conscience—even less than the Jews and Saracens—and will cheat pilgrims if they can.

Article 21. When pilgrims make agreements with Saracens they should not argue with them, swear at them or become angry. Saracens know that such behaviour is contrary to the Christian religion. If they see us behaving in this way, they will immediately exclaim, "What a bad Christian you are!" Everyone can say this in Italian or German! A pilgrim should therefore conduct himself in such a way that he does not bring shame upon the name of Christian in his own person.

Article 22. A pilgrim must take care not to enter mosques, that is, the Saracen temples or oratories. If he is found in one, he will not escape unharmed, even if he manages to escape with his life.

Article 23. Pilgrims should be particularly careful not to mock Saracens when they are praying and using the postures required by their beliefs, since they cannot bear this. They themselves refrain from interfering with us or laughing at us when we are at our prayers.

Article 24. If a pilgrim is detained longer than he would like in Ramleh or elsewhere, he should not assume that it is the fault of the Father Guardian, but rather of the Saracens. They act as they please in these matters, without regard to our convenience.

Article 25. Pilgrims should not object to paying money to save themselves from the many irritations which arise. When money has to be paid, they should pass it over immediately without grumbling. However, you do not need to give money to the driver of your mule, because all of this has been paid by the captain. The only exception is that a pilgrim may give his driver a penny to buy fodder for his mule, although he is not required to do so.

Article 26. The pilgrims should all give something to the keeper of the hospice in which we are lodging, so that it may be repaired and rebuilt.

Article 27. The pilgrims should show respect to the poor convent of the brothers on Mount Sion in Jerusalem. It is with the help of the brothers that the pilgrims are conducted into and out of the Holy Land. Pilgrims' alms support the convent and feed the brothers who live among the infidels to serve the pilgrims according to their means, even waiting on them hand and foot if need be.

Should a pilgrim feel that he has not been dealt with as he would like, or as he might need to be, he should not blame the brothers for this. If they were forced to satisfy everyone with all the bread and wine they were asked for, they would have nothing to live on after the pilgrims depart. Nonetheless they are prepared to nurse sick pilgrims with the utmost care and devotion, and to allow them to convalesce in their own infirmary and rely on the house's charity."

These articles were read aloud to the pilgrims in Latin and German. Now as this homily had lasted such a long time, the Saracens, who were shut outside away from us in the outer court, became impatient. They beat on the gate with stones as though they would break it down. Some mounted up on the roof and peered down into the court-yard where we were, and laughed and shouted. When we looked up at these young men with serious faces and made signs to them to come down, they saw that we were not amused, ceased their shouting, and went away, one after another. We then concluded our entire service in peace, by which time it was about noon....

Ramleh is often mentioned in Scripture—it was here that the holy Samuel was born. Today it is a populous town, with more inhabitants than Jerusalem, and it pro-vides a living for numerous merchants. It has no ram-parts—like many other Saracen towns; there are a good number of mosques within it and in the surrounding area. It is situated in a most pleasant and fertile spot, and all its produce is very reasonable in price, fresh, and of good qual-ity. The residents, however, have very unpleasant charac-ters and show a particular dislike for Christians. Many of them are evil Ethiopians and Moors, or other people with-out understanding....

In the evening of St Procopius' day we got ready for our journey. We left the hospice in the same way as we went in, carrying our luggage slung round our necks. As we went through the town, people ran in from all parts, and the streets were crowded with inhabitants of both sexes who wanted to examine us.

There was a great deal of crowding and this stirred up the dust so much that a man could hardly see the comrade at his side. If he could actually see his shape he was completely unable to recognise him, so thick was the dust. My black hood was so covered that it looked grey rather than black. Even if you needed to open your eyes or your mouth, you could not safely do so. We had to put up with this all across the country, except when we were in stony parts, or when we travelled by night.

In the narrow streets of Ramleh we were in danger of being smothered by the thick dust. In this *melée* I was pressed against the wall of a building near its windows. As the crowd moved very slowly I was kept wedged there. When I looked through the window into the house I caught sight of some women standing there with a number of little children. They made crosses with their fingers and kissed them. In this way they signalled to me that they too were followers of the Crucified. It seemed to me that they were crying.

It is terribly sad that the people of the land where our Lord was crucified, if they are followers of the Cross, cannot wear the Sign of the Cross openly. For in this land the Glorious Cross is hated and despised....As the crowd moved forward I was pushed out from that place and we ended up outside the town where we found our mules and their drivers in a field. Near them was the troop of Saracens who were to be our companions and protect us on our way.

So we mounted our beasts and set off with all speed towards the mountains. Eventually we came to the field of Joshua beside the town of Bethshemesh. This is where fifty thousand men were struck down because they had gazed on the Ark of the Lord when it was set up there. It was in this same field that the Arabs had pitched their tents. There were about three hundred of them.

When we saw their tents we and our escorts were very alarmed. But as we approached the tents we saw just a few very wretched women, some little black, naked children, and a few old men. All the rest of the men were away roaming over the countryside plundering and robbing. When we passed through their camp there was no one to raise a hand against us. However, when we were just on the point of going

up towards the hill country through a valley, we caught sight
of a vast horde of men with camels, mules and horses at the
entrance of the valley. They were getting ready to attack us.

Our escort also got into formation to resist them. They
were alarmed and then got rather panicky, because they
could see that they were Arab bandits, and knew that we
could not pass them by without a skirmish. We could not
turn aside to the right or left, since the route led straight
past them through the narrow valley. When we drew near,
the Arabs formed themselves up to guard the entrance to
the valley and blocked it from us. They had their daggers
drawn, their swords raised, their lances couched ready, and
their bows under tension.

I cannot recall seeing men like them before They were
naked except for a worthless rag about their waist. They
were burnt black by the heat of the sun. Shields hung from
their necks. Their expressions were cruel and savage—a
murderous looking lot they were. When we stared at them,
and then compared them with our Moors and Saracens,
whom we had previously thought scarcely human, we
realised that those escorting us were civilised, God-fearing
men, almost the same as ourselves!

When our escort realised that the Arabs meant business,
they rushed at them in a wave of violence and drove them
out of our way with their weapons. Having opened up a way
through, they called us to push on quickly. We hurried
through the gap which had been prized apart for us.
Whenever a pilgrim made physical contact with an Arab
the latter either grabbed his cloak or his baggage. He then
tugged at it until the pilgrim let it go, or was pulled off his
mule and had to be rescued. Many fell off their mules and
had to picked up; otherwise they would have been robbed.
There was hideous yelling everywhere, and the two sides
rode at each other with great style as though they were
intending to fall on each other and come to blows.

As the fight was going on, the pilgrims passed up
through the valley into the hills. When our enemies saw

this they gathered up rocks from the river bed and threw them after us, aiming at our escort. Yet when they realised that they would be unable to get anything from us by force, they began to ride after us. And now, putting on an appearance of humility and friendship, they begged us to give them something. They did not get much! At last we got away from them. There is no doubt that if we had not been a stronger force they would have robbed us all, despite the safe-conduct of the Sultan.

No pilgrim was seriously hurt; a few were hit with stones. Some, however, lost luggage in the struggle, and some lost their hats. There were no wounds in the skirmish. These easterners have their good side; they shrink from shedding blood. So we went up a shady valley, along a very rough torrent-bed, with high stony mountains on either side of us.

Brother Felix and his party spent the night in an encampment protected by their escort, then went on through rocky terrain passed Shiloh to Emmaus, where our Lord appeared to two disciples on the road. Here the pilgrims visited what was said to be the site of the inn where Jesus had blessed the bread before the disciples. Then they made their way on to the valley of Terebinth, where David killed Goliath. Brother Felix continues:

The chief reason for our wanderings was to reach the most sweet city of Jerusalem, whose fragrance perfumes the whole world, and causes the faithful to hasten there from all parts of the world. As we climbed out of the valley of Terebinth we ceased going eastwards, and went up the slope of a hill facing towards the south. Here, as we travelled among dry stone walls we came to gardens of fruit tress, pot herbs and figs. We looked over to the right, and there, as suddenly as a flash of lightning, was the holy city of Jerusalem shining before us.

What we could see was the part that is joined to Mount Sion, and the holy Mount Sion itself, with all its buildings and ruins. At the highest point we saw Sion's citadel, which is fortified with very strong walls and towers. The light was so clear that the high walls and towers of the citadel seemed to encompass the whole city. A pilgrim or stranger who has never seen Jerusalem would certainly think that the walls of the citadel of Sion were the walls of Jerusalem, which is not the case.

As soon as we saw with our own eyes the Holy City, which was the object of so much of our longing, we immediately dismounted from our mules and saluted her. We bowed our faces to the earth, first greeting her King, the Lord God, with the Sign of the Cross, and then spoke to her in prayer.

…When we had concluded these devotions we remounted our mules, with our eyes full of tears and cheeks wet with joy. The priests and monks among us then all began to sing together *Te Deum laudamus*, but in a low and subdued voice so that we might not offend our escort. Our concern was that our hymn of joy might make them angry if we sang it loudly and clearly. So our song was loud in the voice of our hearts, since our joy was profound and great, far beyond what any words voiced aloud could express.

This joy did not come from emotion, but from our reason. It did not arise from our being in the presence of an object of desire, but of a thing worthy of love, because it was precious. It was not a happiness which leads to sensuality, but rather to seriousness, to a catch in the throat rather than laughter. It is an emotion which does not make the body tremble, but rather bends the limbs; it does not broaden the mouth into laughter, but rather draws the face together into tears. It does not lead to conversation, but silence. It does not make you go off among men, but rather leads you into a quiet corner. It does not make you shout aloud, but rather pray inside you in the words of the psalms.

While in this unexplainable and sweet state of joy we came to the Fuller's field, where Rabshakeh stood and blasphemed against God, and shouted out against those who stood on the walls of Jerusalem. Here in this field, beside the castle which the Sultan has built there, we dismounted from our mules and handed them over to their drivers. Then, taking up our baggage, we walked two by two towards the Gate of the Merchants, or Fish Gate, in silent prayer, with our hands clasped before our breasts. Some of the pilgrims threw away their shoes in their piety, and walked barefoot all the time that we were in the Holy Land. In this way they honoured the glorious footsteps of our Lord, of the Blessed Virgin Mary, and the saints of the Old and New Testaments.

As we came to the gate called the Gate of David, the Gate of Merchants, or the Fish Gate, we passed through it with our heads bowed. By that very act of passing through it we gained plenary indulgences.

From there we proceeded through a long street and came to a great church with closed doors. There was a beautiful courtyard in front of it, which was paved with polished marble of exceedingly vivid whiteness.

When we had all assembled in the courtyard, one of the brothers of the Mount Sion convent got up on a raised place and addressed us. He said that this was the holiest of churches, and venerated by the whole world. Within it was a treasure which was most precious to all Christians, the Sepulchre of our Lord. As soon as we received this confirmation we flung ourselves down on the courtyard before the door of the church, and began to pray and kiss the ground very many times. It really seemed to the pilgrims that virtue was being breathed forth by the ground itself, and was compelling them into prayer.

...I saw some pilgrims lying powerless on the ground; they had lost every bit of their strength; with their strong feeling of devotion they had forgotten their own existence. I saw others wandering hither and thither beating their chests, as though they were being pursued by an evil spirit. Some knelt on the ground with their knees bared, and, holding out their arms in the form of a cross, wept as they prayed.

Others were shaken by such violent sobs that they were unable to hold themselves upright. They found it necessary to sit down and hold their heads in their hands so as to be able to cope with their grief, since their sobs came thick and fast. Some lay so long prostrate on the ground that they seemed to be dead.

Our companions and sisters among the women pilgrims cried out aloud and wept, as though they were in labour. There were also some pilgrims who, out of excessive devotion, lost all control of themselves, and, forgetting how to behave sensibly, made strange and ridiculous gestures from a fervent desire to please God.

It was most interesting to see the very sincere yet different behaviour of the pilgrims as they prayed at the Holy Places. The sites have a marvellous power to move men to tears and make them groan and sigh—the same men who would not be moved by any homily, piece of advice, or passage from Holy Scripture; nor by a painting or carving; nor by promises or threats against them, nor by good or bad times.

Generally, however, those who visit the Holy Places are not affected to this extent, but are merely aroused to an unaccustomed level of devotion and piety. Of course I have seen some people—and I wish that I had not seen them— for whom the pious behaviour of the very devout produced in them quite contrary emotions! When the other pilgrims were at their devotions, these people were unresponsive, and took nothing from the experience themselves. They were rather like brute beasts, without the spirit of God. They stood around and smiled supercilliously at the prayers, tears, prostrations, beatings of breast and the like, which the others were doing. What was particularly objectionable was that these brutes, blind to all piety themselves, devoid of religious feeling, and without a feeling for purity, assumed that the devout were fools, hypocrites and Beghards.

A pilgrimage for such men is completely unprofitable and sacrilegious, since they scorn and misconstrue the behaviour of pious men in such a holy place. These people are worse than Saracens or Jews, who never despise a Christian for acting devoutly. For when we came into this holy courtyard some young Saracens ran there to laugh at us. But when they saw how deeply sincere we pilgrims were, they went off. Yet some even stayed behind and wept with us. There was also a plenary indulgence for visiting this courtyard.

When we had finished our prayer we got up from the ground and went up to the door of the church. We then looked in through the holes through which food is regularly passed to the guardians of our Lord's Holy Sepulchre when they are locked inside. In the middle of the church we could glimpse the Chapel of the Most Holy Sepulchre and the way up to Mount Calvary. Again we were overwhelmed with devout feelings....

After finishing our prayer the Calini led us out of the courtyard or square of the Holy Sepulchre. We crossed the road in front of it and went into the Hospital of St John. This is a large vaulted building, squalid and dilapidated. It is only a part of the ancient hospital, and rather like the great refectories of large monasteries where there are many monks in residence. Here the pilgrims arranged themselves in their groups.

The Suabian nobles, who were my lords, were allocated a place at the end of the building where there was a kind of chamber set apart from the rest and closed off. It was pleasant and respectable. My Lord John, Count of Solms, and his company, went off with Elphahallus, the younger Calinus, to his house and lodged there.

On my first pilgrimage we were not taken to the hospital, but to a great house at Millo at the foot of Mount Sion and we stayed there. During this earlier visit I did not even see the hospital, and was unaware that any traces of it had survived. As soon as the pilgrims had settled in, Saracens, Jews and eastern Christians brought us bread, water, cooked food and fruit, which the pilgrims purchased and consumed.

Two brothers now arrived from the Mount Sion convent, sent by the Father Guardian. They had been told to bring all persons in holy orders to Mount Sion, since it is the custom to lodge them there with the Friars Minor. I joined the party, together with two brothers from my Order of the Preaching Friars. One of these came from the province of the Isle of France, and the other from Naples in the province of Sicily. We were escorted out of the hospital and led up to the convent of the Friars Minor on Mount Sion.

Here we were received most kindly, and the three of us were given a cell to ourselves. So we ate, drank, and served God in their company. I remained in that cell for a good number of days after all the other pilgrims had gone home, enjoying perfect peace and excellent treatment through the kindness of the fathers and brothers of the Friars Minor.

On the thirteenth of July, which was the seventh Sunday after Trinity and the Feast of St Margaret the Virgin, the Father Guardian sent some brothers to the Hospital of St John to invite all the pilgrims to Mass on Mount Sion. All of them, accompanied by the brothers, made their way to the Church of Sion and waited for the time when the service of High Mass began. Although the sun rose early, yet the pilgrims arrived there even before it had risen.

To show their respect for the pilgrim lords, the brothers had adorned the choir, the church and the altars beautifully, covering them with precious hangings. Nowhere have I seen any more exquisite than those here: for women had embroidered on them figures depicting the life and death of Christ.

Important Saracen lords, Turks and Mamluks come from afar and ask to be shown these tapestries. And when the lords, governors and captains of Jerusalem are entertaining important visitors, they conduct them to Mount Sion, and ask the brothers to hang up and display these treasures. They were made for the church as a commission paid for by Philip, Duke of Burgundy, who bestowed many other benefactions on the convent.

The high altar was crowded with gilded monstrances and reliquaries, and over it there was hanging a picture in which St Francis stands alongside our Holy Patron St Dominic. This was particularly well painted. The church itself is not large, because it is only a part of the old Church of Sion.

In the past when Christians ruled the land there was a larger church on this spot. But the Saracens pulled down the section next to the apse or chapel, where the choir of the old church was joined on the right-hand side. The remaining chapel now forms the church, and serves as the choir for the brothers. The ruins of the old choir and church are still plainly to be seen.

When the sun had risen and it was time for Mass, the sacristan beat a wooden board, since they have no bells of any kind....When we were all collected together in the church the brother solemnly chanted the offices of prime and tierce. After tierce the Father Guardian and his attendants, in rich vestments, went up to celebrate High Mass.

The precentor then began one of the songs of Sion, "*Spiritus Domini replevit*," and all the priests and educated pilgrims joined in. And so with joyous solemnity we sang the Mass of the Holy Ghost. This was a service particularly suited to the place, because it was on this spot that the Holy Ghost was sent to the disciples in a visible form. It was appropriate too for the day, because it was the seventh Sunday after Trinity, and the readings for the day mention the seven loaves, that symbolise the seven gifts of the Holy Ghost.

After the service, we priests celebrated our own Masses at four altars which had been prepared for us. I was given a place to celebrate down below in the cloister of the Chapel of St Thomas the Apostle. This is on the spot where the Lord said to Thomas, "Put your finger here," as is written in the twentieth chapter of St John's Gospel.

During High Mass, after the last Gospel, the Father Guardian turned around to the people and preached a beautiful homily in Latin in praise of the Holy Places, and of the importance of visiting them devoutly. This was translated into German by the Venerable Father Paul Guglinger.

During the service the doors were shut, and many Saracens stood outside. After the sermon the door happened to be opened to let someone out. When the Saracens noticed this they pushed forward through the doorway in a disorderly fashion and entered the church. Then they stood near the altar, looking curiously at our mysteries.

Yet they showed no irreverence, apart from standing there in wonderment. The priests, however, immediately stopped the service while the Saracens were led out by the brothers. Yet they did not use force, or drag them along, or argue with them. They simply conducted them out and begged them to stay outside. This was the way our service was brought to an end.

Brother Felix then describes a number of ceremonies and visits to places of interest on Mount Sion. He is particularly struck by the garden of the convent which the Friars had recently purchased. He describes it as follows:

Near the Convent of Mount Sion but beyond its precinct, the brothers have a large garden on a spur of Mount Sion, with views to the south, east and north. With the permission of the Sultan, the brothers acquired it last year from a Saracen for a great deal of gold. When we entered this garden, we first came to the friars' cemetery, where the deceased brothers are buried, and there prayed for their souls.

Then we noticed several deep cisterns. They had been discovered by the brothers after they had purchased the garden and started to cultivate it. They had been filled in with earth and stones, but the friars had cleaned them out, and constructed open channels to lead into them. In rainy weather they collect very good water in these. What is in the cistern in front of the refectory is insufficient to last them through the summer—indeed it failed while I was living there. Before they acquired this garden they used to suffer a good deal from lack of water in hot dry years. But now that they own the garden they cannot be without water, which is considered a precious thing in Jerusalem.

In the garden, in addition to the cisterns, there are trees of many different kinds: figs, pomegranates and similar trees, and vegetables for the use of the convent. The garden is square, and forms part of the Mount Sion spur, with the convent, the church and the ridge of Mount Sion, which are on the level with it, all lying to the west side of it. On all the other three sides there are valleys. The garden is enclosed with a dry stone wall. To the south there is the valley of Aceldama and Mount Gion, to the east the valley of Siloam and the Mount of Offence, and beyond it the valley of Jehoshaphat with the Mount of Olives; to the north is Millo and the Holy City.

We walked all round the enclosure and looked over the wall down into the valleys and across to the mountains beyond. The view is delightful to someone who knows the Scriptures. The wall enclosing the garden stands on the edge of steep stone cliffs, and there may be seen to this day the exceedingly ancient wall of Sion, and the foundation of her towers. Many things lie before one's eyes which are mentioned in Holy Scripture. Indeed what is written there about Millo and Gion and the valleys and other geographical points, cannot easily be understood just by reading about them.

While we were looking about us on this high point, a discussion took place among the lay pilgrim knights which is worth recording. We had stretched ourselves out on the wall and were looking over towards Jerusalem and the valley of Jehoshaphat. These laymen ignored the sights which were immediately in front of them, and concentrated their attention on the building known as Solomon's Temple. They admired this, and expressed a wish to go into it and have a look around. They talked a great deal to one another about how this temple had survived from the time of Solomon to the present day.

While they were talking in this way I listened in silence. But after they had talked inaccurately about it for a long time, I said to them: "My lords and fellow pilgrims, why do you ask no questions, and make no comments on the holy and wonderful sights which are before your eyes, but your sole topic of conversation is about a building quite empty of true worth?"

One of them replied: "We know this Temple of Solomon by common repute, and we have nothing holier or more beautiful in view. As for the mountains and valleys around about us, we do not care for them, and we know nothing about them." They spoke accurately, because they had not yet been to the Mount of Olives. I replied as follows: "The Temple of Solomon is *not* in view. It was destroyed long ago. The building which you now see is the fourth temple built on that spot since Solomon's original temple.

But even if it were the temple of Solomon, why is it of concern to you? In this building Christ is not worshipped; indeed he is blasphemed daily, and Muhammad, who is accursed, is praised. Was it for that abominable and desecrated temple that you came to Jerusalem? Why do you not look across at the valley in front of you, and at the mountain which is to one side of you?"

They replied that they did not know what these places were. I said, "Look, this valley is Jehoshaphat. Into this all people of the world will be gathered on the Day of Judgement. That mountain at your side is the Mount of Olives from which Christ ascended into heaven. Let us discuss these things and admire *them* They are the places which are of concern to *us*. But let us speak no more about that accursed temple!" My intervention resulted in a profitable discussion about the small size of the valley of Jehoshaphat, and related subjects. After this we concluded our pilgrim visit to the places on the top of Mount Sion.

Brother Felix spent a further four months on his second visit to Jerusalem and the other Holy Places. He stayed on after the group to which he was chaplain had left and returned by their galley to Venice. He gives a detailed account of his visits to other places of special significance in Jerusalem and to the sites sacred to our Lord, the prophets and the leading figures of the Old Testament, although much of this covers

*ground also described in the accounts of other pilgrims. The
five passages below have been selected because they record
interesting personal experiences.*

After leaving Bezek, we came to Bethlehem, where we
were welcomed very kindly by the Father Guardian and the
brothers, and were given a good supper. After the meal I
was shown into my cell to rest. But once I was there sleep
fled from my eyes. I lay on my bed wide awake for some
time, then, being bored with resting, I got up.

I had a strong desire to be in the sacred cave of Christ's
birth. But I had no chance of being able to enter it before
midnight since I knew that all the doors were locked.
Nevertheless I crept silently from my cell and entered the
Chapel of St Nicholas where the brothers say their offices.

In this chapel there is a secret way into the Holy Cave
through a narrow doorway. The brothers do all they can to
keep this secret. They are afraid of the Saracens and eastern Christians, who, if they knew of its existence, would
not permit it to be used. I went up to the door without any
hope. But I found it unlocked! So I passed through with a
surge of joy, and made my way along a passage which had
been cut into the rock. I then found the door at the other
end open as well, and went through into the most Holy
Cave itself.

It was lit with many lamps. But I discovered that the two
doors through which people go into the church were locked
fast. When I realised that I was alone in the Holy Cave I
said in my joy: "Blessed be the Lord, and blessed be all the
things which have prevented me from sleeping and lying at
rest on my bed. For this has made me able to keep a most
blessed watch beside the sweet cradle of Christ."

So I kept my personal holy vigil, and passed the hours
according to my ability and knowledge. To speak truthfully
the place is so sweet that it helps you to be devout, and it is
very easy and agreeable to keep watch there.

Early in the morning of the sixteenth day we celebrated

Mass in the most Holy Cave. After this I went to the place of the shepherds out in the fields. Here we sang *Gloria in excelsis* with the angels. Then we went back up to Bethlehem, had a quick look around, and returned to the monastery to dine with the brothers.

Brother Felix managed to fulfil his vow to visit Mount Sinai. His account of the preparation is as follows:

Three things need to be done before setting out on a pilgrimage to Mount Sinai. First, the pilgrims must arrange with the Saracen lords of Jerusalem to draw up an agreement with the guide. Under this the guide shall be obliged to provide an escort and safe-conduct through the desert as far as Egypt. We had already made this agreement. Secondly, it is essential that the pilgrims acquire their own provisions, and have the necessary food to keep them alive during the journey across the wilderness. Thirdly, the agreement should provide that the chief guide should supply camels and camel drivers, donkeys and donkey drivers, and set a fixed day and hour for departure.

All this was done, and the guide appointed the 24th of August, the Feast of St Bartholomew the Apostle, for our departure from Jerusalem, at the hour of vespers. Early in the morning of that day we came out of the Church of our Lord's Sepulchre, and, after breakfasting, all went up to Mount Sion. Here we found both the Calini waiting for us, with camels and camel drivers, and donkeys and donkey drivers.

We made haste, and brought all our baggage out of the brothers' convent. The camel drivers then asked us to pile all of it in one place, so that they could see its full extent, and distribute it evenly among all the camels. Camels must have their loads carefully and finely balanced, and their burdens should be of equal weight. When everything had been carried over into one heap it made a large and heavy pile.

There were many sacks of biscuits, jars full of wine (these were put into sacks made of animal hair so that the Saracens might not see them and criticise us for them), skins full of water, baskets of eggs, coops with live cocks and hens, our bedding and clothes, our knapsacks and trunks, and the baskets which contained our saucepans, kettles, plates and dishes. These and other similar things made a vast mound.

Our drivers were astonished when they saw this. They could hardly believe that twenty men could need such a mass of luggage when crossing the desert. But one needs to make ample provision so as not to be in want during a period of sixty-two days, and to be able to hand out bread and biscuits, smoked meat and cheese to the Arabs and Midianites whom one comes across. This is the way to calm their resentment and be at peace with them. When all our things had been brought forward, the camel-drivers led their camels up to the mound, made them kneel down one after another, and loaded them up.

While this was going on we stood beside them, and carefully scrutinized their hands in case they should steal anything from us! We also watched so as to learn how to load and manage camels. As soon as twenty-two camels had been loaded with a great deal of effort and many arguments, we were summoned by the donkey-drivers to the herd of donkeys. This was to enable each man to choose a donkey for himself on which to ride across the desert all the way to Egypt.

So as to keep the peace, the drivers had agreed among themselves that none should advise any pilgrim to take this or that donkey, or say anything about each beast's good or bad points. We were to be free to choose for ourselves. So anyone who made a bad choice would have no grounds for argument or complaint against anyone. Nor could he have any grounds for paying less than he who was provided with a fine animal. The idea was that when we had finished our selection, he who had in fact chosen the best beast was to pay a tip and drink money to all the donkey-drivers.

The donkey drivers themselves knew which beast was a good one, and which bad. But they were all saddled alike. So my masters the knights ran up and down among the donkeys trying one after another. Sometimes two or three pilgrims would be after one donkey. When I noticed this, I did not wish to offend anyone by making my choice, so I left the crowd, climbed up the stone steps to the door of the Church of Sion, sat down on the door step, and from there looked down on the herd of donkeys.

I watched others choosing their beasts and I carefully considered which I might choose. Among the donkeys there was a big white one, whose ears hung down, and who seemed to have a heavy head and the look of a dull-ish beast. None of the pilgrims would touch him.

I decided on that animal, not because I saw any good in him, but merely so as to give my lords some fun at my expense by choosing one which was despised by everyone! And so when the nobility, after much care and considera-tion, had all chosen beasts for themselves, I went down, and without any examination at all, selected the donkey which had been despised, and led him to a place apart and got ready to mount.

However, the donkey-drivers ran up to me, laughing and shouting, and asked me to give them money. At first I did not understand what they meant, and I was annoyed to be asked for money, since they had not asked for a copper from anyone else. But their interpreter told me that I had chosen the best donkey of all, and that they were therefore asking *me* for the tip. When I understood this, I got out four madi-ni (about one sixth of a Venetian ducat), and handed these over to them. This was the way I ended up with the safest beast of all for the entire journey!

The animal was never tired and had no vices. It never fell down with me on it, never lagged behind, never was frightened, or kicked or bit me. Without any beating it would go on in front of all the others. When I asked the driver how much he would sell it for, he replied that he would not take less than ten ducats for it.

When the camels were loaded, and the donkeys chosen and saddled, we went over to the Church of Sion, and there received the pilgrims' blessing from the venerable Father Guardian of Mount Sion. He embraced each one of us, blessed us and sent us on our way with a kiss. For my part, when I left, I had much more to thank the Father and the entire convent for than anyone else. I had received many kindnesses from them, much greater than all the others. They had indeed been very good to me.

We came out of the Church of Mount Sion and went down to where our donkeys were. When we had mounted, the camels led off and we followed them out of the city. It was not without a great deal of sadness of heart and tears that we left behind the city of Jerusalem, the focus of all our desires. As for me, I have never been happier in any place in the world than in Jerusalem where I had spent such wonderful hours and days.

During their journey the pilgrims and their party called at Gaza, where they had a hot bath. This encouraged Brother Felix to reflect in detail on the rules relating to close association with non-Christians.

On the second day, after Mass, we sent for our guide and begged him to lead us on into the desert to the destination which we were aiming for. He gave his promise that we would set out on the next day. We were delighted with this commitment, and, after we had eaten, we all went together to the Saracen hot-baths where we were bathed and cleansed...

The bath at Gaza is the most sumptuous I have ever seen. In front of the hot-room there is a vaulted building which encircles it like the ambulatory of a cloister. In this building there are many little rooms. They have no beds, but the floors are covered with mats and plaited palm leaves. Each room is closed off merely with a curtain. Here those who wish to take a bath change out of their clothes. In the rooms clean cloths are hanging up, and those wishing to enter the bath wrap these round, covering themselves up from navel to knee. They replace your breeches and belt, so that you are covered in front and behind.

In the middle of the cloister there is a fountain which plays out water from a column of marble through many spouts. All the walls and the pavement both inside and outside the hot-room are faced with different kinds of white marble. This is highly polished so that anyone walking over it needs to take care and tread warily in case he slips, even as one does when walking on ice.

The hot-room itself is like a square tower; it has a dome or vault over it, but there is no ceiling as such. Instead there are a number of round holes about the size of a man's head; these fixed windows are filled with glass of different colours. A soft but adequate light comes through them. There is no furnace in the hot-room, nor does one sense the heat or smoke of a fire; but in one spot there is charcoal being burnt beneath the floor, which heats the marble pavement; and hot water runs along a stone channel which heats the entire room...On the first side there is the extreme heat and the hot water; on the second there is coolness and cold water; the third side is empty and quiet; the fourth side has the door. There is a temperate heat in the middle of the room.

The master of the bath himself waits on those who are bathing in a most kindly and courteous way. He frequently rubs them down, washes them and anoints them with oil and other suitable unguents. The baths are meant to help cure any weaknesses in the limbs. If anyone has any pain, no matter what the cause, the bathman rubs, anoints, presses and stretches the place where the pain is felt until he either cures it or alleviates it. This applies to complaints of pain in the limbs, for instance in the leg, hand, foot or neck—these they treat in a marvellous way.

It is in the bath room that with great skill they rehabilitate arthritic limbs, relieve gout in the hands and feet, and treat gravel and kidney stones. If anyone complains of tightness in the chest or shortness of breath, they work hard at trying to alleviate this. They do this not by just sitting alongside the patient, but they take him and lay him down on the pavement in the middle of the bathroom, either on his back, face downwards, or on his side, as the pain requires. Then the bathman sits on the patient and locates the seat of the pain; then he gently bends the aching arm backwards and forwards, and presses the neck this way and that.

I once saw an Ethiopian ask for a bath cure. He had a tightness in his chest. The bathman laid him on his back on the pavement, sat on his belly and pressed his neck with both hands so hard that his face began to swell so much that his breathing was completely stopped. He held him like this for such a long time that I feared that the man might choke—he had also stopped up his ears with silk. At last he let him go. The man recovered his breath and was exceptionally pleased, saying that from now on he would be well. It is very pleasing to witness such sights as these.

Many illnesses are cured in the baths which we reckon to be incurable, or only treatable by visits to hot springs. There we make huge efforts, at great expense, for days at a time, with the same effect as these men achieve in half an hour! But I believe that the masseurs also use incantations when they are working their cures. For while they are carrying out the remedial treatment that I have described, they continually mutter to themselves, speaking I know not what words into their patients' ears, and carrying on in every way as if they were performing spells.

Men and women never meet in the baths. But the women have their own baths, and the men likewise. Nor do men have women to rub them down, nor women men, but men wait on men, and women on women.

On no account do they permit Jews to join them in the baths, but they permit us to bathe with them. I have often wondered why they allow us to do this without objection, since in other situations they do not associate with us in a friendly fashion. I guess that there are three reasons for it. First, although they do not normally mix with us in an amicable way, yet when they realise that they will obtain some advantage or money from us, they are not only friendly but grovel to us very slavishly. Since they know that we pay the bathman well, they are willing to put up with our company.

Another reason is probably because Saracens have horrible body odour—which is the reason why they are continuously washing themselves, and since we do not smell, they do not mind us bathing with them. They do not extend this indulgence to the Jews, who smell worse than they do...A third reason why they allow us into the bath-house with them is that Muhammad has not actually forbidden them to meet us at the baths, but only in their mosques...

Christians are forbidden to keep company with Jews in many situations; and sharing baths with them is specifically excluded (Gratian's Decretum pars ii., causa xxxviii, quest. I, c.xiii). Anyone who breaks this rule is unfrocked, if he is a priest, or excommunicated, if he is a layman. In this way the rule breaker becomes like the person to whose level he lowered himself by his association; for someone who is excommunicated is the same as an outcast or a Saracen. The same rule applies to pagans as well as Jews. It is for this reason that it is not decent for a Christian to enter the baths of Jews or Saracens.

I hope, however, that we pilgrims did not incur the penalties arising from this piece of canon law. For in time of need we are not even forbidden to eat the unleavened bread of the Jews, nor meat offered to heathen idols. Moreover, there is also the Pope's dispensation. For it was he who gave us leave to travel to the country of the Saracens, and by so doing he necessarily allows us to join the heathen at table, in the bath, and at the doctor's.

Moreover, no danger can arise from such bathing, nor corruption of our faith, nor scandal, nor sin of any kind, since being in their company is neither continuous, nor a reason for familiarity, but is quickly over. Indeed, we were not able to talk with them since we did not understand their language, which is the greatest of all factors of bonding among men.

The last extract is of Brother Felix's account of the small cele-
bration which he held when, after an exhausting and dangerous
journey, his select band of pilgrims climbed St Catherine's
Mount near Mount Sinai.

At this time two of the brothers of the Monastery of St Catherine who were living nearby at the Monastery of the Forty Saints, brought us dried figs, dried dates and water, and these refreshed us. Then, since it was not yet mid-day, we sat down and debated whether we should also climb St Catherine's Mount on the same day, or rest until tomorrow. We concluded that the younger and tougher men, and any who were keen to accompany them, should ascend it there and then, and return from their expedition by sunset. The others—the older and weaker pilgrims— should make their ascent in the cool of the next morning.

Ten of the strongest pilgrims then stood up and made ready to make the ascent in the very intense heat. The party included the Lord John, Count of Solms, Knight, the Lord Harry of Schonberg, Knight, the Lord Sigismund of Marspach, Knight, the Lord Caspar of Siculi, Knight, Master Lazinus, Archdeacon and Canon of the Church of Transylvania in Hungary, Brother Felix of Ulm of the Order of St Dominic, Father Paul Guglinger of the Order of Friars Minor, Brother Thomas, a lay brother of the same Order; and two of the Count's servants named John and Conrad. There were also some Arabs in the party. The group then set off to take the exceedingly steep route up St Catherine's Mount.

We went up the mountain by a long, rough and stony track, through valleys which seemed to have no way through, up sheer cliffs, over-hanging rocks, menacing boulders, frightening inclines and precipitous paths, all this under a strongly burning sun. We had, however, one consolation: we located two springs of cool water during our ascent and refreshed ourselves at these. Nevertheless one knight, exhausted by the vigorous effort needed, gave up completely, and sat down in one of the steepest places unable to go a step further.

We were already more than half way up, and could see the top of the mountain, even though it was a long way above us. When the enfeebled knight saw this he lost confidence in his ability to reach it, and begged us to go on, and let him wait there alone. Our response was to encourage him, and put pressure on him to go on a little further. But when we noticed that he kept falling to the ground after slipping from everyone's grasp, as if he had completely gone to pieces, we tied a long towel to his girdle. With this some of us dragged him along, while others grasped his hands, and pulled him forward by his arms; others got behind and pushed him on. We all put in an amazing amount of effort on behalf of that pilgrim!

At last with God's help we reached the top of the mountain and arrived at the angelic tomb of the most blessed virgin, St Catherine. Here we prostrated ourselves and kissed the place where her sacred body was brought by angels. The first thing we did was to chant the service specified in the *Processional of the Holy Land*, and receive our indulgences.

After prayers we sat down and everyone had a raging appetite for bread and water. They all wished that they had brought their food bag and water bottle with them. I don't know why Providence ordained that I should be the only one to have my basket with me! This contained biscuits, hard-boiled eggs, smoked meat and cheese. I had brought this along for myself alone, whereas everyone else had left their provisions behind with the pilgrims who had stayed down below.

When they saw that I was so well provided they congratulated me, and were annoyed with themselves for failing to bring anything sustaining. Then one of them began to beg a scrap of meat from me, another a crust of bread, another a bit of bread and cheese, and others a drink of wine. When I realised what was going on I was amused. But I gave nothing to anyone. Instead I took my basket and emptied the entire contents on to a hollow rock close by us. It was the actual place where St Catherine's head had lain.

I then issued the following light-hearted invitation to the noblemen and pilgrims: "Look, my masters, Providence has willed that all of you here present should be my guests, and that I alone should cover the costs of your meal. This I would do most willingly were I able to offer you fine entertainment. Yet this is how matters have turned out.

Here in this place, in this very chamber, on this very bed lived and slept my sweetest spouse, St Catherine, for more than thirty years after her passion. She was betrothed to me in my youth, and by Divine appointment she was chosen by me from among all the most precious ladies of the Kingdom of Heaven. It was on this virgin's feast day in the year 1452 that, from love of her, I renounced the world, and took the habit of the Preaching Friars. After one year had elapsed, on the same day, I publicly and solemnly professed obedience to the Order, and bound myself for ever to the service of God and of this virgin. Now come along all of you here and enjoy yourselves in eating what I have brought with me."

At my invitation all of them came forward, and we consumed everything that we had. At this feast of mine there were counts, knights, priests and monks, as well as other secular persons—Christian heretics, Arabs and Saracens. Everyone had a morsel from my basket.

There was plenty of wine, because other pilgrims had brought their bottles, but we were short of water. When one of the guests—an Arab—noticed this, he picked up a jar, then—not running but sliding—he set off down the mountain-side, and soon came back carrying it brimming with fresh water. He had got this from a spring which we did not know existed. So we mixed our wine with water. Our meal did not end until we had completely finished up all the drink, and the food to the last crumb.

Never was my bag so completely emptied and stripped bare as at this spot. By now the sun was setting, and the Arabs warned us to make our descent before it had completely disappeared. So we arose and made a hurried descent. At the Monastery of the Forty Saints we rejoined our comrades just after sunset.

Eleven years elapse before the arrival of our next pilgrim. During this time Mamluk government in the Holy Land became less effective, the lines of authority more uncertain, and the action of the rulers more arbitrary.

By then the Bedouin Arabs seem to have became even more willing to defy authority. The walls of the city of Jerusalem had not been rebuilt since they were razed by al-Mu'azzam in 1219, some thirty years after the city was lost for the first time by the Crusaders. This lack of effective walls made it easier for determined Bedouin bands, when the central authority was weak, to make raids on the citizens living in Jerusalem, as well as on travellers and pilgrims on their way there, so as to extort money and goods.

In 1484 Martin Luther was born at Eisleben in Lower Saxony. Later, as an Augustinian friar, he was to attack the granting of indulgences by the Church to Christians who had confessed their sins and performed acts of penance, such as pilgrimages. According to the Catholic Church's teaching, an indulgence is a remission before God of the temporal punishment in purgatory due to sins whose guilt has already been forgiven. A faithful Christian, duly disposed, may gain these indulgences under certain precribed conditions through the actions of the Church.

Indulgences may be partial or plenary, according to whether they remove either part or all of the temporal punishment of sins. The Church, as the minister of redemption, because of the power granted to it by our Lord to remit sins, is able to dispense and apply with its authority what is seen as a treasury of the satisfaction of Christ, which He won for men on Calvary, and which the saints have won by their holy lives.

Luther was also hostile to the veneration of relics of the saints, which, as we have seen, also forms an important part of the religious spirit shared by those on Brother Felix Fabri's pilgrimage.

In 1492 the forces of King Ferdinand and Queen Isabella in Spain conquered the Arab Emirate of Granada, thus ending all Muslim rule in the Spanish peninsular. Many Jews and Muslims left Spain, and some eventually settled in Palestine. In the same year Columbus reached America. This was later to have great consequence for Christianity: in Latin America to the south where the Catholic Church established a strong presence; and, much later, in the twentieth century, when the power and wealth of the United States became a key factor in the creation and maintenance of a new Jewish State in the Holy Land.

The next account, by Canon Casola, dates from 1494. He was of an aristocratic Milanese family, and became a Canon of the Metropolitan Church of Milan in 1478 at the age of 51. He was 67 when he made the journey to the Holy Land—a remarkable feat for someone of his age. He was a man of the world, widely read and travelled; he also took the Venetian galley tour.

Casola describes the inhabitants of Jerusalem and his visit to the Church of the Holy Sepulchre as follows:

AMONG the inhabitants of Jerusalem there are many of good standing and handsome appearance. All of them go about dressed in the same manner, with robes that look like quilts. Many of these are white, others are made of camlet, or of Moorish silk. They spend as much as they can afford on having carefully fashioned and elaborate white cloth head dresses. This item is called a *sexula* if it is all white, and a *moro naturale* if there are black flecks woven into it.

All the inhabitants live in the same manner, even if they are renegade Christians or true Christians of the Girdle (Descendants of Christians miraculously converted by St Thomas the Apostle, using the girdle of the Blessed Virgin Mary). They take their meals on the ground on carpets. There are some white tablecloths in use, but these are rare.

They do not drink wine—in public that is—but if they get a chance they take a good long swig secretly! They are very partial to cheese, but they will not eat a chicken which has had its neck drawn in our manner. They always cut their chickens' throats. Apart from this they are clean in the way they *cook* their food. They do not sleep anywhere but on the ground. They lie on carpets, of which they have a great many. The way they *eat* is particularly disgusting: even important people thrust their hands into dishes of food. No knives, forks or spoons are used, but their hands go into everything!

I was able to observe some of them at their prayers from a window which overlooked where they were. A number of Moors had slept out in the open air because of the extreme heat. In the morning when they got up they went through a great many prostrations, throwing themselves forward so that they were stretched out at full length. It was amazing to witness this.

When I made further enquiries I learned that when they enter the mosque they do so bare-footed, having first washed themselves in places set apart for the purpose. But they only wash from the waist downwards. In the mosque they uncover their heads, which they never normally do, even in the presence of the greatest lord in the world. It is quite foolish to talk to them about our Faith because they have no rational understanding in them. They are very impetuous, and easily roused to anger; they have no gracious or courteous impulses or actions. In my view no matter how important and learned they are, their ways of behaving make them more like dogs.

I never managed to see a beautiful woman in Jerusalem. In fact they walk about with their faces covered with a black veil. On their heads they wear a contraption which resembles a box, about an arm in length, and, from this, long cloths hang down on both sides, rather like Italian towels.

I know nothing more about these Moorish people, apart from the fact that they have a habit which is very disagreeable to us Italians, and to other kinds of Christians: they pester us for money, which is extremely irritating...

On Thursday the 7th of August all of us pilgrims went to Mount Sion. There many went to confession and also received Holy Communion in that very holy place where the Most Holy Sacrament was itself instituted. Many also said their Mass there. Among us there were sixty-three priests of different Orders. I said Mass myself, and gave Communion to one of our pilgrims from Milan called Bernardino Scotto, and to two men from Ragusa. Then the friars chanted a Mass of the Holy Spirit very solemnly.

One of them preached a most beautiful homily in Latin in which he explained all the sacred places and associations of the Church of Mount Sion in which we were. When Mass was over we formed a procession to visit these places, and, when this was completed, the friars of Mount Sion treated all the pilgrims to a good dinner.

After the meal was over the pilgrims were all advised to go and rest so as to be ready that evening, either to enter the Holy Sepulchre, or to go off to Bethlehem. At a very late hour in the afternoon the order came through that we were to have entry to the Holy Sepulchre. The delay had arisen from a new imposition of a financial charge over and above what was normally exacted. Just before sunset all the pilgrims congregated before the door of the Church of the Holy Sepulchre in a little courtyard very beautifully paved with slabs of marble. In the middle there is a stone which is honoured because it is said that Christ rested there on the way to the place of His Passion.

The representatives who had been appointed to count the pilgrims were now ready. There were ten Moors—men of imposing appearance but not ministers of their religion. They wore robes as white as snow and had very large *sexule* on their heads. It made me feel very hot just to look at them! The men were seated on a small platform about four feet from the ground. This was made of wood, and mats were laid over the boards. On these the men were seating cross-legged, like tailors do at home. They made a very fine picture.

We waited until sunset for the Moor who is in charge of the keys. But he could not be found! You need to understand that although the Sepulchre is administered by the friars of Mount Sion and the other Christian sects, as you will hear later, Christians are not able to go in and out when they wish. They are only allowed to enter at the pleasure of the 'dog' who always keeps possession of the keys. He is the Moor responsible for setting the charges to be paid by the pilgrims, and those to be paid by others who want to enter the Sepulchre at other times. The door of the church has certain slots through which food and other things may be passed to those within when it is locked.

In the end the pilgrims were dismissed with the announcement that they would not be able to enter that evening. The company then began to drift away. But when our ship's captain had already gone some distance away he met the man with the keys! After some argument, and a lot of exchanges which I did not understand, since they were in the Moorish language (but the Prior of Mount Sion understood them), we returned to the Church of the Holy Sepulchre.

Here the door was opened, praise be to God! The representatives whom I have already mentioned began to count the pilgrims in Moorish like sheep, and their interpreter in Italian. Then, with God's grace, we entered that holy church.

Since it was already night every pilgrim lit his candle. Then the friars of Mount Sion began to form up in a procession, because they had come with us for this purpose. They started off at the Chapel of Our Lady, where the church offices are said sequentially by the friars—they take it in turns to be enclosed in the building throughout the year.

The chapel is where Christ appeared to His Blessed Mother after the Resurrection. An anthem was chanted here, and the appointed prayer was said. Then one of the friars explained in Latin all about the wonders that had taken place there, and the relics which were held in the chapel. Apart from this being the place where the apparition appeared to our Lady, a large piece of the Cross of Christ is honoured there. It is placed in a window of the chapel on the gospel side of the altar. It can be viewed, but not touched. On the other side of the altar a large piece of the column at which our Lord Jesus Christ was scourged is honoured. It is an impressive relic because the marks of the blows can be seen upon it. They cannot be touched or they would wear away. The column itself *can* be touched, but only with one hand, and with a few rosaries. In all these places there are important indulgences for being present there.

On leaving the chapel the procession entered the body of the church and proceeded to all the other places usually visited. The first was the place where Christ appeared to Mary Magdalene, and was taken for a gardener. As we processed, the appointed anthems were being sung, and the litanies chanted. Our next visit was to where Christ was held in prison while the hole was being made in the rock in which the Cross was erected. We then went to the place where the garments of Christ were divided, and where lots were cast for them; then on down several steps into the Chapel of St Helena; then down several more steps to view the place below the site of Calvary where the Cross of Christ was found. When we went back up again we came to a chapel in which there is the column to which Christ was bound when the crown of thorns was placed on his head. Finally, with the greatest reverence, we went up by a wooden staircase to the place of Calvary itself.

It was here that one of the friars of Mount Sion preached a lovely homily on the Passion of Christ. His manner of delivery was such that I am convinced that if those Moorish dogs had been there with all the pilgrims they too would have wept. We stayed here for over an hour, then, when the homily was over and the usual prayer had been chanted, we went down to the Holy Sepulchre and entered one at a time.

When the friars had concluded their offices the company set about having some refreshments, that is those who had brought something in with them. The captain, as a man of importance, had made good provision for the occasion, and I went with him to a small place belonging to the friars of Mount Sion and there had supper. The other pilgrims stayed in the church sitting here and there on the floor. When they had had their snack some lay down on the ground to sleep; others did not.

As soon as I saw that the crowding by "people from beyond the Alps" had lessened, I went again with my lighted candle to visit all the sacred places. I was able to touch the major locations and relics with my rosaries without any difficulty. The friars then made a count of the pilgrims and drew up precise lists of those who wanted to say Mass.

The priests were divided into groups to celebrate at three places: the Sepulchre, the place of Calvary, and the Chapel of Our Lady. There was also an option to say Mass where the body of Christ was laid. This is where he was placed when He was taken down from the Cross and anointed with the mixture brought by Nicodemus and Joseph of Rama (according to some authorities Rama is the ancient Arimathea), before being laid in the Sepulchre. Anyone who wished to say Mass here could do so without the need for a special booking on the list. I said my Mass above the Sepulchre under the first arrangement.

On Friday the 8th of August, at nine o'clock in the morning, we were let out of the Church of the Holy Sepulchre and everyone went to his lodgings to rest as well as he could.

Canon Casola made one further visit to the Church of the Holy Sepulchre. On this occasion he was less preoccupied with the ceremonies and his own devotions. He provides this description of the building at the time of his visit.

The church is large. On the west front it has two doors which seem to me to be set in the middle of the church. One of the two is walled up, so that only one can be opened and used. There is no other entrance. On the left hand side of the door there is a beautiful bell tower, but at present there are no bells.

Just as you enter the church there is the place where the body of Christ was anointed when it was taken down from the Cross. To the side of this there is the ascent to the place of Calvary. This site is administered by the sect of Christians called Georgians. Below this there is a dark chapel which is said to be the centre of the world. Here there are two very unprepossessing monuments: one is said to be that of Godfrey, who was the first king after the Christians had rescued Jerusalem from the hands of the Saracens.

On the other tomb there is some Latin lettering in the ancient style, beautiful and still legible. This explains that there lies Baldwin, who descended from Godfrey and was also king. The inscription also reads: "*Baldwin qui fuit alter Machabeus.*" (Baldwin who was a second Maccabeus).

To the side of this there is a chapel which is reached by going down many steps under Mount Calvary; it is administered by another sect of Christians called the Armenians. Then there is another chapel, where our Lord Jesus Christ was bound when the crown of thorns was placed on his head; this is in the hands of the Abyssinians, another Christian sect. There are other places around the body of the church which are administered by various sects of Christians: Syrians, Maronites and Golbites. All of these have different services.

The cupola above the Holy Sepulchre of our Lord Jesus Christ is a very remarkable and magnificent construction. It is truly miraculous that those Moorish dogs have left it standing. But if God does not make some provision for it I believe that it will collapse. A piece has already fallen from the vault near the Latin friars' quarters, and those dogs will not allow it to be repaired. This is despite the fact that the

true Governor of Jerusalem—that is to say, the Usbech—
has obtained permission from the Sultan for its repair. I was
told this by some of the friars who had actually gone to
obtain this permission.

When seen from below, the cupola at first glance resembles that of Santa Maria Rotunda at Rome. This is because
it is rather shallow, is decorated, and has a large aperture in
the centre which provides the light both for the cupola and
for the rest of the church. Upon more careful examination,
however, the cupola can be seen to be constructed on the
same plan as that of San Lorenzo the Greater at Milan. It is
possible to walk around its two galleries, one below and one
above...

The Holy Sepulchre itself is in the middle. It is like a
little round chapel carved in stone which has the diameter of the Sepulchre. It is in this that Mass is said. When
four people are in
the chapel there is
no room for any
more. It is entered
by an aperture,
since there is no
door, and a man has
to stoop consider-
ably to go in. Just
outside there is a
sort of square cell
forming an annex

to the chapel; there is a stone, somewhat raised, in front
of the aperture at the entrance to the Sepulchre. Here it
is said the angel was seated when he told the Maries that
Christ had risen.

In front of this little chapel there is another sort of
chapel served by the Jacobites, one of the Christian sects.
They have an odd way of chanting their offices. During the
night I stood a little while to watch their ceremonies and
listen to their chanting. The general effect this had on the

company was to make them laugh. The *calogeri*, as their priests are called, had little hammers in their hands, and, as they chanted, they beat a piece of iron with these. I was unable to work out why they did this.

In the galleries which are above and below in the cupola some Christian sects have lodgings for their wives and families. Their encampments are marked out with matting and canvas, but everything they do can be seen by all....

The friars have charge of the Sepulchre itself and of the little chapel in front. It is widely reported that St Helena, the mother of Constantine, was responsible for having this marvellous church built. We do not read anywhere that it was built on the initiative of anyone else.

Canon Casola and his party had great difficulties with the authorities in Jerusalem throughout their visit, and on their way back to their ship at the port of Jaffa. The following passage describes events at Ramleh, and the delays and exactions which they had to face as they tried to take their leave from the Holy Land. They are symptomatic of an administration in difficulty.

On Wednesday the 20th of August, the Governor of Gaza, who had come to Ramleh on hearing that the pilgrims had arrived there, devised a further disconcerting extortion. His demands were that

—either the ten Christian slaves, whom we had ransomed on our arrival when leaving our galley for Jerusalem, should be handed back to *him*;

—or we should pay him *five hundred ducats*.

This was a more than devilish scheme. There was no court of justice in Ramleh, and, according to what people said, the Sultan was ten days' march away. It was an impossible situation. Nevertheless, after the Prior had intervened, this extortionate levy was reduced to one hundred and twenty-eight ducats—a great consolation to the pilgrims who were hoping to leave by the following day at the latest.

In the evening the ship's captain went to take the

Governor the money. Yet because his ducats were those called seraphs, that cur-like Governor would not accept them. He wanted ducats from the Venetian Mint!

The captain and all the other pilgrims were in despair because of the delay to our departure. They were experiencing every kind of hardship—they were particularly short of water because the cistern in the hostel where we were lodging was empty, and we had many sick among us.

On Thursday the 21st of August, since the pilgrims had been cheated out of their departure, the Prior of Mount Sion said Mass very early in the morning. Poor fellow, he wanted to comfort our company as well as he could. After a most thorough racking of his brains, he preached a homily in Latin in which he exhorted the pilgrims to have patience under the trials inflicted on us every day by the Moors.

He took the authority for his homily from Holy Scripture and the examples set by the saints: *"Quia opertet per multas tribulationes intrare in regnum Dei."* (For it is necessary to pass through many tribulations to enter into the kingdom of God). In the second section of his address he asked the pilgrims for pardon if he or any of his friars had not shown them all the attention that they had perhaps hoped to receive both in Jerusalem and elsewhere.

In the third section he asked all pilgrims, on their return to their home countries, to beg all those who might be intending to visit the Holy Sepulchre, either because of a vow or out of devotion, to postpone their pilgrimage for the next two years. He gave as his reason the serious persecution now being inflicted by the Moors on pilgrims. He said that they were likely to behave even worse in the immediate future until the Sultan heard all about this and took steps to end it.

After the homily the door of the hostel was opened to admit those bringing provisions to sell to the pilgrims. When the meal was over the Venerable Prior had an interview with the Governor of Gaza. The Prior argued so well that he finally persuaded him to accept the amount of fraudulent exaction already agreed, to take this in whatever ducats could be assembled, rather than in ducats from the Venetian Mint, and allow us finally to leave.

However, when the Venerable Prior went again to pay the agreed sum, the Governor of Gaza began to act like Pharaoh, King of Egypt, did when God wanted Moses to lead the people of Israel into the Promised Land—where we indeed were now. The Governor made a new tyrannical demand. He said that he did not want *money* for the slaves who had previously been redeemed and were now on board our galley, but he wanted them *returned to him!*

At first he said one thing, then another, until the Prior and the captain were thoroughly confused. They did not know what to do to satisfy that mad dog of a Governor of Gaza. At last it was agreed to send a messenger to Jerusalem to the Old Man of Faith (the leading Muslim religious leader in the city) and wait until his opinion on the matter was known.

The messenger was sent on his way, and for the rest of the day there was nothing else to be done. Never was there a day of greater agitation among the pilgrims. The wine and water had run out, and the heat was intense. A great deputation of pilgrims from the other side of the Alps assembled and went to the captain's lodgings. They were shouting at him, as the children of Israel had done at Moses when they had no water in the desert. It was more painful than I can bring myself to say to listen to what the pilgrims were saying, and to witness the distress of the captain who had so many of the men in his care as effective prisoners.

The Venerable Father, Don Fra Francesco, who had a great reputation among the pilgrims, with the Prior, tried to comfort the pilgrims. They said that provision would be made for them to have a drink in the morning. Once they had had supper and the sun had set, the pilgrims began to calm down. But it was at this point that someone—I believe that it was one of the Christians of the Girdle— warned the captain that some Moors were intending to attack the hostel during the night and rob the pilgrims.

The captain summoned the leaders of each national group and explained to them what this Christian had said. He added that he thought that guards should be posted during the night, and this was done.

At about midnight one of the guards thought that he saw armed men near the hostel door. He began to shout out loudly, and his cries penetrated right up to the captain's room. At first we thought that we were all to be cut to pieces... I was sleeping with some others in the captain's room, and was lying on a plank raised perhaps a couple of feet from the floor. When I heard the noise, being half-asleep, I fell off the plank on to the ground. In fact there was only one pilgrim who came to grief as a result of the commotion, and that was Casola who fell off his perch!  There was no real cause for the alarm, even though everyone was very frightened at the time.

When all the company felt able to breathe again I began to laugh. "If there really had been an attack what resistance could we have offered? In the whole hostel there is not a stick of the length of an arm, nor a sword, nor a knife of half an arm's length. In fact there is no weapon of any kind. There are not even any stones, unless we dismantle the hostel itself!" Everyone agreed that I was right. So we went back to rest on our beds till morning.

On Friday the 22nd of August some barrels of wine were brought in and distributed among the company to cheer everyone up until the messenger returned from Jerusalem. While we were waiting expectantly, some messengers came from the Moors. They urged the pilgrims to mount their asses and proceed immediately to Jaffa. Since we thought that Ambrayno had given this order, we got

very excited. But almost immediately afterwards we
learned that the order was false. It was just the Moors
mocking the Christians!

Not long after this the messenger arrived from the Old
Man of Faith in Jerusalem. He had written to the
Governor of Gaza in these terms. On no account should
the Governor let the slaves who had been redeemed and
sent on to our galley depart with *us*, unless *he* was given
the *same number of Moorish slaves* in exchange. If the
Governor had received *money* for the slaves this was to be
returned to us.

This was a terrible blow to us, and a great misfortune for
the men who had been ransomed. The captain was now
required to write in his own hand to the man in charge of
the galley conveying the order that the poor men should be
bound and surrendered to the Mamluks carrying the
Governor's letters.

While the Mamluks went off to the galley, just in case we
should find the wait tedious, a further diversion was
arranged! The Governor of Gaza made an accusation against
a pilgrim from Pavia, Don Giovanni Simone, who had been
created a Knight of the Sepulchre. He was accused of having
stolen a fine parrot in Jerusalem. The Governor sent a
Mamluk to confiscate it forcibly. For some time Fra Antonio
Regna defended this acquisition physically and with argument. But in the end he was compelled to give the bird up
to the Mamluk. Its discovery caused a scandal, and was damaging to the pilgrims. The Moors were always on the look
out for anything which might harm our reputation.

The captain immediately followed the man who had
gone off with the parrot. He sought to make excuses for the
disturbances we had made about this. But Giovanni
Simone insisted on tagging along behind the captain. This
was contrary to the advice of his friends who were unanimously of the view that he should not follow.

Once they were all in the presence of the Governor, the
Moors laid the charge against Giovanni Simone of having

stolen the parrot in Jerusalem. He sought to defend himself by saying that he had bought it. But he was told that he must either name the seller, lose his right hand, or pay fifty ducats! At this point he was put in the "cima" as their prisons are called. In the end, however, the affair was settled for ten ducats of the Venetian mint, which he paid. He also gave some *madini* (a Moorish silver coin) to those responsible for guarding him. But for the present the Governor himself kept the parrot!

Yet the game being played by these dogs had not yet finished! While waiting at Ramleh for the ten slaves to be brought back from the galley we enjoyed more festive times! Events took a turn for the worse after the parrot affair. At the third hour of the night a Frenchman, said to be of royal blood, passed from this life. He was buried in the place set apart by the friars.

On Saturday the 23rd of August, the Mamluks, who had gone to fetch the slaves from the galley, returned empty-handed. The officers of the galley had believed that the captain's letters were extorted under duress, and had therefore refused to surrender the prisoners. The Mamluks had then seized thirteen of the galley's crew who happened to be ashore, and placed them in custody in one of the two Jaffa towers.

When the Mamluks returned to Ramleh without the slaves, there was a huge uproar from the pilgrims. They were now all convinced that they would never escape from the Moors, nor from this land of exile where the only thing that was not lacking was the extreme heat!

The Prior, Fra Antonio Regna, and the captain went once again to see the Governor of Gaza, who was furious at what had happened. They made the excuse that the galley officers had probably refused to surrender the slaves because some of their galley crew had been put in chains. And so, with a lot of difficulty, they persuaded the Governor that a further message should be sent to the officer in charge of the galley.

The Mamluks were sent back this time with a gentleman called Don Giovanni Bernardo. He belonged to the Valessi family—Venetian patricians—and he had been appointed to the galley by the Signoria. The message they took was that if the slaves were not returned by midday on the following day, the Governor of Gaza would extract a fine of two thousand ducats. They left at the twenty-first hour. Don Giovanni Bernardo told us afterwards that they had arrived at the sea at the second hour of the night. He then did everything which he had been commissioned to do by the captain in my presence. He soundly abused the galley officers and threatened them. He was in fact truly worked up by the situation.

Sunday the 24th of August was Saint Bartholomew's day. When all the pilgrims had got up and heard Mass, and we had commended ourselves to God, we waited anxiously to learn the outcome of the mission of the messenger who had gone to the sea. Up on the roof of the hostel we waited in the sun, longing to escape.

Just before the deadline—it was by the will of God—the messenger and the Mamluks arrived. With them were the wretched slaves in chains. These miserable creatures were all sobbing. With good reason! They had been ransomed, and now they were once more in the hands of the Moors. The hardest heart would have been moved at the sight of them. Even the Moors were sorry when they saw their pitiful behaviour.

The men manning the galley had sent word to the captain that he need not hesitate to increase the original ransom sum paid. They said that all extra money would be refunded. According to the ship's officers three of the slaves came from Crete and were well off at home. I spoke to the prisoners and discovered that they knew Italian well. But I did not ask them whether they were from Crete or elsewhere. One thing I did regret, and so did the other pilgrims. When the slaves had originally been ransomed I had contributed a Venetian ducat as my share. Yet when the money was returned, the captain never reimbursed me or the others!

As soon as these poor men in their chains had been handed over to those dogs, we set off on our journey. While the animals were being brought up for us to mount, everyone got ready. Meanwhile, the Governor of Gaza, who had kept the parrot but had received ten ducats from Don Giovanni Simone, sent a message to him to say that he could now take the parrot away. But the Governor also wanted five yards of scarlet cloth in return! On hearing this the Prior and the captain again went to call on the Governor. I did not hear what happened, but the parrot was later taken on board the galley on the captain's orders.

The pilgrims were now mounting in great haste, some on mules and some on donkeys. It had seemed likely that we would never escape from the cruel prison where, contrary to all custom, we had been held for so many days. So we now left without further delay, and arrived at Jaffa in a very short time. If these dogs had been weary of eating our flesh, the pilgrims could have gone aboard straightaway. But they wanted to gnaw our bones as well!

We were exhausted and depressed, and many of us were ill. But the leader of the pack, Abrayno Grasso, forced us to spend the night on the bare hot ground of the sea-shore. I really think that this was our worst night, although we had had many bad ones which we had forgotten. Only the Venerable Father Preacher and his servant were allowed to go on board the galley. The Prior and the captain successfully pleaded for him because the Preacher was ill.

On Monday the 25th of August, the dogs had finally gorged enough on us, and they agreed to let the pilgrims aboard. With God's grace we were all taken by boats at top speed out to the galley. But the captain remained behind on shore for what seemed a good while. It seemed likely that we might well be summoned back to shore again.

On board the galley the officers and crew gave us such warm and affectionate greetings that they could not have done more for us, even if we had been their brothers and sons. Yet once the pilgrims were all aboard, the captain and ship's clerk were detained on shore until the following night. In fact Abrayno did not let the captain leave his tent until he had extracted everything that he wanted from him.

On Tuesday, the 26th of August, when those dogs had at last allowed the captain to leave and he had reached the galley, he was told that one of the German pilgrims—a fellow who had been made a knight at the Sepulchre—had died. Again the captain had to reach an agreement with those dogs, who insisted on him producing ten ducats before they would let us bury the body on land. And so this rich pilgrim, who came of a noble family, ended up being buried there on the sea shore.

As soon as the boat which had carried his body to the shore for burial had returned, we survivors were granted a great act of consolation. For the captain decided to set sail immediately, even before having a meal. The poor fellow had been so mistreated by the Moors that he was now in a tremendous hurry to set off. So, at the fourth hour of the day, he ordered the anchors to be heaved aboard. Then to the praise of God and our Glorious Lady we set sail towards the West.

Despite the privations suffered by the sixty year old canon on his pilgrimage, he returned safely to Milan. On his return he published a breviary for the use of priests when travelling, and a liturgical book of the services for the Three Days of Easter as used by the Church in Milan. Both of these were published in 1494. Later he also published a description and explanation of the ceremonies used for Holy Mass in the Milanese Church. He died in 1507 at the age of eighty.

CHAPTER FOUR

THE FRANCISCANS HOLD ON

THE Ottoman Turks peacefully took possession of Jerusalem from the Mamluks in 1516. With the ending of their long rule, which latterly had been so arbitrary and ineffective, the Holy Land was now adminstered from Istanbul, formerly Constantinople. In 1524 the Franciscans were evicted from the Church of the Cenacle on Mount Sion, and from their convent nearby, by the order of the Turkish Sultan, Sulayman the Magnificent.

Luther and his allies were now beginning to create disunity in the Western Church. In England, Henry VIII broke away from the religious authority of the Pope in 1533. St John Fisher and St Thomas More were executed two years later, and Calvin's theocratic government of Geveva came into being in 1541. The Catholic Church sought to restore its authority, reform its institutions and lay the ground for renewed fervour through the Council of Trent (1545-63). The Society of Jesus, which was to become a powerful force in strengthening the Church, was founded in 1535.

In Jerusalem, Sulayman the Magnificent rebuilt the walls of the city between 1535 and 1541. From the time of their expulsion from their convent the Franciscans lived in a bakery near the Cenacle on Mount Sion. In 1551 Boniface of Ragusa was appointed Franciscan Guardian of the Holy Land. He proved an energetic leader of the friars, and soon acquired new permanent premises. In due course these were extended to include a library, accommodation for lodging and feeding pilgrims, and an infirmary with first class medical facilities.

Boniface also obtained permission from the Sultan to restore the Church of the Holy Sepulchre, which Casola had noted was in disrepair. In 1555 he supervised work on the edicule, or little house, which stood over the tomb of Christ. He was also a witness at the opening of the tomb itself. In 1570, when he

was by now bishop of Stagno he wrote a solemn open letter
describing his work on the edicule, on the opening of Christ's
tomb, and a subsequent miracle. His letter is given below.

IN the year of our Salvation 1555
that most renowned building
which St Helena, the mother of
Constantine the Great, had constructed in circular form around the
tomb was falling down. Indeed it had
almost collapsed, which was an
affront to Christian piety.

Pope Julius III, whose name will
be remembered forever, was grief
stricken at this impending calamity.
And that victorious Roman Emperor,
Charles V, and his renowned son
Philip, who was himself not unpleas-
ing to God, made entreaties to the
Holy Father that action should be taken. The Pope entrusted the task of restoration to us, who at that time had been
given oversight, under Apostolic authority, of the Convent
of St Francis of the Observance in Jerusalem.

We were given the task of rebuilding and restoring the
collapsing sacred structure as soon as possible. The Lord
Francis Varga, his Imperial Majesty's Ambassador to Venice,
urged on the completion of the work with no less enthusiasm, and a great sum of money for the reconstruction work
was provided by him in the Emperor's name. After many
arduous journeys and a great deal of effort and expense we
finally obtained the funding for the project by the good
offices of Sulayman, the Sultan of the Ottoman Turks, and
we then proceeded to attack the task energetically.

In fact it proved necessary to level the structure to the
ground in order that the restored building should stand
more firmly on its foundations and last longer. The demoli-
tion work revealed clearly to our very eyes the Sepulchre of

the Most Holy Lord cut out of the rock. On the top of this two angels could be seen painted. One of these, in a written inscription, was saying: "He has risen! He is not here!" The other was pointing with his finger to the tomb and saying: "This is the place where they laid Him."

Both of these images, as soon as they were exposed to the air, largely disappeared. Now it happened that one of the slabs of alabaster, which St Helena had laid over the tomb so that the Holy Mystery of the Mass could be celebrated there, needed to be removed as a matter of urgency. And so the place where the Son of Man had lain for three days, which no words can adequately describe, was revealed to us.

Then it was that the heavens were clearly opened for us, and the sight was seen by all those with us. In this place the Sacred Blood of the Lord Jesus had been mingled with the ointment with which He was anointed for burial. And the place was everywhere gleaming as if from the rays of the sun. Taking it all in with pious exclamations and a surge of spiritual joy in our souls we gazed in wonder at the place and kissed it.

Present with us as our companions were a number of Christians of the eastern and western traditions. They too were incredibly moved by this heavenly treasure: some wept uncontrollably, some were in a state of profound shock, and others were deeply moved by an ecstasy of the soul.

In the middle of of the sacred place we found that a piece of wood had been placed. It was wrapped in a precious cloth used to wipe away sweat. But when we took this reverently into our hands and kissed it, at the moment when it was first exposed to the air, it dissolved into nothing in our hands, and all that was left was a few gold threads.

Some inscriptions had been attached to that precious piece of wood, but they were so faded over time and by the ageing process that no complete sentence could be made out from the words which were written, except that at the top of a piece of parchment the words 'Helena Magni' in Latin capital letters could be read. From this, although we cannot affirm it with certainty, it is not difficult to guess that the piece of wood which we found is a part of that Most Holy Wood of the Cross which was discovered by the Empress Helena and placed there in Jerusalem by her, as is recorded in Sacred History.

We left one cross made from this wood in the chapel of Holy Mary of the Apparition, near the tomb of the Lord Jesus and above the altar dedicated to the Divine Cross. We took a second piece with us to Rome. This we again divided into several pieces fashioned into the form of crosses. One of these we offered to the Pope —at that time Pius IV held the sacred reins of the entire Church of Christ in his hands. Two other crosses we freely bestowed on two very distinguished and respected cardinals, particularly well known for their Christian piety, named de Carpo and de Ara Coeli. We kept one tiny cross for ourselves, which we were accustomed to use reverently while carrying out our sacred duties.

This is the place to record in a few words a particular miracle of which our very good God was the mighty author, through the agency of the special protection of this cross. It happened that we were once undertaking a difficult journey. It was a dark night, and we had entered into a specially dangerous part of Cilicia called Bachrae. We had reached a certain deep ravine whose surface was thick with mud.

Already in the ravine there were a large number of Muslims who were bound to us as allies. They and their horses had got themselves into a life threatening situation, and we had to go down into the ravine after them. I was seriously worried as soon as I saw the danger that our allies were in. I commended myself to God and His Blessed Mother the Virgin Mary.

Then I took the aforementioned cross in my hands and made the sign of the cross over myself first of all, and then over all the rest of the Christians who were with me, both those in religious orders and priests. It was quite amazing! The darkness of that night was quickly changed into a great flood of light to the great joy of us all, and to the amazement of the infidels who were with us. And so it was that we and all our Christian companions, and the infidels, had the good fortune to be able to escape through that dangerous ravine bathed in the splendour of that most holy light.

We have decided to make all this known to everyone for the glory of Christ our Lord, and for the common consolation of all the faithful. And to give the account greater credibility we have written this out in our own hand and signed it with the greater seal which we are accustomed to use for similar matters of importance.

It was soon after Boniface of Ragusa rebuilt the little house over the tomb of Christ that he was able, in 1559, to acquire from the Georgians the new premises near the Church of the Holy Sepulchre. This has remained the friars' convent to this day. As we shall see in a later account, they needed extraordinary courage and perseverance to survive all the trials that they had to face in their dealings with the Turkish authorities.

However, during the one hundred and forty years which elapses until the time of our next visitor, Turkish dominance and expansion were beginning to be contained elsewhere. Their sea power in the Mediterranean was checked at the Battle of Lepanto in 1570. In 1589, Moscow became a separate Patriarchate of the orthodox churches, thus freeing the Russian Church from the authority of the Patriarchy in Istanbul, which had by now been under the Turkish Sultan's political control for well over a hundred years.

The Œcumenical Patriarch at Constantinople was now the civil as well as the religious head of the Greek nation throughout the Turkish Empire, and the Sultan exacted fees from him on his appointment, and in turn gave him the power to exact fees from his bishops. The Turks continued their territorial advance in the Balkans, but John III Sobieski, King of Poland, finally defeated them on land and saved Vienna in 1683.

The repercussions of the Reformation continued in Western Europe. Elizabeth I consolidated the reformed church in England, and was excommunicated by Pope St Pius V in the same year as the Battle of Lepanto. The religious war between Catholics and Protestants in France lasted from 1562 to 1598. The Thirty Years War (1618-48) was a wider European conflict which often pitted Catholic against Protestant rulers. The Pilgrim Fathers, refugees from these political and religious conflicts, reached America in 1620.

From about the middle of the seventeenth century the Catholic Church in the West was also troubled by an aftershock of the Reformation: a movement within the Church which has become known as Jansenism. This arose initially around the Cistercian convent of women at Port Royal, some seventeen miles from Paris. Its adherents stressed the difficulty of salvation, encouraged a scrupulous sense of sin, and combined this with a belief in restraint in receiving Holy Communion, as a way of expressing penance.

Some intellectual links with Calvinism and Lutheranism can be seen in the way Jansenists interpreted St Augustine's ideas on grace and free will. In due course the Catholic Church acted to correct these tendencies of over-emphasis, but much damage was done to the perception of Western Church unity. Such divisions also perhaps contributed to a strengthening of the spirit of scepticism which had been growing in Western Christendom in the wake of the Reformation and Counter-Reformation.

The next visitor to Jerusalem, Henry Maundrell, was Anglican chaplain to the Aleppo factory, a trading post of the English Levant Company. He visited Jerusalem in 1697. The extract is from his 'Journey from Aleppo to Jerusalem', which was dedicated to Thomas Sprat, the Anglican Bishop of Rochester, who was himself the author of the first 'History of the Royal Society'. Maundrell exhibits something of the rather sceptical but enquiring spirit of members of the Royal Society in his account of his visit to the Church of the Holy Sepulchre, and of his observation of the Easter services in the year of his visit.

THE church is less than one hundred paces long, and not more than sixty wide: and yet is so contrived, that it is supposed to contain under its roof twelve or thirteen sanctuaries, or places consecrated to a more than ordinary veneration, by being reputed to have some particular actions done in them, relating to the death and resurrection of Christ. At first, the place where He was derided by the soldiers: secondly, where the soldiers divided His garments: thirdly, where He was shut up, whilst they digged the hole to set the foot of the cross in, and made all ready for His crucifixion: fourthly, where He was nailed to the cross: fifthly, where the cross was erected: sixthly, where the soldier stood, that pierced His side: seventhly, where His body was anointed in order to His burial: eighthly, where His body was deposited in the sepulchre: ninthly, where angels appeared to the women after His resurrection: tenthly, where Christ himself appeared to Mary Magdalene, &c.

The places where these and many other things relating to our blessed Lord are said to have been done, are all supposed to be contained within the narrow precincts of this church, and all are distinguished and adorned with so many altars.

In galleries round about the church, and also in little buildings annext to it on the outside, are certain appartments for the reception of friars and pilgrims; and in these places almost every Christian nation anciently maintained a small society of monks; each society having its proper quarter assigned to it, by the appointment of the Turks: such as Latins, Greeks, Syrians, Armenians, Abysinnians, Georgians, Nestorians, Cophtites, Maronites &c all which had anciently their several apartments in the church.

But these have all, except four, forsaken their quarters; not being able to sustain the severe rents and extortions which their Turkish landlords impose upon them. The Latins, Greeks, Armenians and Cophtites keep their footing still, but of these four, the Cophtites have now only one poor representative of their nation left: and the Armenians are run so much in debt, that it is supposed they are hastening apace to follow the examples of their brethren, who have deserted before them. Besides their several apartments, each fraternity have their altars and sanctuary, properly and distinctly allotted to their own use. At which places they have a peculiar right to perform their own divine service, and to exclude other nations from them.

But that which has always been the great prize contended for by the several sects, is command and appropriation of the Holy Sepulchre: a privilege contested with so much unchristian fury and animosity, especially between Greeks and Latins, that in disputing which party should go in to celebrate their mass, they have sometimes proceeded to blows and wounds even at the very door of the Sepulchre, mingling their blood with their sacrifices. An evidence of which fury the Father Guardian shewed us in a great scar upon his arm, which he told us was the mark of a wound given him by a sturdy Greek priest in one of these unholy wars.

Who can expect ever to see these holy places rescued from the hands of the infidel? Or if they should be recovered, what deplorable contests might be expected to follow about them! seeing even in their present state of captivity, they are made the occasion of such unchristian rage and animosity.

For putting an end to these infamous quarrels, the French king interposed, by a letter to the grand visier, about twelve years since; requesting him to order the Holy Sepulchre to be put in the hands of the Latins, according to the tenor of the capitulation made in the year 1673. The consequence of which letter, and of other instances made by the French king, was, that the Holy Sepulchre was appropriated to the Latins: this was not accomplished till the year 1690, they alone having the privilege to say mass in it. And though it be permitted to Christians of all nations to go into it for their private devotions, yet none may solemnize any public office of religion there, but the Latins.

The daily employment of these recluses is to trim the lamps, and to make devotional visits and processions to the several sanctuaries in the church. Thus they spend their time, many of them for four or six years together: nay so far are some transported with the pleasing contemplations in which they here entertain themselves, that they will never come out to their dying day, burying themselves (as it were) alive in our Lord's grave.

The Latins, of whom there are always about ten or twelve residing in the church, with a president over them, make every day a solemn procession, with tapers and crucifixes, and other processional solemnities, to the several sanctuaries; singing at every one of them a Latin hymn relating to the subject of each place. These Latins being more polite and exact in their functions than the other monks here residing, and also our conversation being chiefly with them, I will only describe their ceremonies, without taking notice of what was done by others, who did not so much come under our observation.

Their ceremonies begin on Good Friday night, which is called by them the *nox tenebrosa*, and is observed with such an extraordinary solemnity, that I cannot omit to give a particular description of it.

As soon as it grew dusk, all the friars and pilgrims were convened in the Chapel of the Apparition (which is a small oratory on the north side of the holy grave, adjoining the apartment of the Latins) in order to go in a procession round the church. But, before they set out, one of the friars preached a sermon in Italian in that chapel. He began his discourse thus: "*In questa notte tenebrosa* &c.", at which words all the candles were instantly put out, to yield a livelier image of the occasion. And so we were held by the preacher, for nearly half an hour, very much in the dark.

Sermon being ended, every person present had a large lighted taper put into his hand, as if it were to make amends for the former darkness; and the crucifixes and other utensils were disposed in order for the beginning of the procession; after which, the company followed to all the sanctuaries in the church, singing their appointed hymn at every one.

The first place they visited was that of the pillar of fla-gellation, a large piece of which is kept in a little cell just at the door of the Chapel of the Apparition. There they sang their proper hymn; and another friar entertained the company with a sermon in Spanish, touching the scourg-ing of our Lord.

From thence they proceeded in solemn order to the prison of Christ, where they pretend He was secured whilst the sol-diers made things ready for His crucifixion; here likewise they sang their hymn, and a third friar preached in French.

From the prison they went to the altar of the division of Christ's garments; where they only sang their hymn, with-out adding any sermon. Having done here, they advanced to the Chapel of Derision; at which, after their hymn, they had a fourth sermon, (as I remember) in French.

From this place they went to Calvary, leaving their shoes at the bottom of the stairs. Here are two altars to be visited: one where our Lord is supposed to have been nailed to His cross; another where His cross was erected. At the former of these they laid down the great crucifix, (which I but now described) upon the floor, and acted a kind of resemblance of Christ's being nailed to the cross; and after the hymn, one of the friars preached another sermon in Spanish, upon the crucifixion.

From hence they removed to the adjoining altar, where the cross is supposed to have been erected, bearing the image of our Lord's body. At this altar is a hole in the nat-ural rock, said to be the very same individual one, in which the foot of our Lord's cross stood. Here they set up their cross, with the bloody crucified image upon it; and leaving it in that posture, they first sang their hymn, and then the Father Guardian, sitting in a chair before it, preached a passion sermon in Italian.

At about one yard and a half distance from the hole in which the foot of the cross was fixed, is seen that memorable cleft in the rock, said to have been made by the earthquake which happened at the suffering of the God of Nature; when (as St Matthew, ch.27, v.51-52 witnesses) "the rocks rent, and the very graves were opened." This cleft, as to what now appears of it, is about a span wide at its upper part, and two deep; after which it closes; but it opens again below, (as you may see in another chapel contiguous to the side of Calvary); and runs down to an unknown depth in the earth.

That this rent was made by the earthquake that happened at our Lord's passion, there is only tradition to prove: but that it is a natural and genuine breach, and not counterfeited by any art, the sense and reason of every one that sees it may convince him; for the sides of it fit like two tallies to each other; and yet it runs in such intricate windings as could not well be counterfeited by art, nor arrived at by any instruments.

The ceremony of the passion being over, and the Guardian's sermon ended, two friars, personating the one Joseph of Arimathea, the other Nicodemus, approached the cross, and with a most solemn concerned air, both of aspect and behaviour, drew out the great nails, and took down the feigned body from the cross. It was an effigy so contrived, that its limbs were soft and flexible, as if they had been real flesh: and nothing could be more surprising, than to see the two pretended mourners bend down the arms, which were before extended, and dispose them upon the trunk, in such a manner as is usual with corpses.

The body being taken down from the cross, was received in a fair large winding-sheet, and carried down from Calvary; the whole company attending as before, to the stone of unction. This is taken for the very place where our Lord was annointed, and prepared for burial (St John, ch.19, v.39). Here they laid down their imaginary corpse; and casting over it several sweet powders and spices, wrapt it up in the winding-sheet: whilst this was doing, they sang their proper hymn, and afterwards one of the friars preached in Arabic, a funeral sermon.

These obsequies being finished, they carried off their fancied corpse, and laid it in the Sepulchre; shutting up the doors till Easter morning. And now after so many sermons, and so long, not to say tedious a ceremony, it may well be imagined, that the weariness of the congregation, as well as the hour of the night, made it needful to go to rest.

Saturday, March 27.—The next morning nothing extraordinary passed; which gave many of the pilgrims leisure to have their arms marked with the usual ensigns of Jerusalem.

The artists, who undertake the operation, do it in this manner: they have stamps in wood of any figure you desire, which they first print off upon your arm with powder charcoal; then taking two very fine needles tied close together, and dipping them often, like a pen, in certain ink, compounded, as I was informed, of gunpowder and ox-gall, they make with them small punctures all along the lines of the figure which they have printed; then washing the part in wine, conclude the work. These punctures they make with great quickness and dexterity, and with scarce any smart, seldom piercing so deep as to draw blood.

In the afternoon of this day, the congregation was assembled in the area before the holy grave; where the friars spent some hours in singing over the *Lamentations of Jeremiah*, which function, with the usual procession to the holy places, was all the ceremony of this day.

Sunday, March 28.—On Easter morning the Sepulchre was again set open very early. The clouds of the former morning were cleared up; and the friars put on a face of joy and serenity, as if it had been the real juncture of our Lord's resurrection. Nor doubtless was this joy feigned, whatever their mourning might be, this being the day in which their Lenten discipline expired, and they were come to a full belly again.

The mass was celebrated this morning just before the Holy Sepulchre, being the most eminent place in the church; where the Father Guardian had a throne erected, and being arrayed in episcopal robes, with a mitre on his head, in the sight of the Turks, he gave the host to all that were disposed to receive it; not refusing children of seven or eight years old. This office being ended, we made our exit

out of the sepulchre, and returning to the convent, dined
with the friars.

*A little over one hundred years pass before our next pilgrim.
During this time, in the Orthodox East, now largely under
Turkish rule, the churches' aim was survival. The centralisation
of civil power on the Sultanate at Constantinople, and that of
Christian religious authority on the Œcumenical Patriarch, who
also resided there, was consistent with the Islamic view that there
should be no divergence between the structures of religious and
political power.*

*Although the patriarchs of Alexandria, Jerusalem and
Antioch were theoretically independent, they were now in practice subordinate to the Œcumenical Patriarch who also had a
kind of political role as head of all Greeks wherever they resided.
By 1769 the national churches in Romania, Serbia and Bulgaria
were also under the Œcumenical Patriarch's control.*

*Christianity in the East remained fundamentally conservative
under Turkish rule. Some priests and theologians who left the
Sultan's empire to study in the West inevitably came up against
the ideas of the Reformation and Counter-Reformation. This
encouraged some to turn towards those churches which had come
into full communion with Rome, while preserving their own
liturgy. Others absorbed aspects of Protestantism, or of Catholic
spirituality, such as the works of St Ignatius Loyola. But in the
main there were few fundamental changes in Orthodox belief
and practice. Orthodox Christian faith remained a reflection of
that expressed in the unchanging Holy Liturgy which continued
Sunday by Sunday.*

*In the West scepticism continued to grow in the eighteenth
century. Many intellectuals, if not agnostic or atheist, seemed
to feel that some form of deism was more compatible with
their reason than the trinitarianism of traditional Christianity
as found in East and West. Freemasonry, which was at its
heart a kind of intellectual deism, expanded. In 1738 Pope
Clement XII condemned it as incompatible with Christian
faith and tradition.*

The spirit of those involved with the Encyclopédie in France (published 1751-72) was hostile to Christianity. The belief in "reason", which was increasingly personified and deified, seemed to carry all before it. Many of the insitutions in the West, including the Church, the monarchy, imperial rule, and the rigidity of social classes, were increasingly attacked as inconsistent with reason. In Britain, Catholics, who had continued as a tiny fervent minority, often under the patronage of a great family during the days of the brutal persecution of recusants in the 16th and 17th centuries, were also affected by the new spirit. Some leading Catholic families, which had remained stalwart in their Catholic faith for well over a hundred years, now conformed to the Church of England, and were thus able to resume their families' position in public life.

In 1776 the United States of America declared their independence from Britain. In 1789 the revolution in France led to the execution of the king, and a reign of terror against the nobility and church leaders. This was followed by the rule of Napoleon Bonarparte as first consul, and later as Emperor. Yet a reaction against this comparatively recent weakening of a Christian tradition lasting eighteen centuries, and against the breakdown of the social, moral and political order which seemed to some to be the result of this, was not long in arriving.

The French diplomat, author and statesman, Chateaubriand, who became Foreign Minister of France in 1822, visited the Holy Land in 1806. His most celebrated work, the 'Génie du Christianisme' had been published in 1802. It was intended and seen as a counterblast to the deification of reason which many intellectuals of the previous century had seemed to be promoting.

At the time of his pilgrimage Chateaubriand was doing preparatory work for another major work, 'Les Martyres, ou le Triomphe de la Religion Chrétienne.' The journal, which he kept during his eastern pilgrimage, was not originally intended to be published. But when he decided to do so he added a Memoir which describes his conclusions regarding the authenticity of the Christian traditions relating to Jerusalem. A part of this Memoir has been included below before the extracts from his journal.

THE traditions about the Holy Land derive their certainty from three sources: history, religion, and from places or local circumstances. Let us first consider them from an historical point of view.

Christ, accompanied by His Apostles, accomplished at Jerusalem the mysteries of His passion. The writings of the four Evangelists are the earliest documents that record the actions of the Son of Man. The acts of Pilate, preserved at Rome in the time of Tertullian, attested the principal event of that history, the crucifixion of Jesus of Nazareth. The Redeemer expired; Joseph of Arimathea obtained the sacred body and deposited it in a tomb at the foot of Calvary; the Messiah rose again on the third day; appeared to His apostles and disciples, gave them His intructions, and returned to the right hand of the Father. At this time the Church commences at Jerusalem.

It is natural to suppose that the first disciples, and the relations of our Saviour according to the flesh, who comprised this first church in the world, were perfectly acquainted with all the circumstances of the life and death of Jesus Christ. It is essential to remark that Golgotha was outside the city, as was the Mount of Olives; from this it follows that the apostles might the more freely perform their devotions in the places sanctified by their divine master.

The knowledge of these places was not long confined within a narrow circle of the disciples: Peter, in two public addresses, converted eight thousand persons at Jerusalem. James, the "brother" of our Saviour, was elected the first bishop of this church in the year 35 of our era; and was succeeded by Simeon, a cousin of Jesus Christ. We then find a series of thirteen bishops of Jewish race who occupy a space of one hundred and twenty-three years, from the reign of Tiberius to that of Hadrian. The names of these bishops are: Justus, Zachaeus, Tobias, Benjamin, John, Matthias, Philip, Seneca, Justus II, Levi, Ephraim, Joseph and Jude .

If the first Christians of Judea consecrated monuments to their religious worship, is it not probable that they erected

them in preference on those spots which had been distinguished by the miracles of their faith? Can it be doubted
that in those times there existed sanctuaries in *Palestine*,
when the believers possessed such at *Rome*, and in *all* the
provinces of the empire?

When St Paul and the other apostles gave exhortations
and laws to the churches of Europe and Asia, to whom did
they address themselves, unless to a congregation of believers meeting in one common place, under the direction of a
pastor? Is not this even implied by the word *ecclesia*, which
in Greek signifies either an *assembly*, or a *place of assembly*?
St Cyril of Jerusalem uses it in the latter sense.

The election of the seven deacons in the year 33 of the
Christian era, and the first Council held in 51, indicate that
the apostles had particular places of meeting in the Holy
City. We find no difficulty in believing also that the Holy
Sepulchre was honoured from the first institution of
Christianity, under the name of the *Martyrion*, or the
Testimony. St Cyril, Bishop of Jerusalem, preaching in 347
in the Church of Calvary says: "This Temple does not bear
the name of church like the others, but is called *Martyrion
or Testimony*, as the prophet predicted."

At the beginning of the troubles in Judea (before 70),
during the reign of Vespasian, the Christians of Jerusalem
withdrew to Pella. But as soon as the city was demolished,
they returned to dwell among its ruins. In the space of a few
months they could not have forgotten the location of the
sanctuaries, which being, moreover, outside the walls,
should not have suffered much from the siege.

Simeon, the successor of James, governed the church of
Judea when Jerusalem was taken. We find the same Simeon,
at the age of one hundred and twenty years, receiving the
crown of martyrdom during the reign of Trajan. The suc-
ceeding bishops, whose names I have mentioned, fixed their
residence on the ruins of the Holy City, and preserved the
Christian traditions respecting it.

That the Holy Places were generally well known in the

time of Hadrian, is demonstrated by an undeniable fact. This emperor, when he rebuilt Jerusalem, erected a statue of Venus on Mount Calvary, and another of Jupiter on the Holy Sepulchre. The grotto of Bethlehem was given over to the rites of Adonis, a form of idolatry, which in this way advertised by its unwise profanations the fantastic doctrine of the Cross, which it was very much in its own interest to conceal. The Faith made such rapid progress in Palestine during the period before the last insurrection of the Jews, that Barcochehas, the ringleader on this occasion, persecuted the Christians to compel them to renounce their religion.

Moreover, no sooner was the Jewish Church of Jerusalem dispersed by Hadrian in the year of Christ 137, than we find the Church of the Gentiles established in that city. Mark was its first bishop, and Eusebius gives us a list of his successors up till the time of Diocletian: Cassian, Publius, Maximus, Julian, Gaius, Symmachus, Gaius II, Julian II, Capiton, Valens, Dolichian, and Narcissus, the thirteenth after the apostles. There followed Dius, Germanion, Gordius, Alexander, Mazabanes, Hymenaeus, Zabdas, and Hermon, the last bishop before the persecution of Diocletian.

Hadrian, although he was zealous for his gods, did not persecute the Christians, except those at Jerusalem. These latter he doubtless regarded as Jews, since they were in fact of the nation of Israel. The defence of Christianity made by Quadratus and Aristides is thought to have had an effect on him. He even wrote a letter to Minucius Fundanus, governor of Asia, forbidding him to punish Christian believers without cause.

It is probable that the Gentiles who had been converted to the Faith, lived peacably at Ælia, or new Jerusalem, till the reign of Diocletian. This is apparent from the list of bishops of the Church given above. When Narcissus held the bishop's seat, the deacons were in want of oil for the Feast of Easter. We are told that Narcissus performed a miracle on that occasion. Christians at this time were therefore celebrating the mysteries of their religion in public at

Jerusalem, and had altars consecrated for their worship. Alexander, another Bishop of Ælia during the reign of the Emperor Severus, founded a library in his diocese. Such a circumstance must presuppose peace, leisure and prosperity. Where people belong to a proscribed religion they do not open a public school of philosophy.

...There are some writers who go further and assert that even before the persecution of Diocletian the Christians of Judea had regained possession of the Holy Sepulchre. It is certain that St Cyril, speaking about the church of the Holy Sepulchre, positively states: "It is not long since Bethlehem was a country place, and Mount Calvary a garden, the traces of which are still visible."

What then had become of the profane temples? There is every reason to believe that the pagans of Jerusalem, finding their congregations too small to maintain their ground against the increasing numbers of the Christian faithful, gradually withdrew from the temples of Hadrian. Even if the Church, which was still being persecuted, did not dare rebuild its altars at the sacred tomb, it at least enjoyed the consolation of worshipping there unmolested, and of seeing the monuments of idolatry falling into ruin.

We have now arrived at a period when the Holy Places begin to shine with a lustre never more to be darkened. When Constantine had granted the Christian religion royal favour he wrote a letter to Macarius, bishop of Jerusalem. In this he ordered him to cover the tomb of our Saviour with a magnificent church. Helena, the Emperor's mother, went to Palestine herself, and directed the search for the Holy Sepulchre. It had been buried beneath the foundations of Hadrian's buildings.

A Jew, apparently a Christian, who, according to Sozomenes, had preserved the records of his forefathers, pointed out the place where the tomb must have been. Helena thus had the honour of restoring this sacred monument to religion. She also discovered three crosses, one of which is said to have been recognised by its miracles as the cross on which the Redeemer suffered.

...Not only was a magnificent church erected at the Holy Sepulchre, but two others were built by Helena: one over the manger of the Messiah at Bethlehem, and the other on the Mount of Olives in commemoration of the Ascension of the Lord. Chapels, oratories and altars gradually came to mark all the places consecrated by the acts of the Son of Man. The oral traditions were thus committed to writing and thus secured from the treachery of memory.

Chateaubriand then goes on to record brief facts about the main pilgrims to the Holy Land from the fourth to the eighteenth century. His conclusions are as follows.

What an astonishing body of evidence is here! The apostles saw Jesus Christ; they knew the places honoured by the Son of Man; they transmitted the tradition to the first Christian church of Judea; a regular succession of bishops was established, and religiously preserved the sacred tradition. Eusebius appeared, and the history of the sacred places commenced. It was continued by Socrates, Sozomenes, Theodoret, Evagrius and St Jerome. Pilgrims thronged thither from all parts. From this period to the present day, an uninterrupted series of travels for fourteen centuries, gives us the same facts and the same descriptions. What tradition was ever supported by such a host of witnesses?

...To all these historical proofs I shall add some reflections on the nature of religious traditions, and on the local situation of Jerusalem. It is certain that religious traditions are not so easily lost as those that are purely historical. The latter are in general treasured in the memory of but a small number of enlightened persons. They may forget the truth or disguise it according to their inclinations. But religious traditions are circulated among the whole nation, and mechanically transmitted from father to son.

If the principles of religion are strict, as is the case with Christianity; if the slightest deviation from a fact or an idea is treated as a heresy, then whatever relates to that religion will be preserved from age to age with scrupulous fidelity.

...Let us not forget, moreover, that Christianity was persecuted in its cradle, and that it has almost always continued to suffer at Jerusalem. Now it is well known what fidelity prevails among partners in suffering. To these people everything becomes sacred, and the remains of a martyr are preserved with greater respect than the crown of a monarch.

The child that can scarcely lisp, is already acquainted with this treasure; carried at night by his mother to perilous devotions, he hears the singing, he witnesses the tears of his kindred and friends, which become engraved on his young memory; he sees objects that he can never afterwards forget. And, at an age when he might naturally be expected to show nothing but cheerfulness, frankness and a sense of fun, he learns to be serious, discrete and prudent. Adversity is premature old age.

I find in Eusebius a remarkable proof of this veneration for a sacred relic. He relates that in his own time the Christians of Judea still preserved the chair of St James, the "brother" of our Saviour, and the first bishop of Jerusalem. Even Edward Gibbon himself could not refrain from admitting the authenticity of the religious traditions current in Palestine. "They" (the Christians), he says, "fixed by unquestionable tradition, the scene of each memorable event;"—an acknowledgment of considerable weight from a writer so well-informed and at the same time so prejudiced against religion.

...The scene of the Passion, if we extend it from the Mount of Olives to Calvary, occupies not more than a league of ground; and in this little space, how many objects may be traced with the greatest ease! In the first place, there was a hill denominated the Mount of Olives, which overlooks the city and the Temple on the east. This hill is yet there and has not changed. There was the brook of Kidron, and this stream is the only one that passes near Jerusalem. There was a high point at the gate of the ancient city where criminals were put to death; this point is easily located between Mount Sion and the Gate of Judgement, of which some vestiges still remain.

It is impossible to mistake Sion, because it is the highest hill in the city....Golgotha was then a small eminence of Mount Sion, to the east of the mount itself, and to the west of the gate of the city. This high point, on which now stands the Church of the Resurrection, is still perfectly distinguishable. We know that Christ was buried in the garden at the foot of Calvary. This garden, and the house belonging to it, could not disappear at the foot of Golgotha, which is a hill whose base is not so large that a building situated there could be lost.

The Mount of Olives, and the Kidron brook fix the valley of Jehoshaphat; and the latter determines the position of the Temple on Mount Moria. The Temple fixes the position of the Triumphal Gate and Herod's palace, which the historian Josephus places to the east, in the lower part of the city and near the Temple. The Praetorium of Pilate was sited very near Antonia's tower, the foundations of which are known still to exist. The tribunal of Pilate and the site of Calvary being thus ascertained, the last scene of the Passion may be safely placed upon the road leading from one to the other, especially as a fragment of the gate of Judgement is still there to guide us. This road is the *Via dolorosa* so celebrated in the accounts of all the pilgrims.

The scenes of the acts of Christ outside the city are not marked with less certainty by the places themselves. The garden of Olivet, beyond the valley of Jehoshaphat and the Kidron brook, is clearly at this day in the position assigned to it by the Gospel. I could add a multitude of facts, conjectures and reflections to those which I have put forward here, but it is time to conclude this introduction....Anyone who examines the reasoning above, without prejudice, will be bound to admit that, if anything on earth has been demonstrated, it is the authenticity of the Christian tradition concerning Jerusalem.

Later in his work he offers a strong defence of the sincerity of the Crusaders and the value of the Crusades to Christendom and European civilisation.

The writers of the eighteenth century have taken pains to represent the Crusades in an odious light. I was one of the first to protest against this ignorance or injustice. The Crusades were not mad expeditions, as some writers have affected to call them, either in their principle or their results. The Christians were not the aggressors. If the subjects of Omar, setting out from Jerusalem, and making the circuit of Africa, invaded Sicily, Spain, and even France, where they were wiped out by Charles Martel, why should not the subjects of Philip the First leave France to take vengeance on the descendants of Omar in Jerusalem itself?

It was certainly a grand spectacle exhibited by these two armies of Europe and Asia, marching in opposite directions around the Mediterranean, and going forth under the banner of their respective religions, to attack Muhammad and Christ in the middle of their adherents. Those who see the Crusades as nothing but a mob of armed pilgrims running off to rescue a tomb in Palestine must take a very limited view of history.

The point at issue was not simply the deliverance of that sacred tomb, but also to decide which of the two should predominate in the world: a religion hostile to civilisation, systematically favourable to ignorance, despotism and slavery, or a religion which has revived among the moderns the spirit of learned antiquity and abolished servitude.

Whoever reads the speech of Pope Urban II to the Council of Clermont must be convinced that the leaders in these military operations did not have the small-minded views which have been ascribed to them, but rather aspired to save the world from a new flood of barbarians.

The spirit of Islam is persecution and conquest. The Gospel, on the other hand, teaches only toleration and peace. It was for this reason that Christians endured for seven hundred and sixty-four years all the oppressions which the Saracens forced them to submit to. They tried to interest Charlemagne in their cause. Yet neither the conquest of Spain, the invasion of France, the pillage of Greece and the two Sicilies, nor the entire subjugation of Africa, was able for nearly eight hundred years to rouse Christians to arms.

If at last the cries of countless victims slaughtered in the East, if the progress of the barbarians who had already reached the gates of Constantinople, aroused Christendom, and impelled it to rise in its own defence, who can say that the cause of the Holy Wars was unjust? Look at Greece, if you would wish to know the fate of a people subjected to the Muslim yoke. Would those, who at this time exult so loudly about the progress of knowledge, wish to live under a religion which burned the Alexandrian library, and which makes merit of trampling mankind under foot, and holding literature and the arts in regal contempt?

Moreover, the Crusades, by weakening the Muslim population in the very centre of Asia, prevented our falling prey to the Turks and the Arabs. They did more, for they saved us from our own revolutions. For by the Peace of God, they suspended our own internal wars, and opened an outlet for our extra population which can sooner or later cause the ruin of states.

Chateaubriand now describes some of his own experiences in the Holy Places.

I can now account for the surprise expressed by the Crusaders and pilgrims at the first sight of Jerusalem, according to the reports of historians and travellers. I can affirm that whoever has, like me, had the patience to read nearly two hundred modern accounts of the Holy Land, the rabbinical compilations, and the passages in the ancients about Judea, still knows nothing about it.

I paused with my eyes fixed on Jerusalem, measuring the height of its walls, reviewing at once all the recollections of history from Abraham to Godfrey of Bouillon, reflecting on the total change accomplished in the world by the mission of the Son of Man, and in vain seeking the Temple, not one stone of which is left upon another. Were I to live a thousand years, never should I forget that desert which yet seems to be pervaded by the greatness of Jehovah and the terrors of death.

The cries of the drogoman, who told me it was necessary for us to keep close together as we were just at the entrance to the pacha's military camp, roused me from the reverie into which the sight of the Holy City had plunged me. We passed among the tents covered in black lamb-skins: a few, among others that of the pacha, were formed of striped cloth. The horses, saddled and bridled, were fastened to stakes. I was surprised to see four pieces of horse-artillery; these were well mounted, and the carriages appeared to be of English manufacture. Our mean equipage and pilgrims' dress excited the laughter of the troops.

The pacha was coming out of Jerusalem as we drew up to the gate of the city. I was obliged to take off my handkerchief as quickly as possible. I had tied this over my hat to keep off the sun. I did not wish to risk the affront which my servant, Joseph, had received at Tripolizza in Greece. He had been refused admittance to a pacha's palace there because he was wearing a red handkerchief on his head, and this was taken as a pretension to a turban.

We entered Jerusalem by the Pilgrims' Gate, near which stands the tower of David, better known as the Pisans'. We paid the tribute, and followed the street that opened before us; then, turning to the left, we continued along our way until we arrived at the Convent of the Latin Fathers at 12.20 pm. I found it in the hands of the soldiers of Abdullah, pacha of Damascus. They appropriate to themselves whatever they take a fancy to.

Only those who have been in the same situation as the Fathers of the Holy Land, can imagine the pleasure which they received from my arrival. They thought themselves saved by the presence of one single Frenchman. I delivered a letter from General Sebastiani to Father Bonaventura di Nola, the superior of the Convent.

"Sir," he said, "it is Providence that has brought you here. You have official travelling documents (firmans). Please let me send them to the pacha. He will then know that a Frenchman has arrived at the Convent. He will believe that we are under the special protection of the Emperor (Napoleon).

Last year he forced us to pay sixty thousand piastres. According to the normal tradition we only owed him forty thousand, and that is really a customary gift. He wants to extort the same sum from us this year, and is threatening extreme sanctions if we refuse to comply with his demands. We shall be obliged to sell the consecrated plate, since over the last four years we have received no financial offerings from Europe. If this continues we shall be forced to leave the Holy Land, and leave the tomb of Christ in the hands of the Muslims."

I thought myself extremely fortunate to have it in my power to render a small service to the superior. However I asked that he would permit me to make an excursion to the Jordan before sending the firmans. This was to ensure that the difficulties of this journey, which is always attended with danger, might not be further increased: Abdullah might have caused me to be assassinated on the way, and then thrown the blame on the roving Arabs.

Father Clement Peres, the procurator-general of the Convent, a man of wide knowledge, cultivation, understanding and pleasant manners, took me to the state chamber of the pilgrims. My baggage was deposited there, and I prepared to leave Jerusalem, a few hours after I had entered the city. In fact it would have been more sensible to rest than to do battle with the Arabs of the Dead Sea area. I had been travelling for a long time over land and sea on my way to the Holy Places. But no sooner had I reached the destination that I had been longing for than I left it again!

But I decided that this sacrifice was one which I owed to men who are themselves making a perpetual sacrifice of their property and their lives. I could, indeed, have reconciled the interests of the fathers with my own safety by relinquishing my plan to visit the Jordan, since it was up to me to set the limits to my curiosity. But I did not do so.

While I was waiting for the time fixed for my departure, the religious began to sing in the choir of the monastery. I enquired why they were singing, and was told that they were celebrating the festival of the patron of their order. Then I remembered that it was October the 4th, St Francis' Day, and the anniversary of my own birth. I hastened to the church, and there I offered up my prayers for the eternal happiness of her who on this day had brought me into the world. It gave me joy that my first prayer at Jerusalem was not for myself, but for my mother.

It was with great respect that I looked on those religious singing the praises of the Lord. We were within three hundred paces of the tomb of Christ, and I was much affected by the sight of the frail but invincible band which has continued to be the only guard of the Holy Sepulchre since it was abandoned by kings.

A little further on Chateaubriand quotes with approval the following passage from Jean Doubdan, who describes the enormous sacrifices of the friars, and their poverty, in his 'Le Voyage de la Terre Sainte' (Paris, 1657).

"The religious who live there (at the convent of St Saviour), are subject to the rule of St Francis, and keep a very strict poverty. They live entirely upon the alms and benefactions transmitted to them from Christendom, and the gifts given to them by the pilgrims according to their means. But since the pilgrims are far from their own country, and do not know what large expenses they may incur during their return trip, their alms are inconsiderable. Yet this does not prevent them from being received and treated by the friars with great kindness."

Chateubriand himself continues.

Thus those pilgrims to the Holy Land, who are said to leave treasures behind them at Jerusalem, cannot be Catholic pilgrims. Any part of the treasures which falls to the share of the convents, does not come into the possession of the Latin monks. When these religious do receive alms from Europe, the alms, so far from enriching them, are not even sufficient for the preservation of the holy sites, which are everywhere falling into ruin.

Because of this lack of support they are bound to be abandoned by them very shortly. The poverty of these religious is proved by the unanimous testimony of travellers. I have already mentioned their sufferings. If other proofs are necessary, here they are in the words of Father Roger, one of the Franciscan friars, writing in his *Description de la Terre Sainte:*

"As it was a French friar who gained possession of the Holy Places at Jerusalem in 1627, so the first of the religious who suffered martyrdom was a Frenchman, named Limin, of the province of Tourraine. He was beheaded at Grand Cairo. Some time after this, brother James and brother Jeremiah were put to death outside the gates of Jerusalem. Brother Conrad d'Alis Barthelemy, of Monte Politano in the province of Tuscany, was sawn in two from the head downwards in Grand Cairo. Brother John d'Ether, a Spaniard of the province of Castile, was cut in pieces by the Bashaw of Casa. Seven religious were decapitated by the Sultan of Egypt, and two were flayed alive in Syria. In the year 1637 the Arabs martyred the whole community of friars who were on the sacred Mount of Sion. There were twelve in number.

Some time afterwards, sixteen religious, both priests and lay brothers, were taken from Jerusalem and imprisoned at Damascus. This was at the time when Cyprus was captured by the king of Alexandria. They remained there for five years. One after the other they died of their privations. Brother Cosmo was killed by the Turks at the door of the

Church of the Holy Sepulchre, where he used to preach the doctrines of Christianity. Two other friars at Damascus received so many strokes of the bastinado that they died on the spot. Six religious were put to death by the Arabs one night when they were at matins in the convent built at Anathot in the house of the prophet Jeremiah. The building was afterwards burnt. It would be abusing the patience of the reader to enter into the particulars of all the sufferings and persecutions which our poor religious have endured since they have had care of the Holy Places."

Continuing his account of his visit Chateaubriand writes.

The superior sent for a Turk named Ali Aga to conduct me to Bethlehem. He was the son of an aga of Ramah who had lost his head under the tyranny of Djezzar. Ali was born in Jericho, now called Rihha, and said that he was governor of his village. He was intelligent and courageous, and I had every reason to be satisfied with him.

The first thing that he did was to make my servants and myself give up our Arabian dress, and get back into our French clothes. French dress, once so despised by the Orientals, now inspires respect and fear. French bravery has given us back the reputation which we formerly had in this country.

It was French nobles who established the kingdom of Jerusalem, just as it was soldiers of France who gathered the last palms of Idumea. The Turks point out to you king Baldwin's tower at the same time as the camp of the Emperor (Napoleon I). At Calvary you find the sword of Godfrey of Bouillon, still in its ancient scabbard, always on guard in the Holy Sepulchre.

At five o'clock in the afternoon three good horses were brought. We were joined by Michael, the guide to the convent. Ali put himself at the head of our convoy and we set out for Bethlehem, where we were to spend the night and collect an escort of six Arabs.

I had read that the superior of St Saviour's convent is the only one who enjoys the privilege of riding a horse at Jerusalem. I was rather surprised then to find myself galloping along on an Arabian horse. But I have since learned that any traveller is allowed to do the same if he pays money for this!

We left Jerusalem by the Damascus gate, then crossing the ravines at the foot of Mount Sion went up a mountain. On its summit we came upon a plain on which we travelled for an hour. We left Jerusalem behind us to the north. On the west we had the mountains of Judea, and on the east, beyond the Dead Sea, those of Arabia.

We passed the convent of St Elijah. The spot where the prophet rested on his way to Jerusalem is sure to be pointed out to you. It is under an olive tree which stands on a rock by the side of the road. A league further on we came into the plain of Ramah, where you find Rachel's tomb. It is a square structure, surmounted by a small dome. It has the privileges of a mosque, since the Turks, as well as the Arabs, honour the families of the patriarchs. Christian tradition agrees with siting Rachel's tomb on this spot. Historical criticism also favours this view.

Yet, despite the opinion of Thevenot, Monconys, Roger and many others, I cannot myself accept that the actual structure known as Rachel's tomb is an ancient monument. To me it is clearly a Turkish building constructed in memory of a Turkish holy man.

Night had by now come on, and from the mountains we saw the lights of the village of Ramah. A profound silence had come on all of us. It was probably on such a night as this that Rachel's voice suddenly rang out in their ears. "A voice is heard in Ramah", crying out and sobbing bitterly: it was Rachel weeping for her children, and refusing to be comforted because they had gone for ever. In this the mothers of Astyanax and Euryalus are outdone; Homer and Virgil must yield the crown for pathos to Jeremiah.

It was by a narrow and rugged road that we came to Bethlehem. We knocked at the door of the convent. Those within were somewhat fearful because our visit was unexpected. Ali's turban was at first a cause for alarm. But matters were soon explained to their satisfaction.

Bethlehem received its original name from Abraham. The word means *House of Bread*. It has the additional name of *Ephrata*, which means The Fruitful, which it received because of Caleb's wife. This distinguishes it from another Bethlehem in the territory of the tribe of Zebulon. Bethlehem Ephrata belongs to the tribe of Judah; it also went by the name of the City of David, because that king was born and tended sheep during his childhood there. Natives of Bethlehem also include Abijan, the seventh judge of Israel, Elimelech, Obed, Jesse and Boaz. It is the place where the events of the charming story of Ruth took place. Later the apostle St Matthias was born there, in the same town as his Saviour.

The first Christians built an oratory over the manger of our Saviour. The Emperor Hadrian ordered it to be demolished, and had a statue of Adonis erected there instead. St Helena had the idol destroyed and a church built on the spot. The original structure is now blended with the various additions made by the Christian princes. St Jerome, as every reader knows, retired to the solitude of Bethlehem. Later it was taken by the Crusaders, and then returned under the yoke of the infidels. Yet throughout the whole time it has been an object of veneration for pilgrims. For seven centuries pious religious, accepting a life of continuous martyrdom, have been its guardians.

At four in the morning I began my tour of the monuments of Bethlehem. Though the structures have been often described they are so interesting that I cannot prevent myself from giving some particulars.

The convent of Bethlehem is connected with the church by a court enclosed with high walls. We crossed the court and were admitted by a small side-door into the church.

The building is certainly of great antiquity, and, though often destroyed, and as often restored, it still keeps signs of its Greek origin. It is built in the form of a cross. The long nave, or, if you like, the lower upright part of the cross, is furnished with forty-eight columns of the Corinthian order, in four rows. These columns are two-foot six inches in diameter at the base, and eighteen feet high, including the base and capital. As there is no roof as such to the nave, the columns support nothing but a frieze of wood. This occupies the place of the architrave and of the whole entablature. Open timber work rests on the walls, and rises into the form of a dome to support the roof that no longer exists, or perhaps was never completed.

The wood-work is said to be of cedar, but this view is mistaken. The windows are large, and were formerly adorned with mosaic paintings and passages from the Bible in Greek and Latin characters. Some traces of these are still visible…The remains of the mosaics to be seen here and there, and some of the paintings, are of interest for the history of the arts. In general they show figures in full face, upright, stiff and without movement or shadows. Yet their effect is majestic, and their character dignified and austere.

The Christian sect of the Armenians is in possession of the nave which I have just described. It is separated from the other three branches of the cross by a wall, which destroys the unity of the building. When you have passed beyond this wall you find yourself opposite the sanctuary, or the choir, which occupies the position of the top of the cross. This choir is raised up two steps above the nave. Here there is the altar dedicated to the Wise Men of the East. On the pavement, at the foot of this altar you see a marble star.

This corresponds, as tradition claims, with the point of the heavens where the miraculous star that conducted the three Magi became stationary. This much is certain: the spot where the Saviour of the world was born is exactly underneath this marble star in the subterranean church of the manger, about which I will speak below. The Greeks are in occupation of the choir of the Magi, as well as the other two transepts formed by the transom of the cross. These last are empty and without altars.

Two spiral stairs cases, each composed of fifteen steps, are in view on the side of the outer church; they lead down to the subterranean chapel beneath the choir. Here is that place, which will be revered for all eternity, where our Saviour was born. Before I went down, the Superior put a taper in my hands, and gave me some brief instructions. The sacred crypt is irregular in shape, since it occupies the irregular shape of the stable and the manger. It is thirty-seven feet

six inches long, eleven feet three inches wide, and nine feet high. It is hewn out of rock. The sides are faced with beautiful marble, and the floor is covered in the same material. These embellishments are ascribed to St Helena.

The church receives no natural light from the outside. It is illuminated by thirty-two lamps sent there by different princes of Christendom. At the far end of this crypt, on the east side, is the place where the Virgin brought forth the Redeemer of mankind. The spot is marked in white marble, encrusted with jaspar, and surrounded by a circle of silver, having rays like those with which the sun is depicted. Around this are inscribed the words:

HIC DE VIRGINE MARIA
JESUS CHRISTUS NATUS EST.

A marble table, which serves for an altar, rests against the side of the rock, and stands over the place where the Messiah came into the world. It is lighted by three lamps, the handsomest of which was given by Louis XIII.

At a distance of seven paces to the south, after passing the foot of one of the stair-cases leading to the upper church, you come to the manger. You go down two steps

to it, for it is not on a level with the rest of the crypt. It is
a low recess, hewn out of the rock. A block of white marble, raised about a foot above the floor and hollowed out
in the form of a manger, indicates the very spot where the
Sovereign of Heaven was laid upon straw. Two paces further on, opposite the manger, stands the altar which occupies the place where Mary sat when she presented the
Child of Sorrows to the adoration of the Magi.

Nothing can be more pleasing, or better calculated to
arouse sentiments of devotion, than this underground
church. It is adorned with pictures of the Italian and
Spanish schools. They represent the mysteries of the place:
the Virgin and child after Raphael, the Annunciation, the
Adoration of the Wise Men, the coming of the Shepherds,
and all those miracles of mingled grandeur and innocence.

The usual furnishings of the manger are blue satin,
embroidered with silver. Incense is continually smoking
before the cradle of the Saviour. I have heard an organ,
touched by no ordinary hand, play during Mass the sweetest
and most tender music of the finest Italian composers.

This music charms the Christian Arab, and often he
leaves his camels to graze, while slipping away to adore the
King of Kings in his manger, like the shepherds of old in
Bethlehem. I have seen one of these desert dwellers receive
communion at the altar of the Magi with a fervour, a piety
and a devotion unknown among the Christians of the West.

Father Neret writes: "No place in the world excites more
profound devotion. The continuous arrival of caravans from
all the nations of Christendom, the public prayers, the prostrations, even the richness of the gifts sent there by
Christian princes, all this produces feelings in the soul
which it is much easier to imagine than understand."

I may add that the effect of all this is heightened by the
extraordinary contrast. For on leaving the crypt where you
have encountered the wealth, arts and religion of civilised
nations, you find yourself in profound isolation among
wretched Arab huts, half-naked barbarians and faithless

Muslims. Yet this is the place where so many miracles were manifested. Now the sacred land, however, no longer dares express its joy, and it keeps locked away in its heart the memories of its glory.

After his visit to Bethlehem, and a dangerous expedition to the Dead Sea, Chateaubriand returned to Jerusalem. Below is his description of the convent of the Friars—now situated in Jerusalem itself since their expulsion from Mount Sion, and of the hospitality which they provided.

You reach it (the convent of the Latin fathers) by a covered way that leads to another passage of considerable length, which is very dark. At the end of the passage you arrive at a courtyard formed by the wood-house, cellar, and pantry of the convent. Here on the right you see a flight of twelve to fifteen steps, which ascends to the cloister. This is immediately above the cellar, wood-house and pantry, and as result overlooks the courtyard from where you came in.

The cloister's east end opens out into a vestibule from which you enter the church. This is very attractive, with a choir fitted out with stalls, a nave lit by a dome, an altar in the Roman style, and a small organ. Everything is contained in a space of only twenty feet by twelve.

At the west end of the cloister there is another door which leads into the convent. Jean Doubdan describes it simply and accurately as follows.

"The convent is very irregular in shape and built in the ancient style. There are several floors. The offices serving the convent are small and concealed from view. The apartments are simple and dark; there are several little courtyards and two small gardens, the largest of which may be about eighty to ninety square yards. These open spaces are bounded by the city walls. The only recreation in the convent is to go up to the terrace of the church where you may have a view of the whole city which slopes away down the hill to the valley of Jehoshaphat.

From there you can see the church of the Holy Sepulchre, the court of Solomon's Temple, and, further off to the east, the Mount of Olives; to the south you can see the castle of the city and the road to Bethlehem, and to the north the cave of Jeremiah. Such is the plan and description of the convent. It has very much the simplicity and poverty of Him, Who though rich, yet on this very spot became poor for our sakes.

The apartment which I occupied is called the Pilgrims' Great Room. It looks out on a courtyard enclosed by walls on all sides. The furniture consisted of a hospital bed with curtains of green serge, a table, and a box. My servants had two cells at a considerable distance from me. A pitcher of water and an Italian-style lamp completed the furnishing.

My room was large but dark because it had only one window. Thirteen pilgrims had written their names inside on the door. The first was Charles Lombard, who had visited Jerusalem in 1669, and the last John Gordon, who came in 1804. Of the thirteen travellers only three had French names.

The pilgrims do not eat with the fathers, as at Jaffa. A separate meal is made for them, and they go to whatever expense they please for this. If they are poor, they are supplied with food. If they are rich, they pay for those things which are bought for them. As a result the convent receives not a single farthing from pilgrims for food. Lodging, a bed and linen, lighting and a fire, are always provided free as part of their hospitality.

A cook was placed at my disposal. I hardly ever dined before it was dark after returning from my excursions. Lentil soup, dressed with oil was the first dish. Then came veal, stewed with cucumbers or onions, broiled kid, or mutton, boiled with rice. Beef is never eaten here—buffalo meat has a strong taste. I had some roast fowl: pigeons, and sometimes partridges—white ones known as partridges of the desert. Game is very plentiful in the Ramah plain and in the mountains of Judea: partridges, woodcocks, hares,

wild boar and antelope. The quails of Arabia, which fed
the Israelites, are almost unknown in Jerusalem, though
you sometimes find them in the Jordan valley. The only
vegetables ever brought to my table were lentils, beans,
cucumbers and onions.

The wine of Jerusalem is excellent. It has the colour and
taste of the wines of Rousillon, and is still supplied from the
hills of Engaddi near Bethlehem. I had the same fruit here
as at Jaffa: large grapes, dates, pomegranates, water-melons
and apples. The figs were of the second season, since those
of the sycamore, or Pharaoh's fig-tree, were over. The bread
made at the convent was good and well-flavoured.

*Before he left Jerusalem the Fathers decided to confer an hon-
our on Chateaubriand for his services to Christianity through his
writing, especially for the 'Génie du Christianisme.' His
account of the ceremony at which this honour was bestowed,
and of his departure from the Holy City, follows:*

The Fathers of the Holy Land determined to confer on
me an honour which I had neither solicited nor deserved.
They asked me to accept the Order of the Holy Sepulchre.
It was in consideration of the feeble services which I had
rendered to religion. This Order, of high antiquity in
Christendom, though its origins may not date back to the
time of St Helena, was formerly very common in Europe. At
present it is scarcely ever encountered, except in Spain and
Poland. The Superior of the Latin convent, as Guardian of
the Holy Sepulchre, has the sole right to confer it.

We left the convent at one o'clock and went to the
Church of the Holy Sepulchre. Here we proceeded to the
chapel belonging to the Latin Fathers. The doors were carefully shut in case the Turks should catch sight of the arms.
This might well cost the religious their lives.

The Superior put on his pontifical robes; the lamps and
tapers were lit. Then all the brothers formed a circle around
me, with their hands folded on their breast. While they

sang the *Veni Creator* in a low voice, the Superior stepped up to the altar and I fell on my knees at his feet. The spurs and sword of Godfrey de Bouillon were taken out of the treasury of the Holy Sepulchre.

Two of the religious, standing one on each side of me, held the venerable relics. The Superior recited the custom-ary prayers and asked me the usual questions. He then attached the spurs to my heels, and struck me three times over my shoulders with the sword. At this moment the reli-gious began to sing the *Te Deum* while the Superior pro-nounced prayers over my head.

All this is but a shadow of the ceremony of days gone by. Yet there are other considerations. I was at Jerusalem, within a dozen paces of the tomb of Jesus Christ, and thirty from that of Godfrey de Bouillon. I had been equipped with the spurs of the Deliverer of the Holy Sepulchre, and had touched that sword, both long and broad, which so noble and brave an arm had once wielded. If anyone  reading this bears in mind these circumstances, as well as my own life of adventure and wanderings over land and sea, he will easily understand that I could not but be moved.

Nor was the ceremony without effect on me. I am a Frenchman. Godfrey of Bouillon was a Frenchman. His ancient arms, when they touched me, passed on to me an increased ardour for glory and for the honour of my country. My certificate, signed by the Guardian and sealed with the seal of the convent, was delivered to me. Along with the splendid diploma of knighthood, I was also given my humble passport as a pilgrim. I have kept them both, a record of my visit to the land of that ancient traveller, Jacob.

Now that I am about to bid farewell to Palestine I must ask the reader to accompany me once more beyond the wall, so as to take a last look at this extraordinary city.

When seen from the Mount of Olives, on the other side

of the valley of Jehoshaphat, Jerusalem presents an inclined plane, descending from west to east. A wall with battle-ments, fortified with towers and a Gothic castle, surrounds the city. However, it excludes part of Mount Sion which it enclosed of old.

In the western quarter, and in the centre of the city towards Calvary, the houses stand very close; but in the east-ern part, along the Kidron brook, you see empty spaces. These include the area around the mosque built on the ruins of the Temple, and the nearly deserted spot where the castle of Antonia and the second palace of Herod once stood.

The houses of Jerusalem are heavy, square masses, very low, and without chimneys or windows. They either have flat terraces or domes on top, and look like prisons or sepul-chres. To the eye, all the buildings would appear as one uninterrupted level, if it were not the case that the towers of the churches, the minarets of the mosques, the tops of a few cypress trees and clumps of cacti, break up the unifor-mity of the vista. When you look at these stone buildings, surrounded by a stony countryside, you are ready to ask yourself whether they might not be the disordered monu-ments of a cemetery in the midst of a desert.

When you *enter* the city there is nothing to compensate for the lack of inspiration in the view of the city from a dis-tance. You become lost among narrow, unpaved streets. Here you go up, there you go down on the uneven ground, walking amid clouds of dust and loose stones. The canvas which is stretched from house to house increases the gloom of this labyrinth. The bazaars, roofed over, and a breeding ground for infection, completely exclude natural light from the desolate city.

A few mean shops have poor displays of shoddy goods; but even these are frequently closed, since the owners fear a visit from a passing cadi (a magistrate/inspector). There is no one to be seen in the streets, and no one at the city gates, except an occasional peasant gliding through the gloom. He takes care to conceal the fruits of his hard work under his garments, since he is afraid of being robbed of his earnings by a thuggish soldier.

A little way off, in a corner, an Arab butcher is slaughtering some animal; it has been suspended by the legs from a ruined wall. From the man's haggard and ferocious expression, and his bloodstained hands, you would rather suppose that he has been cutting the throat of another human being rather than killing a lamb. In this city which murdered God the only noise heard from time to time is the galloping of a horse returning from the desert. It is the janissary, bringing the head of one of the Bedouin, or on his way back from plundering the unfortunate Fellahin.

In this extraordinary desolation you should pause and reflect for a moment on two circumstances which are even more remarkable. Among these ruins of Jerusalem there are two classes of independent people who find in their religion sufficient strength to survive these complex horrors and wretchedness. Here live communities of Christian monks whom nothing can compel to abandon the tomb of Christ: neither robbery, nor personal ill treatment nor death threats.

Night and day they chant their hymns around the Holy Sepulchre. Stripped in the morning by a Turkish governor they are found that night in prayer at the foot of Calvary, on the very spot where Christ suffered for the salvation of mankind.

Their faces are serene, their lips present a continuous smile; they receive the stranger with joy. Without power, without soldiers, they protect whole villages from injustice. Women, children, flocks and herds, when driven from where they live by batons and swords, seek refuge in the cloisters of these recluses.

What is there to prevent the armed bullies from pursuing their prey and breaking down such feeble defences? It is the charity of the monks. They deprive themselves of all their resources in life to provide financial aid to those who seek their help. Turks, Arabs, Greeks, Christian schismatics, all throw themselves on the protection of a few poor religious who have not the means to defend themselves. It is at this point that we must acknowledge the truth of what Bossuet has said: "Hands raised to heaven disperse more battalions than hands armed with javelins."

While this type of the new Jerusalem rises from the desert with a bright splendour, turn your eyes now to a spot between the Temple and Mount Sion. Here is another tribe, cut off from the rest of the inhabitants of the city. They are the object of every kind of degradation. They bow their heads without complaining; they put up with every kind of insult without demanding justice. They sink under repeated blows without murmuring. If their head is required, they offer it to the scimitar. When any member of this proscribed community dies, his companions go at night and bury him secretly in the valley of Jehoshaphat, in the shadow of Solomon's Temple.

If you go into these people's houses you will find them in the extremes of poverty teaching their children to read a mysterious book. They in their turn will teach their children to read it. These people still continue to do what their forefathers did five thousand years ago. Seventeen times they have seen the destruction of Jerusalem, yet nothing can prevent them from turning their face towards Mount Sion.

To see the Jews scattered all over the world must surely arouse wonder. But to be struck with a supernatural astonishment you need to see them at Jerusalem. You must see these rightful masters of Judea living as slaves and foreigners in their own country. You must witness how under all the oppression they suffer they continue to expect a king who is to deliver them. This great and pitiful longing remains with them: bowed down by the cross which condemns them and which is planted on their heads, they cower near their Temple of which no stone remains upon another.

The Persians, the Greeks and the Romans are swept from the earth; and a tiny tribe, whose origin preceeded those of the great nations, still exists, unmixed, among the ruins of its native land. If anything among the nations has the character of a miracle, that character, in my opinion is here revealed. Even to a philosopher what can seem more amazing than the sight of ancient and new Jerusalem together at the foot of Calvary? The former is bowed down with dejection at the sight of the Sepulchre of the risen Jesus; the latter rejoices before the only tomb which will have no body to render up at the end of time.

I thanked the Fathers for their hospitality. I wished them most sincerely a happiness which they never expect to enjoy here below. As I was about to leave, my heart was overwhelmed with sadness. I know of no sufferings that can be compared with those suffered by these unfortunate religious. The state in which they live resembles that which existed in France during the reign of terror.

I was about to return to my country, to embrace my relations, to see my friends again, to enjoy once more the sweet things of life. These Fathers, who had relations, friends and country as I did, remained in exile, in this land of bondage. Not all of them possess the strength of mind which makes a man impervious to privations. I have heard expressions of regret, which convinced me of the greatness of their sacrifice. Did not Christ, on this same spot, find the cup bitter? And yet he drank it up to the dregs.

On the 12th of October I mounted my horse, with Ali Aga, John, Julian and Michael the guide. We left by the Pilgrims' Gate on the west, and passed through the pacha's camp. Before we decended into the Terebinth valley, I stopped once more to survey Jerusalem. Never again will it be saluted by the pilgrim as it once was, for it no longer exists, and the tomb of Christ is now exposed to the elements.

There was a time when all of Christendom would have eagerly contributed towards the rebuilding of this sacred monument. But today nobody thinks of such a thing, and the smallest sum spent for such a meritorious purpose would seem an absurd superstition. I gazed on Jerusalem for some time, then went on my way into the mountains. It was twenty-nine minutes past six when I lost sight of the Holy

City. Thus a navigator records the moment when he stops seeing a distant region which he will never see again.

At the bottom of the Terebinth valley we found Abou Gosh and Giaber, the chiefs of the Arabs of Jeremiah, waiting for us. We arrived at Jeremiah about midnight. Abou Gosh insisted on our eating a lamb which he had provided for us. I offered some money, but he refused. His only request was that I should send him two measure of Damietta rice when I arrived in Egypt.

I cheerfully promised to do this. But I did not remember my promise till the moment when I was embarking at Tunis. As soon as communications with the Levant are restored, Abou Gosh shall certainly have his Damietta rice! He shall see that, though a Frenchman's memory may fail him, yet he keeps his word! I hope that the little Bedouins of Jeremiah will mount guard over my gift, and that they will yet say: "Forward! march!"

At noon on the 13th, I arrived at Jaffa.

CHAPTER FIVE

THIS IS WHERE HE WALKED

CHATEAUBRIAND had come to realise the importance of the
Christian past and its value for the new century. He sensed a
change in the intellectual climate. The spirit of the eighteenth century had tended to be hostile or indifferent to religion. As the nineteenth century got under weigh, Christianity began to be valued
again in the West, both for itself, and for its moral influence.
Romanticism in literature and art, and the revival of interest in
chivalry both pointed this way. Men were turning away from an
exclusive reliance on human reason, which seemed in part to have
led to the French Revolution and the Terror. Chateaubriand both
noted the new mood and contributed to the change by his writings.

In the East the Greek Orthodox Church in Jerusalem was
given permission by the Turkish Sultan to restore the Church of
the Holy Sepulchre after a serious fire in 1808. This had brought
down the roof of the rotunda on to the cupola over the little
house above the tomb of Christ. The morale of Orthodox
Christians was later boosted by the successful War of Greek
Independence against the Turks (1821-30).

In England Catholic Emancipation in 1829 was a practical
result of this change of climate, even though there were also
other political reasons for it. The successes of the Oxford
Movement, which sought to revive pre-Reformation belief and
practice in the Church of England, were another sign of change.

John Henry Newman's conversion to Catholicism, which was preceded and followed by that of many other Anglican clergymen and important lay figures in British society, was symptomatic of this renewed interest in religion.

The Papacy, which had been very weak at the time of Napoleon's imperial rule (1804-14), gained new confidence after the Congress of Vienna which settled the shape of Europe after his defeat. Pope Gregory XVI condemned political liberalism in the encyclical 'Mirari vos' in 1832, and Pius IX, in the 'Syllabus of Errors' of 1864, contested many of the aims, principles and ideals of modern society. In 1870 the First Vatican Council defined the doctrine of papal infallibility in relation to church doctrine.

This renewed confidence of Christianity, which in the West was shared by Catholics and Protestants alike, was reflected in a new missionary age in Asia, Africa and Latin America. Britain and most other major European powers had been consolidating empires abroad in the eighteenth and nineteenth centuries, and Christian missionaries followed in their wake.

Despite their territorial rivalries overseas, Britain and France co-operated in the construction and operation of the Suez Canal which opened in 1869. In due course this made the journey easier for pilgrims to the Holy Land from Asia and Australia.

In Europe, Prussian and French rivalry culminated in the Franco-Prussian War of 1870 which ended the monarchy in France. British economic and military power was at its height in the latter part of the nineteenth century, but the United States, which grew strongly economically, and in population through immigration after the American Civil War (1861-65), was beginning to overtake it. Yet for the Holy Land's future, perhaps the most important event was the first Zionist Congress in 1887.

It was against this background that the following accounts of pilgrimages were written by two women within a few years of each other in the eighteen nineties. One was English, a fashionable painter of military subjects. She was part of that stream of nineteenth century English converts to Catholicism. The other was an ordinary Italian woman, whose book describing her simple response to the Holy Places caught the imagination of millions.

The artist, Elizabeth Butler, visited the Holy Land with her husband, Major-General (later Sir William) Butler, in the spring of 1891. He was Commandant of the British forces in Alexandria. Although Palestine was still part of the Ottoman Empire at this time, Britain's power in the Near East was such that this safari in Palestine by a British general and his wife was granted every facility by the Turkish civil authorities, and by the different religious leaders. Lady Butler's account was written for her mother, and subsequently published as 'Letters from the Holy Land.'

AT sunrise this morning the throbbing of the screw suddenly ceased, and as I went to the port-hole of our cabin I beheld the lovely coast of the Land of Christ, about a mile distant, with the exquisite town of Jaffa, typically Eastern, grouped on a rock by the sea, and appearing above huge, heaving waves, whose grey-blue tones were mixed with rosy reflections from the clouds. Here was no modern harbour with piers and jetties, no modern warehouses, none of the characteristics of a seaport of our time.

Jaffa is much as it must have looked to the Crusaders; and we approached it, after leaving the steamer, much as pilgrims must have done in the Middle Ages. The Messageries ship could approach no nearer on account of the rocks, and we had to be rowed ashore in open boats—very large, stout craft, fit to resist the tremendous waves that thunder against the rocky ramparts of Jaffa. How often I have imagined this landing, and have gone through it in delicious anticipation!

Everything was made as pleasant as possible to us, Mr.—— coming on board to direct the proceedings, and a Franciscan monk also boarding the steamer with greetings from Jerusalem at the request of the Archbishop of Alexandria.

As our boat was the last to leave the steamer I had time to watch the disconcerting process of trans-shipping the other tourists who all went off in the first boats, and nothing have I ever seen of the sort could compare with what I beheld during those breathless moments.

The effect produced by brawny Syrian boatmen tussling with elderly British and American females in sun-helmets and blue spectacles, and at the right moment, when the steamer heaved to star-board and met the boat rising on the crest of a particular wave, pushing them by the shoulders from above, and pulling them into the boat from below, was a thing to remember. (To go down the ladder was quite impossible, so violent was the bumping of the boat against the ship.) To miss the right moment was to have to wait till the steamer which then rolled to port, and the boat which then sank into the trough of the sea, met again with the next lurch. The poor tourists said nothing; they hadn't time given them for the feeblest protest, but looked quite dazed when stuck down in their seats.

Thanks to our kind friends we had a boat to ourselves and we were not worked off so expeditiously, being thus able to submit with something more approaching grace. We had a large crew of rowers, and being only ourselves, the monk and Mr ——, we went light. Three or four times the helmsman had to be extra vigilant as a huge roller, which hid everything behind it, came racing in our wake, and lifting us as though we were so much seaweed, carried us forward with dizzy swiftness. Woe betide that boat which such a wave should strike broadside on! At each crisis the "stroke oar" sang out a warning, and redoubled his work, the perspiration coursing down his face. The whole crew sang an answer to his wild signal in a barbaric minor.

Nothing could be more invigorating than this experience; one moment when hoisted on the crest of a wave one saw Jaffa, the Plain of Sharon, and the hills of Judea ahead, and astern the Messageries steamer and small craft riding at anchor, and the next moment nothing between one and the sky but jagged and curling crests of wild billows! On landing at the rocks we were hoisted up the slippery steps in more iron grips. On such occasions it is useless to hesitate—indeed they don't let you, you had much better at once surrender your individuality and become a passive piece of goods if you don't want a broken limb.

We immediately found ourselves in such a picturesque crowd as even my Egypt-saturated eyes took new delight in, and we passed through the Custom-House with the agent obligingly clearing all before us, and got into a little carriage after climbing on foot the steep part of the town. What a town! No description I have yet read does full justice to its tumbled-down picturesqueness. Those black archways like caverns, those crooked streets filled with people, camels and donkeys—all this to me is fascinating.

I am too hurried to pause here long enough to try to define the difference between life here and life in Egypt. There is not here the barbarism of the latter's picturesqueness, and one feels here more the beauty of the true East. I don't see the abject squalor of Egypt, and the people's dresses are more varied. All this stone masonry is very acceptable after the brick and mud of the Egyptian hovels. Here is the essence of Asia—there of Africa. I am afraid these remarks are crude, but I think the definition is a just one.

As we drove to the little German inn in the outskirts of town, we noticed the air getting richer with the scent of orange-flowers, and soon we passed into the region of the orange-orchards. The trees were creamy white with dense blossom, and the ripe fruit was dotted about in masses of white. The honey they gave us at breakfast was from these orange flowers. Here our drogoman, Isaac, met us.

I made my first sketch—the first I trust, of a series I marked down before leaving Alexandria. It was of Jaffa, seen over the orange trees from the inn garden, and charming it was to sit there in the cool shade, with birds singing overhead as never one hears them in Egypt. Fragments of classical pillars stood about and served as seats under the chequered shade of flowering fruit-trees along the garden paths.

The Mediterranean appeared to my right, and overhead sailed great pearly clouds in the vibrating blue of the fresh

spring sky. I must say I felt very happy at the reality of my
presence on the soil of Palestine.

At 2 pm we started in a carriage like our dear old friend,
the "*Vetturino*", for Ramleh, our halting place for the
night. How can I put before you the scenes of loveliness
we passed through? The country was a vast plain of rolling
wheat, bordered in the blue distance with the tender hills
of Judea.

This land of Philistines far surpassed my expectations in
its extent, its grand sweep of line, its breadth of colour and
light and shade. It was some time before we came out on
the Plain of Sharon, and we drove first along the way
between orange-orchards bordered along the roads by
gigantic hedges of prickly pear.

Our *Vetturino* was drawn by three horses abreast, all with
bells, and it was exhilarating to set out at a fast trot along
with other jingling and whip-cracking vehicles, and escorted by horsemen in brilliant Syrian costumes dashing along
on their little Arabs, and carrying their long ornamental
guns slung across their backs.

I had just one horrible glimpse (of which I said nothing,
as of some guilty thing), just as we started, of a railway
engine under some palm-trees. It is awaiting there the completion of the line to Jerusalem to puff and whistle its beau-
ty-marring career to the Holy City. I am thankful my good
luck has brought me here just in time to escape the sight of
a railway and its attendant eyesores in this sacred land.
Why such rush through this little country, every yard of
which is precious? An express train could run in two hours
"from Dan to Beersheba" —and what then?

*After spending the night at Ramleh Elizabeth Butler and her
party went on towards Jerusalem. Her account continues.*

At 9.30 am we left the plain and at once entered the
hills of Judea, which are more uniformly stony than one
would suppose them to be from a distance. We soon

stopped at a wayside khan, about a half-a-dozen *Vetturinos* being assembled in the yard, and all the horses were rested. We then began the ascent of the dear Hill Country, fragrant with memories of Mary on her journey made in haste from Nazareth.

I did not expect such a long and high ascent, having failed to realise from descriptions the immense altitude of the land that holds Jerusalem. "Things seen are mightier than things heard." The wildflowers increased in beauty and variety, chief, I think, amongst them being the crimson anemonies with a black centre which tossed their gay heads everywhere in the mountain breeze. Olives and stones, stones and olives on all sides. Here and there a carob tree or a clump of tamarisk at a tomb.

As we crested the first pass and looked back we saw the plains of Philistia, with Ramleh white in the sunshine and the sea beyond shining in a long flash of silver. Before us to the right soon loomed against the clouds the greatest tombs of the Maccabees, and away to our left, on a high cone, appeared, remote and awful, the "Tomb of Samuel," a dominating feature over all the land.

As we descended on the other side of the pass we came in sight of Ain Kareem, the reputed birthplace of John the Baptist, on the side of a high hill. The words of the Magnificat sounded in one's mind's ear. It is a grand situation and most striking as seen from the road. At the bottom of the valley formed by the hill of Ain Kareem runs the dry bed of the brook from which David chose his smooth stone for Goliath. William (General Butler) went down and selected just such a smooth white stone as a memento.

At the bottom of the valley we halted at a Russian khan and I took a little sketch of a bit of hill-side and a pear-tree in blossom. You must have seen this land with "second sight," for you have always seen a flowering fruit-tree in your mental pictures of it at Eastertide and Lady Day. Palestine is essentially the land of little fruit-trees.

On leaving the Russian khan, where we beheld chromo-lithographs of the late and present Czars on the walls, and were interested in the high Muscovite boots of our host, we had another great ascent, and soon after reaching the top my feelings became more and more focussed on the look-out ahead. I saw signs that we were approaching Jerusalem.

There were more people on the road, and a detachment of the Salvation Army was marching along with a strangely incongruous appearance. Yet only incongruous on account of the dress, for, morally, those earnest souls are among the fittest to be here. I stood up in the carriage, but William from the box saw first. He raised his hat, and a second after I had the indescribable sensation of seeing the top of the Mount of Olives, and then the Walls of Sion! It was about three o'clock.

We left the carriage outside the Jaffa Gate, for no wheeled vehicle can traverse the streets of Jerusalem, and we passed in on foot. We had first to go to the hotel, of course, a very clean little place facing the Tower of David. Thence we soon set out to begin our wonderful experiences.

I had what I can only describe as a qualm when we reached, in a few hundred steps, the Church of the Holy Sepulchre. It was all too easy and too quick. You can imagine the sense of reluctance to enter there without more rec-ollection. I had a feeling of regret that we had not waited till the morrow, and I would warn others not to go on the day of their arrival.

We reached the Church through stone lanes of inde-scribable picturesqueness, teeming with the life of the East, and there I saw the Jerusalem Jews I had so often read of—extraordinary figures in long coats and round hats, a ringlet falling in front of each ear, while the rest of the head is shaved. They looked white and unhealthy, many of them red-eyed and all more or less bent, even the youths. No greater contrast could be seen than between those poor creatures and the Arabs who jostle them in these crowded alleys, and who are such upstanding athletic men, with

clear brown skins, clean-cut features, and heads turbaned
majestically. They stride along with a spring in every step.

There are Greeks here too, and Russians in the crowds,
and Kurds, Armenians, and Copts—in fact samples of all
the dwellers of the Near East, wearing their national dresses; and through this fascinating assemblage of types and
costumes, most distracting to my thoughts, we threaded our
way to-day, ascending and descending the lanes and
bazaars, up and down wide, shallow steps, till we came in
front of the rich portal of the Church of churches.

With our eyes dazzled with all that colour, and with the
sudden brilliance of the sunshine which flooded the open
space in front of the facade, we passed in! Do not imagine
that the church stands imposingly on an eminence, and
that its proportions can strike the beholder. You go down
hill to it from the street, and it is crowded on all sides but
the front by other buildings.

But its gloomy antiquity and formlessness are the very
things that strike one with convincing force, for one sees at
once that the church is there for the sake of the sites it
encloses, and that, therefore, it cannot have any architectural symmetry or plan whatever, and its enormous extent is
necessitated by its enclosing the chapels over Calvary and
the Holy Sepulchre and many others besides, which the
empress Helena erected over each sacred spot whose identi-
ty she ascertained with so much diligence.

It is very natural to wish that Calvary was in the open
air,—lonely, under the sky that saw Christ suffer on the
Cross. But already, in the year 326, St Helena found the
place of execution buried under mounds of rubbish purpose-
ly thrown upon it; and where would any trace of it be today
had she not enclosed it—what with man's destroying acts
and the violence of the storms that have beaten against this
rock for nineteen centuries and more? It was, to begin with,
but a small eminence close outside the walls.

On entering the church you discern in the depths of the
gloom of the tortuous interior the rough steep steps cut in

the rock that lead to Calvary, on your right hand. On climbing to the top, groping in the twilight, you find your-self in a chapel lined with plates of gold and hung with votive lamps. The sacred floor, which is the very top of Calvary, is entirely cased in gold, and under the Greek altar is shown the socket of the Cross, a hole in the rock. Our altar stands to the proper left of the Greek, which has the post of honour.

Descending from Calvary there is a long stretch of twilight church to traverse before we come to the Sepulchre. Again I had not realised, from the books I had read, the great dis-tance that separates the two, and, indeed, many writers in their scepticism have done their best to belittle the whole thing. I confess that before today I was much under the influ-ence of these writers, but I have now seen for myself, a privi-lege I am deeply thankful for. It was an overwhelming sensa-tion to find the spaces that separate the sites so much vaster than I had expected, and to have, at every step, the convic-tion driven home that after all the modern wrangling and disputing the old tradition stands immovable.

It certainly would be hard to believe that when St Helena came here the dwellers of Jerusalem should have lost all knowledge of where their "Tower-hill" stood in the course of three centuries. She was commissioned, as you know, by her son, Emperor Constantine, that ardent con-vert to Christianity, to seek and secure with the utmost per-severance and care all the holy sites, and to her untiring labours we owe their identification to this day.

The great central dome of the church rises above the chapel of the Holy Sepulchre, which chapel stands in the vast central space, a casket enclosing the rock hollowed out into our Lord's Tomb and its ante-chamber. You enter this ante-chamber and, stooping down, you pass on your hands and knees into the sepulchre itself. On your right hand is the little low, rough-hewn tomb, covered with a slab of stone worn into hollows by the lips of countless pilgrims throughout the long ages of our era. A monk keeps watch there, and besides him there is only space enough for one person at a time. I have made many attempts to tell you my thoughts and feelings during these bewildering moments of my first visit, but I find it is impossible, and you can understand why.

Elizabeth Butler's account includes a description of her expedition to the Bethlehem region and Galilee.

Towards evening we drove from this place of rest (a German khan in Hebron) a long way back on the road to Jerusalem, but not far short of Bethlehem we came in sight of our camp! How charming and inspir-iting that sight was—three snowy tents pitched by the  Pools of Solomon under the walls of a Crusader Castle, with some sixteen saddle and baggage animals picketed close by, and the dear old Union Jack flying from the central tent! I was delighted at the fact that our camp life was to begin that night.

Everything struck us as in excellent order, our horses, saddles and bridles, the tents, the servants and all. Those Pools of Solomon are three immense reservoirs of water which the Wise King made to supply the Temple at Jerusalem. Myriads of frogs were enlivening the evening air with their multitudinous croakings which increased to deafening proportions as night closed in. I took a hasty sketch. Much hyssop grows there, "*Asperges me, Domine, hyssopo et mundabor.*"

I was greatly pleased with my first night under canvas. To have grass and stones and little aromatic herbs for a bedroom carpet was a new and delightful sensation for me. We started this morning at sunrise, my sketching things handily strapped to my saddle by William's directions, in a flat straw *aumonière*. Isaac had swathed his tarboush in a magnificent *cufia*, and our retinue wore the baggy garb of Syria. William

rode a steel-grey Arab, I a silver-grey, Isaac a roan-grey, and the man whom we called the "flying column," because he is to accompany us with the lunch bags, while the heavy column with baggage, tents, etc., goes ahead by short-cuts, rode a chestnut.

We passed through Bethlehem and down to the Field of the Shepherds, where I completed, as well as I could in the heat and glare, my sketch begun here the other day. A group of some twenty Russian pilgrims arrived as we did, and we saw them in the grotto of the sheepfold, each holding a lighted taper and responding to the chant of their old priest, who had a head which would do admirably for a picture of Abraham.

These poor men were in fur coats and high clumsy boots, and one told us he had come from Tobolsk, and had been two years on that tramp. He assured us he could manage his return journey in no time, only ten months or so. Their devotion was profound, as it always is, and was utterly unselfconscious. I think we English are too apt to suppose that because devotion is demonstrative it is not deep. Great pedestrians as we are, how many Englishmen would walk two years to visit this sheepfold? That two years' test borne by the Russian peasant must have gone very deep.

I remember reading with much approval, when a child, with a child's narrow-mindedness, Miss Martineau's shocked description of the demonstrative piety of a noble Russian lady on Calvary, who repeatedly laid her head in the hole where the Cross had been, weeping and praying and behaving in a most un-English manner. The memory of that passage came back to me today as I saw these rough peasants, so supremely unconscious of our presence, throwing themselves heart and soul into their adoration of God, and I thought of Mary Magdalene and *her* prostrations and tears.

After the service for the Russian pilgrims "father Abraham" fell asleep under an olive-tree, with his hoary head on a stone which he had cushioned with dock leaves, and the younger priest who had taken part in the service went back to his ploughing, which he had left on the approach of the pilgrims. They both had their Fellaheen clothes under their cassocks, and they wore the tall Greek sacerdotal cap. They were natives of Bethlehem.

"Abraham" blessed our meal, but refused to partake of it, except the fruit, as this is the Greek Lent. We had a long talk with him through Isaac, and a lively theological argument, which had the usual success of such undertakings, enhanced by its filtration through a Mahometan interpreter converted to Protestantism by the American Baptist Mission at Jaffa!

That old patriarch was a magnificent study as he sat, pointing heavenwards under the olive-trees and discoursing of his Faith, with Bethlehem rising in the distance behind his most venerable head. He made some coffee for us, a return civility for the fruit, and as we rode off many were the parting salutations between us and the group of people who had been the audience of our theological arguments, made unintelligible by Isaac. Among the crowd was an ex-Papal Zouave who turned out to have been orderly to a friend of ours in the old days at Rome.

We rode along a track in the field of Boaz, now knee-deep in corn, a cavalry soldier, who had been sent to escort us through the "dangerous" region, leading the way. His escorting seems to consist of periodical "fantasia" manoeuvres, when he shakes his horse out at full gallop, picking a flower in mid-career and circling back to present it to  me,—a picturesque proceeding in that floating caftan and white and brown striped burnous. I was pleased to see this

figure in our foreground caracoling, curveting, and career-
ing. He is in such pleasing harmony with his native land-
scape. He and Isaac are all over pistols and weapons of various sorts, but William says that the necessity for arms in
Palestine is now a thing of the past, and only a bogey.

*Several days later they had reached the foot of Mount Tabor
where they camped.*

Off again at sunrise over the saddle of Mount Tabor. Very
rough riding through dells of oak, where the honeysuckle
hung in masses and scented the air. Tabor itself is scarcely
beautiful in outline, and like the magnified mounds that the
old masters intended for mountains. In their pictures of the
Transfiguration their Tabors are very like the original.

This was our most glorious day's journey, for it took us to
the shores of the Lake of Galilee. Hermon in distant
Lebanon was visible ahead of us throughout. We rode up to
near the top of the "Mount of the Beatitudes," and then on
foot reached the very top, and had our first view of the
Sacred Sea from that immense height. Here Christ
preached the Sermon on the Mount, and down there,
intensely blue, lay that dear lake whose shores were so often
trodden by His feet. Hermon arose above the majestic land-
scape, and a warm, palpitating light vibrated over all.

In a scrap of shade from a rock we made our halt, and I
had an hour and a half for a sketch. Then we rode down to
Tiberias, descending into a furnace, though when once on
the shore the breeze was sweet off the water. Tiberias is a
dreadful little town, and we were glad to thread its alleys as
quickly as possible. Our camp was on the pebbly strand
about half a mile south of this, the only town on these
shores that once held such brilliant cities. I made an
evening sketch, and before retiring for the night we strode a
long time by those sacred waters in the light of the full
moon. The waves were strong, and sounded loud in that
great stillness. At such time as this the sense of our Lord's

presence is almost more than one's mortal heart can hold.

We picked up hundreds of shells, which will make suitable rosaries, mounted in silver, the cross made out of olive wood which I have brought from Gethsemane. I will send you one.

On Thursday the 23rd of April we went by boat three hour's row to near the mouth of the Jordan, at the north end of the lake, where grassy slopes are supposed to be the scene of the miracle of the Loaves and Fishes. It is very difficult to describe to you my enchantment at seeing one after another these places I have longed to see from early childhood, when our beloved father used to read  us the Bible every Sunday. The lake was pale and calm, delicately tinted, and there was a heat-haze over everything in the early part of the day.

We disembarked under some thorny acacias which gave deep shade, and I had the delight of making a sketch there of the coast, looking westwards, whilst William went on by boat to the Jordan. Rosy oleanders fringe the water as far as the eye can reach; the "Mount of Beatitudes" and top of Tabor are in the distance, and the site of Capernaum in the middle distance. God has trodden these scenes with human feet; the feeling of sketching them is scarcely to be put before you in words.

The boatmen were very angry at being kept, whilst I finished the sketch, from returning at the right time, for they told us that if the west wind sprang up we should never be able to get home that night. Surely enough we were only able to get as far as Capernaum with hard pulling against a strong west wind, which suddenly changed the whole face of the lake.

Its pale blue was now dirty green and the choppy waves lashed with foam, and so wild did the waves become that progress of the boat was almost impossible. These sudden and violent gusts that come through the gullies between the mountains are dreaded by the fishermen of today as they were in Peter's time. Fortunately William had in the morning ordered that our horses should be sent round to meet us here in case the wind arose, and we gladly got on them at this point, having an enchanting ride back and being able to canter our horses. We heard afterwards that the boatmen did not get back in till one in the morning.

In the spring of the following year, an Italian woman, Matilde Serao, made a visit to the Holy Land. Her account of this, 'Nel Paese di Gesú,' was one of the most popular books ever written on the pilgrimage. There were thirty editions within a year of its publication in 1897.

In the Introduction to her book she explains the purpose of her account: "I have endeavoured, in my journey through Palestine, humbly and honestly to seek out the soul of the Blessed Land where Christ dwelt and where His voice was heard. I found it in the clear skies of Samaria, in the tiny violet and yellow flowers that bloom where once stood the home of Martha and Mary, and by that fountain at Nazareth where the Virgin Mother bathed her gentle hands. I found it on the shore of the lake of Gennesareth, on whose waters Jesus walked, and where He commanded the storm to cease; and, indeed, in every place where the Son of God lived, suffered, and preached the words of peace and hope. I have sought to chronicle my impressions of the Holy Land even as I felt them whilst still vibrating with the intense emotions I experienced, as I trod the paths He had passed along and visited the scenes hallowed by His Life and Passion."

Below are some extracts from her account.

A LINE of railway now runs from Jaffa to Jerusalem, a journey which takes three and a half hours to complete, the only train starting at half-past two in the afternoon. Every vessel that touches Palestine, be it Egyptian, Austrian, French, or Russian, does so before noon; whereby travellers have barely the time on landing to rush up to the Jerusalem Hotel, wash their hands, swallow a cup of boiling coffee, and start off again for the Holy City.

Very few people find time to visit Jaffa, and yet it is a very interesting and quaint city, whose harbour is always ruffled by crested waves. A dry sea-wind is ever blowing which carries off that unhealthy dampness that is so dangerous elsewhere in the East. The gardens of Jaffa are magnificent, and the sight of their abundance of golden oranges and pale yellow lemons, glowing amid glossy leaves, reminded me, with a sigh, of lovely Sorrento.

Jaffa is a rich prosperous city, with picturesque old streets, and rows of small, modern houses in the old quarter. The women of Jaffa, unlike other Orientals, are extremely fair; they all wear long, white muslin cloaks clasped at the throat, and they are, for the most part, veiled: the more orthodox with a thick yashmac, having a pattern upon it, completely concealing the face. Some, however, who have acquired European tastes, have discarded the yashmac altogether, and their dark, almond-shaped eyes glance at you with a sweet yet proud expression. But, owing to the awkward hours fixed for landing and departing, no one can see much of Jaffa. To do so one would have to remain at least a day and a night here, which very few can do; the English, having seen quite enough of Jaffa in two hours, never rest till they have started off again.

The journey, considering it is so short, is distinctly expensive, costing twelve shillings. There are only two classes, first and second, but even in the first-class carriages the seats are of unpolished wood, and there are no cushions or anything to rest your elbows on. In a word, they are a great deal less comfortable than our third-class carriages.

The train starts three-quarters of an hour after time, as the Turks, never quite sure how many people may arrive, generally get confused and completely lose their heads, only to become more indolent than ever, while the passengers protest and shout in every language under the sun. At the last moment one or two carriages have to be added, and finally the train starts amid a veritable hubbub, as is always the case in these countries, people apparently quarrelling at the top of their voices.

There is usually some stoppage or other on the line; we were kept, for instance, for forty minutes at Sejed. Water had to be fetched for the engine. Once we started again afresh the driver had to go at full speed to make up for lost time. It was the reverse of pleasant, we were so terribly jolted. The carriages are small and badly built, and the surface, always on an incline, is not much wider than the permanent way, and is flanked on one side by a steep hill and on the other by a deep, precipitous ravine with a torrent rushing along at its foot. The line, moreover, curves continually, and the engine and carriages jostle and sway in a most terrifying manner. It is wiser not to look out of the windows, but to confine one's attention to the interior of the carriage and patiently await events.

Not infrequently the train runs off the rails! But so far no very serious accident has occurred. There are five stations between Jaffa and Jerusalem, and the latter should be reached at six o'clock, though it is generally half-past six or even seven, before the train runs into the terminus.

You cannot conceive of anything more unromantic than this railway journey, which entirely wipes away all previous pleasant anticipations, peaceful thoughts, holy aspirations or poetical fancies about the Holy Land which the sea journey had evoked. I do not mean, of course, to belittle the advantages of railway travel as a most necessary, practical and useful means of travel—anywhere else but in Palestine.

The contrast between its practical methods and the stupendous tradition of the Holy Land is too great. It causes a feeling of positive revulsion to see the name of the Sion of the Psalmist, the scene of the Birth and Passion, which should move every Christian heart in its depths, printed on a commonplace green railway ticket! It is simply intolerable and, indeed, quite horrible, to find oneself in a railway carriage full of fat, smoking, somnolent Turks, seated in their favourite attitude, with a shoeless foot in one hand. No Turk will ever keep on his shoes a moment longer than he can help!

To be driven at full speed through the beautiful plain of Sharon, where the Philistines conquered the Children of Israel and carried off the Ark of the Covenant, is positively dreadful; or to be "rushed" through the valley of Sorve, where Delilah overcame Samson, and whence she sent him, a blinded prisoner, to Gaza. Is that not where the tomb of the faithful old Simeon is, who so tenderly took the Holy Child in his arms and then begged to depart in peace, for he had beheld the Messiah?

And is not that the Hill of Bad Counsel where the Pharisees, with Caiaphas at their head, deliberated how Jesus should be put to death? The train goes so fast that, although you may recognise, you cannot *distinguish* anything through the smoke and steam. Your eyes are tired and your spirit weary, and you sink back on your hard, wooden bench disappointed and discouraged.

By the time you reach Jerusalem you are altogether demoralised. Fancy arriving at the gates of the City of David and of Solomon at this tearing, puffing rate! Imagine seeing the City of Jesus for the first time in all this confusion, without even having a moment to collect your thoughts and to call up the slightest feeling of devotion! To those happy travellers who visited Jerusalem in other ages, after overcoming great difficulties, much fatigue and strange adventures, it must indeed have appeared a haven of divine peace.

The knights who followed Godfrey de Bouillon and fought before its holy walls, saw the Holy City in a different light to us. Even a few years ago the good people who arrived leisurely in carriages, on horse-back, or on foot, could still kneel in its sacred dust as they passed under its time-honoured gates.

All is changed, and we up-to-date folks dash into Jerusalem in a stuffy railway carriage, amid oaths of railway porters and a thousand distracting sounds and scenes, just as if we were mere commercial travellers bent on the most commonplace sort of business. In this way we pass under the shadow of the Mount from where the Light of the Cross has spread to the uttermost ends of the earth!

What an abomination of desolation! This horrible railway was not made for the likes of me, but for those who are always in a hurry, who must see everything in the shortest possible time, even the Holy Sepulchre, or the House of Mary at Nazareth. It has been made for the ever-restless Anglo-Saxons—they would only marvel at our emotion, and feel amazed that we should manifest it outwardly— since it is by *them* that Palestine lives, and the railway has been built expressly for their benefit. Under these altered and unfortunate circumstances it is quite impossible to repeat, as Christians were expected to do in bygone days on beholding the Towers of David, the beginning of the noble 122nd Psalm,

> I was glad when they said to me,
> "Let us go to the house of the Lord!"
> Our feet have been standing
> Within your gates, O Jerusalem!

Jerusalem, built as a city
Which is bound firmly together,
To which the tribes go up,
The tribes of the Lord,
As was decreed for Israel,
To give thanks to the name of the Lord.

In old days it was the rule that the pilgrim to Jerusalem should never enter any house until he had visited the Holy Sepulchre. But this can no longer be done, for now it closes at sundown, and the train only arrives after sunset! Thus we have no choice anymore but must go straight to the Grand Hotel and prepare for the *table-d'hôte* dinner, as if we had arrived at Monte Carlo instead of Jerusalem!

THE WAY OF THE CROSS

Anyone who wants to follow the "The Way of the Cross" should not begin his pilgrimage from the house of Annas, the high priest (who deliberated and determined to put our Lord to death); nor from the palace of Caiaphas (who was only an instrument in the hands of his father-in-law, Annas); but from the house (or lithostratos) of Pontius Pilate, the humane Roman governor, who made several unavailing efforts to save Jesus.

The pilgrim who selects this path, every step of which is associated with some incident in the closing act of the fatal Tragedy, and who wishes to examine and meditate on each point of interest, will have to employ rather more than an hour to reach Golgotha, the place of death in the Church of Calvary.

In many places the road is still fairly steep, while in others it consists of a series of steps—as, for instance, in front of the Coptic Bishop's house, where Jesus fell under the weight of the Cross for the third time; and again, before the house of Holy Veronica. Like all the roads in Jerusalem, it is paved with long narrow stones which make walking exceedingly troublesome and tiring.

The *Via Dolorosa*, since it is far more precipitous than an average country road, takes the Christian pilgrim rather more than an hour to cover from end to end. How much longer must it have seemed to the Martyr! At that time it must have been much steeper than now, and was probably not paved at all. Moreover, it would have been in very bad condition, as were all the roads in those days.

He was laden with the weight of His Cross! He had passed the preceeding days in vigil and profound emotion; the last two nights must have been especially terrible: for He had been so lately bound to the column, scourged and outraged. His Soul was full of anguish and His strength was failing.

Death upon the cross was one of the most terrible punishments conceivable, lasting sometimes as many as three days, when the legs and arms of the condemned, if still living, were broken. To Jesus, as He dragged Himself along the cruel Way of the Cross, the way must have seemed interminable.

The Praetorium of Pontius Pilate is now a Turkish barracks, filled with Muslim foot-soldiers. The Turks, with their habitual courtesy to those who give them money, offered no opposition to our visiting the exact spot where the *Via Dolorosa* begins. Every Friday the Franciscan Fathers, followed by a band of pilgrims and other devout people, start the "Way of the Cross" from this point, pausing to pray before each of its fourteen "stations." A flight of twenty steps leads up to the Turkish barracks.

When the door is opened, you pass beneath a broad flag bearing the White Star and the Crescent, and enter a large courtyard. This place, stacked with guns, is where the soldiers clean their cooking utensils and wooden bowls; it was the Praetorium, or *lithostratos*, where Jesus was condemned.

Who can forget Pilate's last word after he had washed his hands: "I am innocent of the blood of this just person."? Well, they were uttered from the wall immediately opposite you. It was in this very courtyard, where the guns shine so brightly in the sunlight, and the Turkish soldiers polish their buckles, that the Jews cried out tumultuously, "His blood be on us, and on our children!"

Then Jesus descends into the roadway, the full weight of His Cross upon His shoulders: the site of the stairway is marked by a white stone set in the wall. The actual steps have been taken to Rome, where they still stand close to the Lateran Basilica.

The ascent begins. The soldiers surge round the two thieves, Cosmas and Dismas, while He Who has been mocked as "King of the Jews," reviving by a superhuman effort, momentarily recovers His strength. His Face is dead-ly pale. His exhausted Frame is bathed in sweat. Blood streams from the Wounds inflicted on His Head by the Crown of Thorns. But when He comes to the spot where the street from the Praetorium enters the Damascas road, He sinks to the ground for the first time—the exact place is still indicated by a split column.

Here the road is wide and filled with foot passengers, heavily laden camels and donkeys, and half-naked Arabs going to the neighbouring bazaar. The Martyr rises, and about a hundred yards further on a group of women come forward. Among them is the Virgin Mother seeking her Son. He says to her, "Salve Mater!"

But she does not answer Him. Overcome with horror and grief, she falls back fainting into the arms of the other women. This heart-rending incident happened, according to ancient tradition, in a narrow and little frequented lane. Beyond stands a little chapel dedicated to "Our Lady of the Swoon." After this meeting with His mother, Jesus's strength fails rapidly.

But the soldiers are in haste to finish their appalling task, for the Passover is at hand, and they wish to enjoy the feast at their leisure. So, finding a countryman nearby called Simon of Cyrene, they load him with the Cross. This occurs before a grey house where the road turns: the Cyrenian lightens our Lord's burden for a little, thereby relieving His aching Shoulders.

From this point onwards the road grows steeper and the steps begin. And while the Sufferer, fainting and bathed in Sweat and Blood, ascends them, at each step calling on death to release Him, a woman comes forward out of her house. She is called Berenice and is Jewish. Without fear the tender-hearted woman comes forward through the soldiers. Then, with a cloth, she wipes the emaciated Face of Christ. On that linen the impress of the Divine Face still remains, and from that day she is no longer called Berenice, but *Vera-icon*, the "true image".

Her little house is still standing at the top of steps under a dark archway. It is very gloomy, being cut into the living rock—perhaps some day a chapel will be built here in her honour to commemorate this tender act of charity.

About sixty-yards beyond the house of Veronica, along a street which was the Road of the Gate of Judgement, Jesus falls for the second time. A number of little white houses enclose the place. On the window ledge of one is a white rose bush in bloom. It is probably watered by some dark-eyed woman of Jerusalem, on whose doorstep lads are playing and chattering in Arabic.

Under a shower of blows, our Lord again tries to rise. His agony excites such profound pity, that, at the sight of it, a group of women standing by are moved to tears. Then the great prophesy falls from His Lips, and He exclaims, "Daughters of Jerusalem, weep not for Me, but weep for yourselves and for your children." Having said this, He resumes His weary journey.

The road is long and steep. Already the place of infamy and death, Golgotha, looms in sight; but to reach it yet another effort is needed. In our time this road is shut in by buildings of a later date. If you want to follow Jesus all the way, you must make several turns, even retracing your steps, in order to reach one of the last "stations"—a high platform, close to Calvary, where Jesus falls the third time. This place, forming the corner of the Bazaar, is one of the dirtiest and most overcrowded in Jerusalem...

The last scene of all took place within what is now the Church of Calvary, opposite the rock which was to receive our Lord's body. A large stone, placed on the ground, marks the spot where Jesus was stripped, and where soldiers cast lots for His garments. A little further on, in the same church, a square of mosaic indicates the place where He was actually crucified. A few yards beyond, towards the east, is a cylindrical hole lined with silver, which indicates the spot where the Cross was raised. It was turned towards the West, and thus the Eyes of the dying Christ were fixed upon that part of the world where His faith was to be founded.

And now the sad scene is nearly over. The seven words are spoken; He has pardoned the good thief; He has made his farewell to His mother and to John, and has yielded up His Spirit to His Father. It is finished!

Here stands the altar of the *Stabat Mater*. It was erected by pious Christians to commemorate the place where Jesus Christ was taken down from the Cross, and where His body was laid across His mother's knees. Upon that marble slab over there, the Stone of Anointment, His Body was washed and embalmed with myrrh and aloes. Twenty paces further on is the little garden of Joseph of Arimathea. Here in a newly-made tomb, He was laid.

Night is falling!

The *Via Dolorosa* is ended...

THE CHURCH OF THE HOLY SEPULCHRE

The centre of Christian Jerusalem, the most modern and most essentially English centre, is the broad populous square on which stands the new Grand Hotel, where those mighty rivals, Cook and Gaze, have their offices, and on which there are four or five large European shops, and even a livery stable located under the Jaffa Gate!

From this essentially modern centre starts the road lead-ing to the Church of the Holy Sepulchre—a narrow alley running through one of the Turkish bazaars of Jerusalem, with little dark shop windows in which it is impossible to distinguish the wares displayed behind them. On either side are crowds of Turks smoking their *narghilehs*, camels squatting on the ground, donkeys laden with corn, and Arabs everlastingly arranging their own and other people's affairs whilst smoking their inevitable cigarettes.

Once past the bazaars the lane-like, ill-paved road makes one or two bends and then descends to a lower level by a series of very wide steps. The religious influence of the surroundings now begins to assert itself. Little shops come into sight where every kind of wax candle, bedecked with gold and silver foil, or painted blue and red, is exposed for sale; from the slender taper costing three Turkish piastres, to the enormous candles, the weight of which only the mightiest candelabras can bear.

Here cartloads of rosaries of every description and shape are sold: from the tiny ones intended for the hand of a little child, to those made of great carved beads the size of a walnut, which a giant might use with advantage! Here too are rosaries composed of glass beads, fragrant amber, polished cherry stones and lapis lazuli.

The dark shops are literally lighted up with pictures of Palestine painted vividly on wood, or Byzantine fashion on a gold ground like the icons of the Panagia that once upon a time blazed in Sancta Sophia at Constantinople, but even more gaudy. Sometimes the profile of the saint in these icons is outlined in the most quaint manner. All these objects, if you can believe the pale-faced shopkeeper, have touched the Holy Sepulchre and have been consecrated thereby.

Now we approach the Sacred Tomb. At the fourth bend of the road, after mounting sixty steps of the little square where it stands, the beautiful facade of the church—the only really artistic part of the ancient building—comes into view. It has two large Gothic doors, one of which is always shut. Above each door is a pure Gothic window, also invariably closed and choked up with creepers, among which hundreds of chattering birds have built their nests.

On the little square a few poor itinerant merchants expose their wares on a strip of dirty carpet: little medals, rosaries and faded photographs. On all sides pop-corn sellers call attention to their succulent grain, and water-carriers attract notice by clinking their little brass disks.

An utter confusion of thoughts and objects overwhelms the Christian at the very door of the church wherein stands the Holy Sepulchre. He has scarcely made the Sign of the Cross, after passing beneath its portals, before he becomes aware of the extraordinary agglomeration of ill-assorted things and people that surround him.

First of all, to your left on entering, stands what may be called the Porters' Lodge. It consists of a floor, or wooden platform, covered with carpets and cushions on which are sitting, or lying, two or three Muslims, the custodians of the chief church of Christendom!

The Sultan has preserved his right of possession over these Holy Places, but without any show of arrogant discourtesy. These Turkish porters drink their coffee out of little cups, smoke cigars or pipes, but very rarely speak to each other, though they noiselessly and incessantly pass the amber beads of their *combolois*, or Turkish rosaries, through their brown fingers.

They appear to be lost in Oriental contemplation, and look very picturesque, with their long tunics of striped red and yellow silk or satin, their feet enclosed in the whitest of socks, their slippers beside them. On their heads they wear turbans, the folds of which go twice round their fez. They never seem to pay the least attention to the people who enter the church, and pass their days in stolid contemplation of nothing at all!

After duly observing this group of Muslims squatting at the very door of the Temple where Jesus was buried, you perceive, exactly opposite to you, the Anointing Stone, upon which the Body of our Lord was washed and sprinkled with myrrh and aloes. Each pilgrim on reaching the Sacred

Stone prostrates himself. Some extend their arms in an attitude of supplication. Others beat their forehead against it. Others kiss it with effusion or else sit by it for hours wrapt in silent devotion.

Here the varied forms of religious adoration are plainly manifest, each with a different individual manner and expression. Upon this Stone, before which every Christian bends the knee, the various Churches begin to show their curious and diverse ways of manifesting religious zeal. Eight lamps burn above it, suspended by a silver chain which is linked to two side candelabras. Of these eight lamps, three belong to the Latin Church, three to the schismatic Greek Church, one to the Armenian, and one to the Coptic. Each of these churches belongs to Jesus and is dedicated to His service, and is a sign of His Redemption; and each demands its share in the place where He lived, suffered, and was buried.

Anxiously we look round the Church of the Holy Sepulchre in an endeavour to grasp its outline, and to imprint an early, general, and enduring picture of it on the memory and imagination. All kinds of architectural form are blended in it harmoniously.

In the centre stands a circular-shaped building which marks the crypt that contains the Holy Sepulchre. It is surrounded by a colonnade and a wide, dark corridor. On one side of the apse, which is an elongated oval raised some three yards above the pavement, on a sort of platform, stands the entrance to the chapel belonging to the schismatic Greeks.

The part nearest to the Chapel of St. Mary Magdalene, where it appears to become rectangular, belongs to the Latins. One small section, however, is the property of the Armenian Christians under the patronage of St. James. On all sides, even in the darkest nooks and corners, we perceive churches and chapels, large and small. Some of these ascend to the first floor on one side, whilst others are underground. They form such a confused and irregular collection as to be quite bewildering. You feel almost afraid to move.

There is, moreover, a long uncovered outer gallery where the rain comes in, and which connects the two farthest sections of this most singular church. In this half-ruined labyrinth, built in every style of architecture, and belonging to all nations—it has been destroyed and rebuilt eight times—are united under one roof every one of the sites rendered famous for ever by the Passion. Among the different Christian sects who worship here there reigns a fair amount of good fellowship on ordinary occasions. But sometimes it is otherwise, and the holiest spot in Christendom not infrequently becomes the scene of scandalous disorder and riot.

In the colonnade surrounding this venerable pile may be seen groups of Coptic women, dressed in blue rags, crouching for hours on the ground with their children in their arms. They have a curious fixed gaze in their wild, beautiful eyes, which seem to watch the passer-by without quite seeing him.

As you move into the church you hear the slow nasal tones of the schismatic Greek priests chanting their rite; it is coming from the higher gallery ornamented with gold and gems. You then enter the underground chapel where St Helena found the Holy Cross in a well. A dark-bearded Armenian priest, robed in black, with a hood over his head, advances and sprinkles you with holy water scented with attar of roses.

This strangest of churches is so shapeless, but at the same time so majestic, that its general outline entirely escapes you—an effect doubtless due to the confused variety of its architecture. Its mystical manifestations are so complex, it has such a varied and heterogeneous character, that the image left on the mental retina, even after many visits, soon becomes blurred.

One part of it is clean and well-ordered, and another is ill-kept and almost dirty. There, it is rich and sparkling with jewels. Here, poor and quite simple. In one place it is European; in another Oriental. Everything depends on the country, nation, condition, and customs of the various owners of that particular part of the building. And according to true devotion or fanaticism, it becomes a church, a room, or a public square.

On one altar are artificial flowers, whilst real fresh-cut blooms adorn another. Lights are everlastingly burning in heavy silver lamps, or in simple coloured glasses. There are shining metal balls suspended from the roof in which your face is reflected awry; and also big, white cocoa-nut mats, with knots of red ribbon and white beads, such as you see hanging in mosques.

In the midst of all this medley of the beautiful and the ugly, you vainly endeavour to concentrate your thought on the real meaning of this holiest of places, and seek to do homage to its Lord. The four Christian Churches have a common proprietorship in this great Shrine, and take good care to manifest their differences on every possible occasion. There are five Latin, five Greek, three Armenian priests, and one Coptic priest, sharing the same altars. You look in vain in this strange church for a unifying idea, to find only confusion, spiritual revolt and dissension.

The Holy Sepulchre itself is quite different...Its chapel is completely separated from the rest of the Church, and has been built upon the living rock, which formed the tomb of Joseph of Arimathea, in which Christ was buried. It is still adorned with the rich marbles presented by Helena, mother of the Emperor Constantine, on whom the Christian peoples of all ages have conferred the well-deserved title of Helena the Great.

The sacred building measures about twenty-seven feet in length by eighteen feet in breadth, and eighteen feet high, and is raised about half a yard above the level of the pavement. Four steps lead up to it. It is an elongated chapel from east to west, being square towards the west, and shaped like a pentagon towards the east. The interior is composed of two little cells or chambers, almost quadrangular, joined together by a low narrow opening, through which one has to stoop to enter.

The first little cell, on entering, is called the Chapel of

the Angel. The beloved disciple tells us that very early in the morning of the first day of the week after our Lord's death, Mary of Magdala came to the Sepulchre. She found the stone rolled back and the tomb empty. Not knowing where they had taken and laid Him, she began to weep bitterly. She then saw two young men wearing white garments, which frightened her. They said to her, "You are looking for Jesus of Nazareth, who was crucified. He is risen; He is not here."

In the centre of the Angel's Chapel, raised on a marble stand and surrounded by a marble balustrade, and worn by the kisses of countless pilgrims, is a piece of the stone which the Magdalene and other pious women found rolled back. For, as the Evangelist tells us, "it was very large."

This cell, which may be called the vestibule of the Holy Sepulchre, is kept in almost total darkness, save for the faint glimmer of the fifteen silver lamps hanging from the roof, which, as usual, belong to the four principal Churches. All the burial places of the Jews had that sort of vestibule or entrance, and the one belonging to Joseph of Arimathea was doubtless constructed like the rest.

The Sepulchre was still quite new, and had been erected by this worthy man in his garden, just outside Jerusalem, near the hillock called Golgotha. Not far from this place, in an underground corner of the church, other tombs belonging to the family of Joseph of Arimathea have been found. The Holy Sepulchre was isolated from the rest by St Helena. The topography could not be more evident, simple or accurate.

The Holy Sepulchre is in the second small room. The entrance to it is through an arched opening, and is very low, less than a yard and a half high by three-quarters of a yard wide. One person can pass through at a time, and then only by bending nearly double. This archway is cut out of solid rock.

The cell of the Sacred Tomb is smaller than the one where the Angel appeared. It barely measures six and three-quarter feet in width, by six feet in length. It has been entirely encased in marble, for both pilgrims and tourists were in the habit of breaking off bits of the stone, which otherwise would soon have been carried away piecemeal. Through certain chinks in the slabs of marble can be seen the rock itself.

The Holy Sepulchre has one long side next to the wall. It is excavated in the rock in the form of an arch, measuring a little over three feet in width by six feet in length...The Holy Sepulchre being raised only a few feet from the ground, it is easy for a person to kneel and kiss it; and since there is always a priest watching, only one or two people besides him can enter at a time, and then only with difficulty.

The throng remains in the church for hours before being able to enter the ante-chamber of the Angel, then afterwards into the Holy Sepulchre itself. Every now and then, as one pilgrim comes out, walking backwards in token of reverential respect, another enters. Suspended over the tomb from the arch are forty-three superb silver lamps burning day and night. The first series of these, and the more central, thirteen in number, belong to the Roman Catholics—that is to say the Franciscans of the Holy Land; thirteen belong to the Schismatic Greeks, thirteen to the Armenians, and four to the Copts.

Above the tomb is a very dark indistinct picture representing the Resurrection. On either side of this, on two little projecting parapets, the Franciscans have been able to place a movable altar, upon which they daily celebrate the "Mass of the Holy Sepulchre." The chamber is light, as the Greeks made an opening in the roof at the beginning of the nineteenth century, but is blackened by the fumes of the forty-three lamps.

As it is now, so has it ever been described by the pilgrims of all ages who have come and worshipped before it, and have written their impressions about it. All speak of the living rock encased in marble; of the dark, smoke-blackened vault, and of the special shape of the sarcophagus against the wall. The rock of which the tomb is made is whitish in colour and veined with red; it is called by the Arabs *melozi*, or sacred stone. The sarcophagus was covered with marble before the thirteenth century, the walls being lined in the same way at a much later date, though otherwise everything has remained untouched and unchanged...

Here adoraton is perpetual. The inmates of those convents which have their gratings and choirs opening into the church watch night and day. Every hour of the day foreign pilgrims are constantly joined by the Christians who live in Jerusalem itself and its environs, and by those who come from the most distant parts of Syria. Here is a woman of Jerusalem, enveloped in her long white cloak which falls over her forehead. Her veil, which is often quite transparent, discloses her dark irregular features, and her magnificent dull black eyes. She kisses the stone with dignified reverence.

Then comes a peasant from Bethany, draped in a long linen tunic and ample black and white cloak, with a hand-kerchief wound twice round his head like a Bedouin. Before the tomb he signs himself hurriedly, and beats his forehead against the marble in an outburst of devotion.

A beautiful Bethlehemite woman from the happy land where Jesus was born is dressed in a blue woollen gown embroi-dered in red. She is wearing a white kerchief worked in yel-low, blue and red, folded in a point over forehead and shoul-der. With stately grace she bends her noble head with its regular features, brilliant com-plexion and fine eyes.

Next comes a little peasant-woman from Ain Kareem, St John of the Mountain, the land of the Forerunner. She is a small, thin, charming little woman, dressed in dark blue, with tiny bare feet and hands. She draws her white, silk-like

linen cloak over her brows to hide the three rows of gold
and silver coins which encircle her hair. With her baby in
her arms half hidden in the folds of her shawl she bends
foward, and both mother and child kiss the Sepulchre.

The *beghina* of the Russian colony settled in Jerusalem
now enters. She is dressed in black, with a large white
handkerchief folded against her chest, and a tight white
kerchief like a cap on her head. You can easily detect that
she is an orthodox nun by the exaggerated manner in
which she makes the Sign of the Cross, and by her profound prostration.

Then follows a crowd of Turks, Arabs, Egyptians,
Europeans, in turbans, fez, caps, hats, rich, poor, even beggars. They bend over the Sepulchre, genuflect and depart.
And now come members of the various religious orders:
browned-cloaked Franciscans, white-robed Dominicans,
Greek priests in high black hats, Armenian priests with
great black silk hoods under which glitter their flashing eyes
and waving black beards, the Latin missionaries, nuns of St.
Joseph, European women dressed in dark habits, who live in
Jerusalem and lead a sort of monastic life, all throng in to
venerate the tomb of their Lord.

Mingled with these good people is a crowd of children:
boys and girls, large and tiny, belonging to all nationalities.
They come there to kiss the Sepulchre. They are especially
numerous during the hours when schools are closed. It is a
touching sight to watch these little creatures come in
silently and push their way on tiptoe through the throng of
grown-up people, in their childish endeavour to kiss the
Sacred Stone where He who bade little children come unto
Him was laid.

I remember one day seeing a tiny brown mite. He was
wearing a yellow and red tunic tied round the waist with a
ribbon. He had no shoes or stockings on, and he laughed as
he vainly tried, being too short, to reach and kiss the tomb.
Twice he tried to jump up and touch it with his lips, and
twice he fell back. At last I raised him in my arms, and with

joy he kissed the marble with a number of little resounding kisses. Yalla! yalla! (Go away! go away!) cried the Armenian priest sharply, who was on watch; though I noticed he smiled all the same. And as the child with his bare feet ran quietly way the priest sprinkled him with rose-scented holy water!...

As the day declines the women of Jerusalem return to their houses, enveloped in their cloud-like muslin cloaks, one end of which is invariably kept tightly pressed to the mouth by a brown hand. On their fingers they wear coarse silver rings, and on their slender wrists light blue glass bracelets, made in Hebron, the land of Abraham. They, too, have been upon their pious errand to the tomb.

At sunset even the sunburnt, dirty, deformed, weather-beaten Christian beggars go back to their mud huts under the shadow of the Mount of Olives outside the walls of Jerusalem. As they trudge along the dusty road they twist, in their dried-up fingers, the cheapest of cigarettes, their one and only luxury, without which the meanest and poorest of human beings could not exist in this strange country.

In the soft twilight hour you will see the pilgrims returning for the night from the Valley of Jehoshaphat, the Tomb of the Kings, or the Fountains of Solomon, to the Latin, Greek, Armenian or Russian hospices. The rich European leaves the Sepulchre at sundown to rest in the English hotels. The great church becomes silent and empty. On the side of the rotunda belonging to the Copts a woman prays motionless beside some pillar, or prone upon the ground. Presently she rises and slowly departs.

Outside on the square those who walk about selling rosaries, scapulars, little crosses, and medals in imitation silver, gather up their goods into bags with two pouches, and disappear. The crowd of sunburnt sellers and water-carriers follow. Not a soul now descends the little steps by which half the town of Jerusalem had come down to the Piazza. No one now lingers under the archway of the Templars; the chirrup of the birds is hushed.

The sun sets. A dull thud re-echoes through the deserted arches and chapels of the church. The doors are closed until dawn. Within the gloomy church, pilgrims who have obtained the privilege of remaining in adoration by the Sepulchre throughout the watches of the night are left alone with their Lord.

Night gradually falls over the whole building. First it effaces the marked outline of the massive columns of the rotunda, then obliterates the upper gallery, and, lastly, even the peep of blue skylight that shows through the narrow windows of the clerestory. The pillars round each chapel and the quaint architectural features of this strange structure are soon lost in the sepulchral gloom. Here and there are a few faint glimmers of light.

Beside the apse, the second church, Calvary, which forms part of that of the Holy Sepulchre, and to which it leads up by two steep flights of marble steps, is merged in utter darkness. Only the occasional flicker of a lamp lingers on that part of Golgotha where the Cross was driven into the earth. Here and there a dim light flickers in the Chapel of St Saviour, and in St Mary Magdalene, the chapel belonging to the Franciscans.

The small underground chapels cut out of the solid rock, where are the tombs of Joseph of Arimathea and his family, and where the Holy Cross was found, look like so many dark caverns ready to engulf you. The harassed and penitent soul who has been given permission to stay in this mysterious church during the long watches of the night realises, in this weird darkness, his intense longing to converse, as it were, with his Maker and examine his conscience as, possibly, he has never thought of doing before.

His senses soon become almost atrophied, and he falls a prey to strange hallucinations. Leaning against the door of the sacred building, not venturing to enter or to stir a step forward, he loses himself in a profound, dreamy reverie.

The proportions of the great building seem to expand and become colossal, limitless, in the darkness. If a breath of air disturbs the faint light of the lamps, the watcher fancies some spirit has passed over them and made them quiver. Isn't that a step lightly treading the pavement? Is that white figure down there human? Perhaps those whispers that disturb the silence are mere creations of the imagination...

The watcher's heart is heavy, and he fancies himself haunted by ghosts, some sad, others wrathful, that have risen from their graves to hover about the tomb of tombs. The ear may hear nothing, but the quickened imagination conjures up strange sights and sounds. It peoples the lonely church with voices wailing with sorrow or ringing with reproach, the voices of the lost ones who are gone before! Presently the darkness seems filled with hazy, vanishing figures, with livid, dying faces, and shadowy skeleton hands, waving blessings or beckoning farewells.

The place is indeed haunted—with memories, with sadness, with fear. The awful silence is only broken by the muttering of some bitter ejaculation, stifled sob, yes, even with the rattle of the dying!

Then, wild with horror and repentance, the keeper of this vigil staggers into the mortuary chamber to prostrate himself by the tomb, even as a child sinks on its mother's breast. To him this stone is the last refuge, where he shall find shelter and love.

Then the trembling, fevered lips kiss the marble, and in the dead of night repeat again the everlasting question that rises, during the hours of greatest exhaltation or of profoundest depression, to the lips of the suffering believer, the question a son asks his father, the question a Soul asks its God, but louder, more fervent, more insistent: "Now that we are alone together in the night, O Lord, and that Thou seest all I think and feel—since I come here desiring to remain in Thy presence one night before Thy Sepulchre—tell me, oh! tell me, what is the Truth and which the Way?"

The Soul waits on. And here, in the clear light of the forty-nine lamps which burn perpetually above the Holy Tomb, a new-born peace falls upon the restless conscience, soothing its vain terrors. In this holy place all the falsehood, meanness, poverty, cupidity, false pride, and hypocrisy of the soul crumble to pieces, like some dense wall that has kept out the light of Heaven. The heavy chain that fettered the human being to the vainglory and pleasures of this world is loosened, and the unclean spirit cast out. The Soul is freed. For Jesus Christ, Who was buried here, desires that souls, liberated by repentance from evil, should come to Him and be healed by the touch of His tomb.

Would that the proud, the unjust, the frivolous, who live for this world only, the brutal and the sensual, could pass one night alone with Him in this sacred spot, where stands his funeral couch, the slab on which His divine and bleeding form rested! Then would they see light; and the evil that binds them down would pass from them by mere contact with the tomb of the God of Love and Unselfishness, Who died that His lofty ideal should live and be eternal.

Thus the Soul communes, listens, and remembers. How many profound, never-to-be forgotten words He uttered during His life! Yet one, especially vibrates here more clearly than elsewhere: "Martha, Martha, you are anxious and troubled about many things; one thing is needful." Only one? Is it no matter, then, if our wishes are unfulfilled, if our dreams are not realised?

Does it not matter that our love should be unrequited and our hatred should be vain? Is all this of no importance? No, or but very little. One thing *only* is necessary. He who lay two nights in the grave has said it. Are the ties of family affection nothing? The reverence of children for their parents; the gratitude of friends; faith and loyalty: are not these things needful? May we not weep and bemoan the incompleteness of our work, and the scorn with which our best intentions are so often met? Are we not to complain or trouble ourselves if our heart and mind cannot reach their goal? If we fall fainting by the way, without wish, desire, or hope, should we seek consolation in ourselves alone? "One thing only is needful": the Life of the Spirit.

The Soul sees and knows. He lived the great life of the Spirit, and desires that all, through Him, should also live, even as He did. All those who are suffering, oppressed, infirm, miserable, the weak through age, sex, or condition, women, old men, children, the sick and the poor, all received from Him those spiritual consolations which elevate and purify: those suffering from the effects of terrible misfortune, oppressed by misery, the sad and abandoned, all have felt in their inward conscience the sublime idea of a future recompense, the pure fount of all comfort.

That spiritual life, which, in Him, assumed a divine form, setting aside all human calculations, pardoning all offences in pity for the humble and penitent sinner, in love for the suffering ones—He has given this boon to all who believed or will believe in Him. The divine gift for the cure of souls has only been given in order to complete the most wonderful of hidden miracles.

This life of the Spirit, however humble and simple, is always consoling: it may be great and powerful, lifting men to the sublimest heights, to the ideal of heroism and martyrdom. It gives youth its joy, manhood its strength, and it is the blessing of old age. For is it not the legacy of Him Who was born in Bethlehem and died in Jerusalem?

The Soul, now quiet and calm and at peace from now on, exclaims: "Thou hast spoken to me, O Lord, during this terrible yet glorious night, and hast answered thy servant. I now know what is the Truth, and wherein lies the Way."

From the round space in the cupola, the light of dawn descends in radiance on the sacred tomb: and the bright sun enters the church in a triumphant burst of glory.

*At the end of the account of her visit to the Holy Places
Matilde Serao describes her feelings on the day of her departure.*

Among travellers who come to this sacred city there is a
pious custom: the first thing to do on arrival and the last
before leaving is to visit the Holy Sepulchre. Next morning, therefore, feeling more than usually nervous and disturbed, I went for the last time to the church which contains the most venerated tomb in the world.

It was a glorious day and the streets of Jerusalem looked
bright and full of life in the clear sunshine. The birds twit-
tered, even as they had done six weeks before when I first
saw the great windows of the facade of the church. Inside
there was the same coming of priests of all nationalities,
monks, visitors, and mendicants.

Suddenly all my enthusiams seemed to leave me and I
became cold and unmoved. In vain did I try to collect my
thoughts with my brow pressed against the cold marble of
the Holy Sepulchre and lose myself in prayer. It was useless:
a thousand and one foolish commonplace details about my
journey crowded into my brain: the closing of boxes,
telegrams to send, what hotel to go to in Constantinople
etc., etc.—impossible to excite the least feeling of interest
and emotion: I remained untouched, frozen.

Thus did I kneel for some time, asking for grace to feel at
least some sorrow at parting. This was not the first time I
had experienced such stagnation and incapacity to raise my
spirit in fervent prayer, and thereby conquer my horrible
and sterile indifference. Sometimes it comes after a period
of much fervour and entreaty for spiritual communion. I
had, of course, been lately through a time of great excite-
ment during my stay in the Land of Jesus, and I had been
much agitated by mystic impressions, so that perhaps I was
now incapable of bearing any more.

Rising from my knees, I left the Holy Sepulchre and
walked out of the church as cooly as if I were leaving a tele-
graph office. Then I returned to the hotel like an ordinary

tourist who is pleased at the thought of having plenty of time in which to make all the final arrangements for departure.

All went smoothly without a hitch: my luggage was packed, my bill paid, I had not forgotten the servants, and my good friend Issa was beside the carriage which was waiting to drive me to the station, standing a little way off outside the great stone archway Bab-el-Khalil.

Everything was complete. I took a last look round my room to see that I had left nothing behind, counted my packages, felt that I had my keys—yes, everything was in perfect order.

But still I could not get over the impression that I had forgotten something. What could it be? I turned over in my mind all that I should have done: my passport was stamped: I had telegraphed to the hotel at Constantinople: my place was booked on the steamer. A silent voice in my heart seemed to whisper, "You have forgotten something, you have forgotten something."

Slowly and troubled I descended the staircase, amid the salutations and farewells of everyone, and was just about to enter the carriage, when lo! I suddenly remembered that I had forgotten to take a *real* farewell of the Sepulchre of our Lord. So I returned to the great church for a few last moments of meditation and prayer.

Thus, hurried and agitated, I re-entered the Church of the Holy Sepulchre, only a few moments before the train was to start, driven there as if by some irresistible force. As I approached the Holy Tomb I felt all the anguish of separation. While, prostrate beside it, my lips pressed the cold marble with passionate kisses, my arms stretched across it, and my eyes rained tears upon it, I recalled that I should never return again. After all you only go to Jerusalem once in a lifetime. I realised that my feet would never again pass beneath its gates, or my heart be filled with such an anguish as this.

Only once before had I experienced anything approaching this emotion. That was when, during the most terrible and desolate night of my life, I had thrown myself sobbing and inconsolable, upon the body of my dead mother. So now I was torn and heartbroken at leaving the place where He had lain.

I may have excited surprise in some who witnessed my grief. But others may have sympathised with my feelings at being separated from this sacred spot. They may have even joined their tears to mine. But I neither looked up nor noticed them. When I reached the threshold I glanced back, as you do towards the human form of someone greatly loved.

Then the thought came to me that this great church would endure when I was no longer alive. Like some living thing this tomb would continue to watch over Christian souls and hearts; but I should never see it again. Then, with bowed head, I slowly went out. I can remember nothing more, nor how I reached the station or left the city. I only remember that I was silently sobbing and my heart was very heavy.

As the train carried me away I looked back at the high hills of Sion. I was glad that I was alone with my sorrow, and that I had had the courage to refuse to allow anyone to see me off.

In the carriage with me were some English people who evidently thought me either ill or demented. Their words came back to me long afterwards. At the time, however, I did not heed them, for I was trying to impress upon my mental vision the last view of Jerusalem, to carry away with me every line, colouring, and detail so that I could recall it all when far away...

Jerusalem disappeared before my eyes, though I still tried to catch a last glimpse of the Holy City as the train rolled swiftly on. It was indeed all over now. The Tower of David was the last thing I saw. As it faded into nothing I made a vow.

I swore that for Jesus's sake, and for that of this land made blessed by His Life and Death, I would write a book. It would not perhaps be the best or most skilful, but the most human and sincere. I promised to write it with the faith and humility of a true Christian, for other trusting and hopeful Christians to read. My vow is now fulfilled. Today I lay my work at the foot of the Cross. As I stretch out my arms towards it I murmur for myself and those dear to me the words so often uttered by the early Christians: "*Ave Spes Unica!*" (Hail, our sole Hope!)

CHRONOLOGY

FIRST CENTURY

8-4 B.C. Birth of Jesus Christ

14 A.D. Death of Emperor Augustus

14-37 Tiberius, emperor

30 Death and Resurrection of Jesus

34 Martyrdom of St Stephen and conversion of St Paul

44 Death of Agrippa I, last of the Herodian rulers of Judea

45-46 Paul called by Barnabas to supervise the missionary work in Antioch

47-48 St Paul's first missionary journey to Cyprus and Galatia.

49 Apostolic Council in Jerusalem

49-50 St Paul's second missionary journey to Galatia, Philippi, Thessalonica, Athens etc

50-52 St Paul in Corinth

52 St Paul visits Jerusalem and Antioch and begins third missionary journey

56 St Paul's last visit to Corinth

58 St Paul arrested in Jerusalem

61-63 St Paul captive in Rome

62 Martyrdom of James, first Bishop of Jerusalem, a kinsman of Jesus Christ; he is succeeded by Symeon, son of Clopas (mentioned in St John's Gospel); according to tradition he was a brother of St Joseph)

64 Gessius Florus becomes last Roman prefect of Judea

64 Burning of Rome and persecution of Christians there

64-67 Probable martyrdom of St Peter and St Paul in Rome

70 Siege and destruction of Jerusalem by Titus; ruins become garrison town

95 Domitian's persecution of Christians

SECOND CENTURY

98-117 Trajan, emperor; during his reign Jerusalem becomes a pagan city

110 Martyrdom of St Ignatius of Antioch in Rome

117-38 Hadrian, emperor

132-35 Jewish revolt of Bar Cochebah; expulsion of Jews and Christians of Jewish origin from Jerusalem

135 Hadrian begins reconstruction of Jerusalem as Colonia Ælia Capitolina, celebrating both Emperor's name and patron god, Jupiter Capitolinus. Erection of statue of Venus on Mount Calvary, of Jupiter on site of the Holy Sepulchre; rites of Adonis celebrated at grotto of Bethlehem

140 Beginning of crisis of Christian gnosticism

c.155 Martyrdom of St Polycarp at Smyrna

c.180 Foundation of catechetical school of Alexandria

c.185 St Irenaeus' *Against Heresies*

197 Tertullian's *Apology*

THIRD CENTURY

203 Origen begins directing school of Alexandria

212 Emperor Caracalla grants Roman citizenship to all inhabitants of the Empire except those who had surrendered unconditionally

222-35 Alexander Severus, emperor

c.232 Origen expelled from Alexandria; founds school of Caesarea in Palestine

249-50 Emperor Decius' persecution of Christians

258 Emperor Valerian's persecution; martyrdom of St Cyprian in Carthage, and Pope Sixtus II in Rome

284-305 Diocletian, emperor

296 Birth of St Athanasius

FOURTH CENTURY

303-05 Major Christian persecution under Diocletian

306-37 Constantine, emperor (full sovereignty from 324)

310 Constantine victor at battle of Milvian Bridge; death of emperor Maxentius

311 Galerius' edict of toleration of Christians

312 Donatus at Carthage argues that those who had surrendered the scriptures during Diocletian persecution were disqualified from episcopal office; later argues that validity of sacraments depends on disposition of their administrator

313 Edict of Milan grants religious freedom to Roman citizens; Pope Melchiades condemns Donatism

314 Council of Arles condemns Donatism

325 First Council of Nicaea condemns Arianism

c.325/326 Constantine's mother, St Helena, visits Palestine and begins supervision of building of churches at principal sites concerned with life of Jesus Christ. Sozomen, a Palestinian, in his Church History records that she also located Cross of Christ and of those crucified with him. Macarius, Bishop of Jerusalem, discerns which was Christ's Cross through healing of a sick woman

328-73 Athanasius, bishop of Alexandria

329-30 Constantine greatly enlarges Byzantium on the Bospherous and makes it eastern capital of the Roman Empire.

333 BORDEAUX PILGRIM visits Jerusalem

335 Dedication (on 17 September) of the Holy Sepulchre complex, consisting of little house (edicule) over the tomb of Jesus, shrine of Calvary, and immense Basilica, the Martyrion

336 Death of Arius at Constantinople

337 Death of Constantine

337-79 Pro-Arian successors of Constantine

c.347 ST CYRIL BECOMES BISHOP OF JERUSALEM

354 St Augustine born in Numidia, North Africa

367-378 ST CYRIL banished from see by Arian emperor, Valens

c.374 St Jerome visits Syria

374 St Ambrose becomes bishop of Milan

381 First Council of Constantinople

381-84 EGERIA visits the Holy Places

382-385 St Jerome acts as Secretary of Pope Damasus in Rome

386 St Jerome settles in Bethlehem with ST PAULA and St Eustochium

387 St Augustine baptised in Milan at Easter

395 Arcadius and Honorius become emperors of east and west respectively

396 St Augustine becomes bishop of Hippo

FIFTH CENTURY

c. 404 St Jerome completes his Latin version of the Bible (The Vulgate); death of ST PAULA at Bethlehem

406 Barbarians cross Rhine and invade Gaul

410 Rome captured by Alaric the Goth

c 410 British monk, Pelagius, in commentary on St Paul's Epistles, denies doctrine of original sin; argues that man can be perfected by his own efforts

410 Goths sack Rome

410-507 Visigoth kingdom in Gaul and Iberian peninsular

416 Pelagianism condemned by synod at Rome under Pope Innocent I

420 Death of St Jerome at Bethlehem

c.428 Nestorius, bishop of Constantinople, argues that there are two person and two natures in Jesus Christ, and that the Blessed Virgin Mary was only mother of the man Christ, and not mother of God

430 Death of St Augustine at Hippo

431 Council of Ephesus condemns Nestorianism and proclaims Mary Mother of God

438 Empress Eudocia visits Jerusalem; Jews permitted to return to Jerusalem to pray at site of the Temple; riots between Christians and Jews in Jerusalem

438 Birth of St Sabas near Caesarea in Cappadocia

440-461 St Leo the Great, pope.

443/444 Empress Eudocia returns to Jerusalem, after a public break with Emperor Theodosius II; lives in Jerusalem until her death in 460; devotes herself to building churches and embellishing Christian sites

451 Council of Chalcedon defines two natures of Christ and condemns Monophysitism

455 Rome taken by the Vandals under Genseric

457-61 Death of St Patrick; Christianity well established in Ireland

478 St Sabas founds lavra (monastic communities) in wild gorge between Jerusalem and the Dead Sea

c. 480 Birth of St Benedict

493 St Sabas given oversight of all monks in Palestine by Patriarch of Jerusalem

493 Ostrogoth kingdom of Italy

497/8 Baptism of Clovis at Rheims and the conversion of Franks

SIXTH CENTURY

507 Victory of the Franks over the Visigoths

527-65 Justinian, emperor of the East

530 Antoninus Pius visits the Holy Land

531 Justinian, on advice of St Sabas, funds building of hospital for sick pilgrims in Jerusalem, and church dedicated to the Mother of God, and endows them; provides garrison to protect Palestinian monasteries

533 Power of the Vandals in North Africa destroyed by Emperor Justinian

543 Justinian dedicates Church of Mother of God in Jerusalem

c 547 Death of St Benedict

553 Second Council of Constantinople

587 Conversion of Visigoth king in Spain from Arianism to Catholicism

590-604 Gregory the Great, pope

597 St Augustine of Canterbury arrives in England to evangelise Anglo-Saxons

SEVENTH CENTURY

610 Muhammad appears in Mecca as a prophet of Allah

614 Persians capture Jerusalem, with the aid of the Jews within the city; destroy its Christian churches, and massacre and enslave many Christians (but Holy Sepulchre itself may not have been damaged); Holy Cross sent to Ctesiphon, the Persian capital, to be cared for by Persian Queen, Meryem—a Nestorian Christian. Church of the Nativity at Bethlehem spared because of depiction of Magi in Persian dress in mosaic over its entrance

622 Flight of Muhammad to Medina (the Hegira)

627 Emperor Heraclius defeats Persians at Nineveh

630 Restoration of Holy Cross to Jerusalem by Emperor Heraclius

632 Death of Muhammad

638 Arabs under Caliph Omar capture Jerusalem; before this the Holy relics had been sent to Constantinople

642 Alexandria captured by the Arabs

638-750 Ummayad Caliphate rules Palestine from Damascus

680 ARCULF visits the Holy Places

680-1 Third Council of Constantinople; doctrine of the two wills of Christ proclaimed; condemnation of monothelitism

690 Beginning of St Willibrord's English mission to Germany

692 Dome of the Rock at Jerusalem completed by Caliph Abd al-Malik

695 St Willibrord consecrated bishop of the Frisians by Pope Sergius

698 Carthage taken by Arabs

EIGHTH CENTURY

c. 700 ST WILLIBALD born in Wessex

711-12 Conquest of Spain by the Arabs and destruction of Visigoth kingdom.

717-18 Pope Leo II defeats Arabs at Constantinople and saves Eastern empire.

724 ST WILLIBALD visits the Holy Land

726-80 First period of iconoclasm

732 Charles Martel defeats Arabs at Poitier

740 Earthquake in the Holy Places

750-1258 Abbasid Caliphate in Baghdad

751 The Carolingian Empire in France begins

754 Martyrdom of St Boniface in Germany

754 Recognition of the Pope's temporal rule from Rome to Ravenna by Pepin the Short, son of Charles Martel

768-814 Kingdom of Charlemagne

774 Destruction of Lombard kingdom in Italy

785-809 Caliphate of Haroun al Rashid, correspondent of Charlemagne, to whom he made concessions in Jerusalem

786 Death of ST WILLIBALD at Eichstätt

787 Second Council of Nicaea permits the veneration of icons

794 Council of Frankfurt adopts the addition of the *filioque* to the Creed

800 Charlemagne crowned Emperor in Rome

NINTH CENTURY

815-43 Second period of iconoclasm

847-86 Patriarchs Ignatius and Photius occupy the see of Constantinople in turn

858 Nicholas the Great, pope

864 Baptism of Prince Boris of the Bulgars

869-70 Fourth Council of Constantinople

867 Patriarch Photius writes to other eastern patriarchs denouncing the addition of the *filioque* to the Creed

TENTH CENTURY

909 Foundation of Monastery at Cluny by William of Aquitaine

923-24 Muslim mobs destroy Christian churches in Ramleh, Askelon, Caesarea & Damascus

929 Martyrdom of St Wenceslaus, duke of Bohemia

936-73 Otto I, king of Germany

962 Otto I crowned by Pope John XII; restoration of the Western Christian Empire

966 Baptism of Prince Miesko and beginning of conversion of Poland

969-1171 Fatimid dynasty rule in Egypt

970 Fatimid dynasty conquers Palestine

985 Baptism of Gézo, duke of Hungary

988 Baptism of prince Vladimir and beginning of conversion of Russia

1000 St Stephen crowned king of Hungary

ELEVENTH CENTURY

1009 Destruction of the Church of the Holy Sepulchre on the orders of the Fatimid Caliph of Egypt, al-Hakim; it is likely that much of the rock-cut tomb survived; almost total destruction of the Martyrion

1012-23 With the support of al-Hakim's Christian mother, Maria, (sister of Orestes, who was Patriarch of Jerusalem from 984-1005), Christians do some restoration work on the Church of the Holy Sepulchre

1039-56 German Emperor, Henry III, exercises control of papal elections

1052 Patriarch of Constantinople, Michael Cerularius, demands that Latin churches there adopt Greek practices, which they refuse

1054 On a mission from Pope Leo IX about recognition of Greek and Latin usage, Cardinal Humbert lays a Bull of Excommunication on the altar of Church of Sancta Sophia, excommunicating Patriarch Cerularius and denouncing the omission of the *filioque* from the eastern churches Creed

1056-1106 Henry IV, German emperor

1073-85 St Gregory VII, pope; he campaigns against the investing of ecclesiastical power by secular rulers

1095 Pope Urban II preaches the first crusade at Piacenza and Clermont; Byzantine Emperor seeks western aid for a crusade against the Turks in Anatolia

1096 Beginning of First Crusade

1098 Turks take Antioch

1099 Crusaders take Jerusalem; large-scale massacre of Muslims

1099-1187 Jerusalem effective capital of the Latin kingdom in Palestine

TWELFTH CENTURY

1101 Latins replace Greeks as resident clergy in the Church of the Resurrection (now known as the Church of the Holy Sepulchre)

1102 SAEWULF visits the Holy Places

1115-53 St Bernard, abbot of Clairvaux

1119 Foundation of the Templars

1120 Hospitallers become a military order

1122 Concordat of Worms ends the lay investiture conflict between rulers and the Western Church

1123 First Council of the Lateran

1139 Second Council of the Lateran

1149 Consecration of the Crusaders' additions and embellishments to the Holy Sepulchre complex

1159-90 Frederick Barbarossa, emperor

1159-81 Alexander III, pope

c.1159 Peter Lombard's *Book of Sentences*

1170 Birth of St Dominic, founder of the Dominican Order

1179 Third Council of the Lateran

1181 Birth of St Francis, founder of the Franciscans

1187 Jerusalem falls again into Islamic hands after Latin defeat by Saladin; Latin clergy leave the city and Holy Places revert to Greek, Syrian and Armenian control

1191 Latins capture Acre in the Third Crusade

1198-1216 Innocent III, pope

THIRTEENTH CENTURY

1204 Fourth Crusade; capture of Constantinople by the Crusaders and creation of a Latin empire in Constantinople and on Greek mainland

1209-29 Albigensian Crusade

1215 Fourth Lateran Council

1216 Pope Honorius III approves Dominican order

1219 St Francis accompanies the Crusaders on the Fifth Crusade to Egypt

1223 Pope Honorius III approves the Franciscan Order

1226 Death of St Francis

1226-70 St Louis, king of France

1229 Frederic II, king of Germany and Sicily, retakes Jerusalem

1241 King Bela of Hungary defeated by the Mongols at Mohi

1244 Jerusalem finally lost by the Crusaders

1245 First Council of Lyons

1250 St Louis defeated by the Sultan of Egypt at Mansourah

1254 St Louis leaves the Christian east

1258 Mongols sack Baghdad, but spare the Christian community

1260 Damascus falls to the Mongols; Mamluks defeat the Mongols at Ain Jalud

1261 End of the Latin empire of Constantinople

1261-1520 Mamluk dynasty in Egypt

1266-73 Dominican, St Thomas Aquinas, writes the *Summa Theologiae*

1268 Antioch falls to the Mamluks

1274 Second Council of Lyons

1291 Fall of Latin state of Acre to the Mamluk Sultan Qalawun

1294-1303 Boniface VIII, pope

FOURTEENTH CENTURY

1305 Election of French pope, Bernard de Got, as Clement V

1309 Popes establish themselves at Lyons

1311-12 Council of Vienne; Knights Templars suppressed

1347-53 The Black Death

1377 Gregory XI returns from Avignon to Rome

1378-1417 The Western Schism; rival popes in Rome and France (Avignon)

1382 Condemnation of Wycliffe

FIFTEENTH CENTURY

1415 Death of John Hus at the stake

1417 End of the Western Schism; Martin I the sole pope

1427 Birth of CANON CASOLA

1439 Union of Greeks with the Catholic Church at the Council of Florence

1453 Constantinople falls to the Turks and the Christian Eastern Empire ends

1455 Invention of printing

1474-1516 Isabella and Ferdinand, rulers of Spain

1480 BROTHER FELIX FABRI, a Dominican friar of Ulm, goes on his first visit to the Holy Places

1483 BROTHER FELIX FABRI makes his second visit to the Holy Places

1484 Martin Luther born at Eisleben in Lower Saxony

1492 Conclusion of the Spanish reconquest of Granada from Arabs, and discovery of America

1494 CANON CASOLA visits the Holy Places

SIXTEENTH CENTURY

1507 Death of CANON CASOLA at the age of 80

1509-47 Henry VIII, king of England

1512-17 Fifth Council of the Lateran

1515-47 Francis I, king of France

1516-56 Charles I, king of Spain; from 1519, known as Charles V, Emperor of Germany

1516 The Turk, Selim Shah, takes peaceful possession of Jerusalem from the Mamluks; rule administered from Istanbul, formerly Constantinople

1516-1918 Turkish rule in Palestine

1517 Martin Luther publishes 95 propositions relating to the doctrine and practice of the Catholic religion

1520 Luther and his allies excommunicated

1524 Franciscans expelled from the Cenacle church on Mount Sion by order of Sulayman, Turkish Sultan at Constantinople, and lose their convent there

1527 Sack of Rome by the troops of the emperor Charles V

1533 Henry VIII breaks with the Papacy

1535 Execution of St John Fisher and St Thomas More

1535 Foundation of the Society of Jesus

1535-41 Sultan Sulayman the Magnificent rebuilds the walls of Jerusalem

1541-64 Calvin's theocratic government of Geneva

1545-63 Council of Trent

1546 Death of Luther

1555 Rebuilding of the edicule over the tomb of Christ in the Church of the Holy Sepulchre; opening of the tomb itself witnessed by BONIFACE OF RAGUSA OFM

1556-98 Philip II, king of Spain

1558-1603 Elizabeth I consolidates the Reformation in England

1559 Franciscans under BONIFACE OF RAGUSA OFM acquire a new convent located near the Holy Sepulchre from the Georgians

1562-98 Wars of religion in France

1566-72 Pontificate of St Pius V

1570 Battle of Lepanto; Christian navy defeats the Turks; Pius V excommunicates Queen Elizabeth I

1589 Moscow becomes separate Orthodox patriarchate

1598 Henry IV of France guarantees toleration to the Huguenots (edict of Nantes)

SEVENTEENTH CENTURY

1618-48 The Thirty Years War

1620 Pilgrim fathers reach America

1624-42 Richelieu's government in France

1627 Franciscan friars re-establish their tenure in the Church of the Holy Sepulchre

1633 Trial of Galileo

1643-1715 Louis XIV, king of France

1648 Treaty of Westphalia confirms the religious division of Europe

1649-58 Cromwell's Commonwealth in England

1653-1713 Jansenist crisis

1683 John III Sobieski, king of Poland, defeats the Turks and saves Vienna

1685 Revocation of the edict of Nantes

1688-89 Flight of James II from England; William of Orange becomes William III of England

1690 Franciscan friars regain privilege of celebrating Holy Mass in the tomb of Christ

1697 HENRY MAUNDRELL, chaplain to the Aleppo company, visits Jerusalem

EIGHTEENTH CENTURY

1702-13 War of the Spanish succession

1715-74 Louis XV, king of France

1738 Pope Clement XII condemns freemasonry

1740-58 Benedict XIV, pope

1740-86 Maria Theresa, ruler of the Habsburg empire

1751-72 Publication of the *Encyclopédie* in France

1751-72 Catherine II, empress of Russia

1765-90 Joseph II, ruler of Austria

1773 Clement IV suppresses the Society of Jesus

1776 Declaration of Independence by the United States of America

1778 Death of Voltaire and Rousseau

1781 Kant publishes the *Critique of Pure Reason*

1789 French revolution

1792-4 Abolition of the French monarchy; execution of Louis XVI; the Terror

1799 Pius VI, pope, dies a prisoner in France

1799-1804 Napoleon, first consul in France

1800-23 Pius VII, pope

NINETEENTH CENTURY

1801 Concordat between France and the Holy See

1804-14 Napoleonic empire

1806 CHATEAUBRIAND visits the Holy Places

1808 Fire damages the Church of the Holy Sepulchre; roof of the rotunda collapses on edicule; cupola and much cladding destroyed

1809-10 Greek Orthodox Christians, with permission of Sultan, restore the Church of the Holy Sepulchre

1810-25 Spanish colonies in south and central America gain independence

1814-15 Congress of Vienna and Holy Alliance

1814-30 Restoration of the Bourbons in France

1821-30 Greeks gain independence from Turkish rule in war

1822-24 CHATEAUBRIAND, foreign minister of France

1829 Roman Catholic Emancipation in England

1832 *Mirari vos*, papal encyclical against liberalism

1837-1901 Victoria, queen of England

1845 John Henry Newman received into the Roman Catholic Church

1846-78 Pius IX, pope

1848 Karl Marx's *Communist Manifesto*; civil unrest in many European countries

1854 Pius IX defines the dogma of the Immaculate Conception of the Blessed Virgin Mary —that she was without sin from her conception

1859 Charles Darwin's *On the Origin of Species by Natural Selection*

1861-65 Civil War in the United States

1864 Pius IX's *Syllabus of Errors*

1868 Rebuilding of the dome in the Church of the Holy Sepulchre

1869 Opening of the Suez Canal; owned by company with French and British government shares

1869-70 First Vatican Council; papal infallibility defined

1870-71 Franco-Prussian War

1873 Egypt becomes independent from Turkey, but remains under British and French financial control

1887 First Zionist congress

1890 ELIZABETH, LADY BUTLER, visits the Holy Land

1891 Papal encycical *Rerum Novarum*, on social questions

1893 MATILDE SERAO visits the Holy Land

BIBLIOGRAPHY

SOURCES OF THE TEXTS OF THE ACCOUNTS

The sources are listed in the order in which the accounts appear. The first date in brackets gives the year in which the writer's pilgrimage took place, or, in the case of the description of the opening of the tomb of Christ by Bishop Boniface, the year in which this happened.

Seven of these accounts were first published by the Palestine Pilgrims' Text Society (PPTS) in the nineteenth century. The translations are largely based on those accompanying these texts, but a number have been substantially modified and, where appropriate, retranslated, in order to clarify the sense, take into account later research, and make them easier to read. Punctuation and paragraphing have also been amended where this seemed desirable. The other translations have also been modified in a similar way.

St Matthew, Chapter 2:1-9 of his Gospel, *Revised Standard Version of The Holy Bible*, London, 1973.

St Luke, Chapter 2:41-52 of his Gospel, *Revised Standard Version of The Holy Bible*, London, 1973.

The Bordeaux Pilgrim, *Itinerary from Bordeaux to Jerusalem* (c.333), tr. Aubrey Stewart, PPTS, London, 1887.

Egeria, *Pilgrimage of S. Silvia of Aquitaine to the Holy Places* (c.385), tr. John H. Barnard, PPTS, London 1891. Recent scholarship has shown that this work is by Egeria, a nun from Spain, rather than the purported S. Silvia.

St. Paula, *Letter of Paula and Eustochium to Marcella, about the Holy Places* (c.386), tr. Aubrey Stewart, PPTS, London, 1889.

St Cyril of Jerusalem, *Catechetical Lectures Vol II, Lecture XXIII (On the Mysteries)*, (c.347), tr. Rev. R W Church, ed. J.H. Newman, Library of the Fathers, Oxford, 1838.

Arculf, *Pilgrimage of Arculfus to the Holy Land* (c.670), tr. Rev. J. R. Macpherson, PPTS, London, 1889.

St Willibald, *Hodoeporicon* (c. 724), tr. Rev. Canon Brownlow, PPTS, London, 1891.

Saewulf, *Pilgrimage of Saewulf to Jerusalem and the Holy Land*, (1102-3), tr. Rev. Canon Brownlow, PPTS, London, 1892.

Brother Felix Fabri OP, *The Book of the Wanderings of Brother Felix Fabri*, (1480-1483), tr. Aubrey Stewart, 2 Vols., PPTS, London, 1892.

Canon Pietro Casola, *Canon Pietro Casola's Pilgrimage to Jerusalem*, (1494), tr. Margaret Newett, Manchester, 1907.

Bishop Bonifacio Stephano of Ragusa, OFM, *Liber de Perenni Cultu Terrae Sanctae et de Fructosa eius Perigrinatione*, (1550), 2nd Edition, Venice, 1575, tr. Antony Matthew, 1999.

Rev. Henry Maundrell, *Journey from Aleppo to Jerusalem at Easter*, (1697), London, 1810.

François Auguste,Viscomte de Chateaubriand, *Travels in Greece, Palestine, Egypt and Barbary*, (1806-7), tr. Frederic Shoberl, 2 Vols., London, 1811.

Elizabeth, Lady Butler, *Letters from the Holy Land*, (1891), London, 1903.

Matilde Serao, *In the Country of Jesus*, (1892), tr. Richard Davey; first published in Italian in 1899; English edition, London, 1905.

SECONDARY WORKS

Attwater, D., with John, C.R., *The Penguin Dictionary of Saints*, London, 1995.

Anwad, Sami, *The Holy Land*, Jerusalem, 1993.

Bainton, R.H., *Penguin History of Christianity, Vol.* 1, London, 1967.

Barraclough, Geoffrey, *The Medieval Papacy*, London, 1967.

Bede, *History of the English Church and People*, tr. L. Shirley-Price, London, 1955.

Brooke, Christopher, *The Twelfth Century Renaissance*, London, 1969.

Biddle, Martin, *The Tomb of Christ*, London, 1999.

Cotterell, Paul, *The Railways of Palestine and Israel*, Abingdon, 1984.

Devos, P., "La Date du Voyage d'Égérie", *Analecta Bollandia*, Vol.28 (1967).

El Hassan, HRH Princess Sumaya, and Piccarillo OFM, Fr. Michele, *The Mosaics of Jordan*, London, 1993.

Freeman-Grenville, G.S.P., *The Beauty of Jerusalem and the Holy Places of the Gospel*, London and the Hague, 1983.

Hubert, Jean, Porcher, Jean and Volbach, W.F., *Europe in the Dark Ages*, tr. Gilbert and Emmons, London, 1969.

Knox, Ronald A., *Enthusiasm*, London, 1987.

Lane, Frederick, C., *Venetian Ships and Shipbuilders of the Renaissance*, London, 1934.

Larousse Encylopedia of Byzantine and Mediaeval Art, English edition, London, 1963.

Lockyer, Roger, *Habsburg and Bourbon Europe*, 1470-1720, London, 1974.

Moore, Elinor A., *The Ancient Churches of Old Jerusalem*, Beirut, 1961.

Morton, H.V., *In the Steps of St Paul*, London, 1934.
—— *In the Steps of the Master*, London, 1936.

Norwich, John Julius, *A History of Venice*, London, 1983.
—— *Byzantium, The Early Centuries*, London, 1988.

Orlandis, José, *Short History of the Catholic Church*, tr. Michael Adams, Dublin, 1985.

Peters, F.E., *Jerusalem*, Princeton, 1985.

Rice, David Talbot, *Byzantine Art*, London, 1962.
——*The Byzantines*, London, 1962.

Runciman, Steven, *A History of the Crusades*, 3 vols., Cambridge, 1955-1957.

Southern, R.W., *Western Society and the Church in the Middle Ages*, London, 1970.
—— *The Making of the Middle Ages*, London, 1973.

Treharne, R.F., and Fullard, Harold, *Muir's Historical Atlas: Ancient and Classical*, London, 1963.

Ware, Timothy, *The Orthodox Church*, London, 1963.

Wilkinson, John, *Egeria's Travels*, London, 1971.

LIST OF ILLUSTRATIONS

Jerusalem

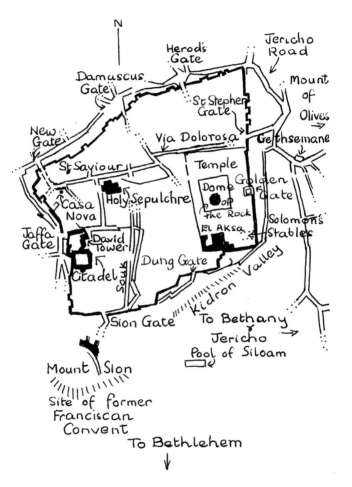

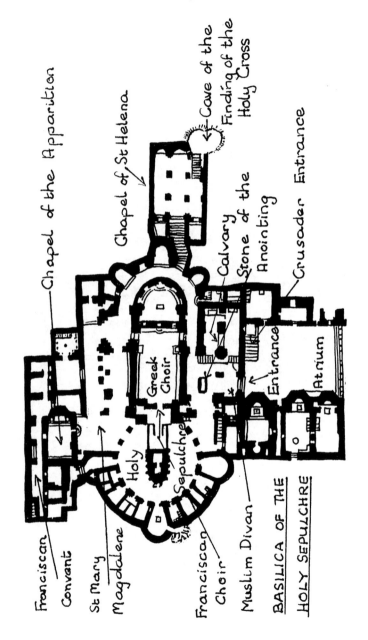

Chapel of the Apparition

Chapel of St Helena

Cave of the Finding of the Holy Cross

Calvary

Stone of the Anointing

Crusader Entrance

Greek Choir

Holy Sepulchre

Entrance

Atrium

Franciscan Convent

St Mary Magdalene

Franciscan Choir

Muslim Divan

BASILICA OF THE
HOLY SEPULCHRE

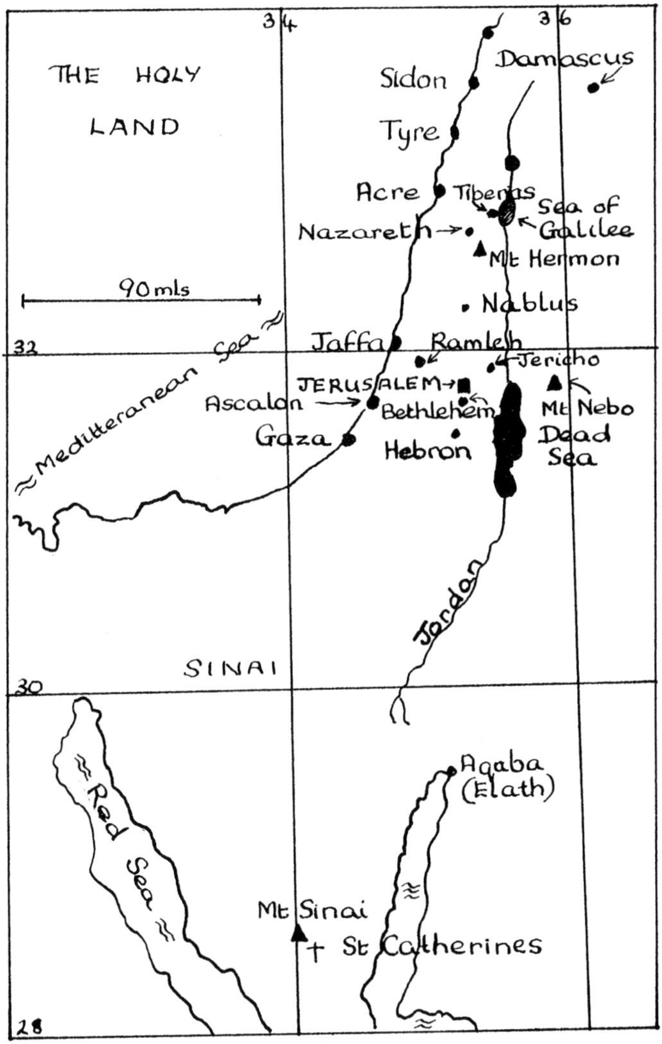

THE HOLY LAND
34
36
Sidon
Damascus
Tyre
Acre
Tiberias
Sea of Galilee
Nazareth
Mt Hermon
90 mls
Nablus
Mediterranean Sea
32
Jaffa
Ramleh
Jericho
JERUSALEM
Ascalon
Bethlehem
Mt Nebo
Gaza
Hebron
Dead Sea
Jordan
SINAI
30
Red Sea
Aqaba (Elath)
Mt Sinai
St Catherines
28

Pray for the peace of Jerusalem!
    "May they prosper who love you!
Peace be within your walls,
    And security within your towers!"
For my brethren and companions' sake
    I will say, "Peace be within you!"
For the sake of the house of the Lord our God,
    I will seek your good.

From Psalm 122